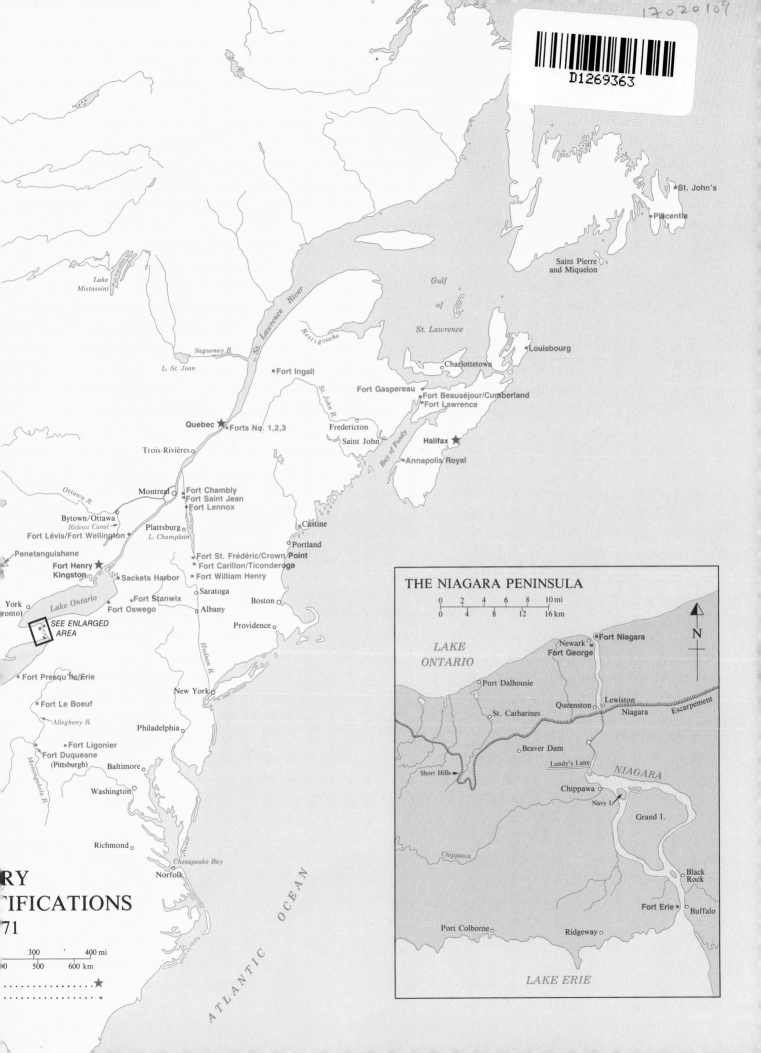

St. John's
Placentia

Saint Pierre
and Miquelon

*Lake
Mistassini*

St. Lawrence River

Saguenay R.

Restigouche

*Gulf
of
St. Lawrence*

L. St. Jean

Fort Ingall

Fort Gaspereau

Charlottetown

Louisbourg

Fort Beauséjour/Cumberland
Fort Lawrence

Quebec ★ Forts No. 1,2,3

St. John R.

Fredericton

Halifax ★

Trois-Rivières

Saint John

Bay of Fundy

Annapolis Royal

Ottawa R.

Montreal
Fort Chambly
Fort Saint Jean
Fort Lennox

Bytown/Ottawa
Rideau Canal
Fort Lévis/Fort Wellington

Plattsburg
L. Champlain

Castine

Portland

Penetanguishene

Fort Henry
Kingston

Sackets Harbor

Fort St. Frédéric/Crown **Point**
Fort Carillon/Ticonderoga
Fort William Henry

York
(ronto)

Lake Ontario

□ SEE ENLARGED
AREA

Fort Stanwix

Saratoga

Fort Oswego

Albany

Boston

Providence

Fort Presqu'ile/Erie

Hudson R.

New York

Fort Le Boeuf

Allegheny R.

Philadelphia

Fort Ligonier
Fort Duquesne
(Pittsburgh)

Monongahela R.

Baltimore

Washington

Richmond

Chesapeake Bay

Norfolk

ATLANTIC OCEAN

RY

TIFICATIONS

71

300   400 mi
500   600 km
. . . . ★
. . . . ■

THE NIAGARA PENINSULA

0   2   4   6   8   10 mi
0   4   8   12   16 km

N

*LAKE
ONTARIO*

Newark **Fort Niagara**
Fort George

Port Dalhousie

Lewiston
Queenston
Niagara

St. Catharines

Escarpment

Beaver Dam

Short Hills

Lundy's Lane

NIAGARA

Chippawa
Navy I.

Grand I.

Chippawa

Black
Rock

Fort Erie Buffalo

Port Colborne

Ridgeway

LAKE ERIE

Previously published:
René Chartrand
Canadian Military Heritage
Volume I
1000-1754

CANADIAN MILITARY HERITAGE

Volume II

1755-1871

RENÉ CHARTRAND

CANADIAN MILITARY HERITAGE

Volume II

1755-1871

ART GLOBAL

Canadian Cataloguing in Publication Data

Chartrand, René

    Canadian military heritage.
    To be completed in 3 v.
    Includes bibliographical references and index.
    Contents: v. 1. 1000-1754 - v. 2. 1755-1871.

    Translation of: Patrimoine militaire canadien.

    ISBN 2-920718-44-4 (v. 1) - ISBN 2-920718-45-2 (v. 2)

    1. Canada – History; military. 2. Armies – Canada –History. 3. Soldiers – Canada.
I. Title.

FC226.C42 1993   355' .00971   C93-096593-0
F1028.C42 1993

This work was published at the initiative and under the auspices of
Communications M. C. Stratégiques
and the Directorate of History, Department of National Defence of Canada

Project Coordinator: Serge Bernier

Design and Production: Art Global, Montreal

Computer Graphics: Stéphane Geoffrion, Cabana Séguin design

Printed and bound in Canada

Cet ouvrage a été publié simultanément en français sous le titre:
PATRIMOINE MILITAIRE CANADIEN – D'hier à aujourd'hui
Tome II
1755-1871
ISBN 2-920718-45-2

© Art Global Inc., 1995
384 Laurier Avenue W.
Montreal, Quebec H2V 2K7

ISBN 2-920718-50-9
2nd quarter 1995

I would like to thank the following historians, curators, collectors and illustrators who opened their doors to me and shared the fruits of their research:

Francis Back, Montreal – William Y. Carman, Sutton – Brian L. Dunnigan, Old Fort Niagara – Gerald A. Embleton, Onnens – Bruce Ellis, Halifax – John R. Elting, Cornwall-on-Hudson – Edward Denby, Toronto – Paul Fortier, Ottawa – S. James and Joyce Gooding, Bloomfield – Michelle Guitard, Hull – Albert W. Haarman, Washington – John Houlding, Rückersdorf – Sheldon Kasman, Toronto – A. Ulrich Koch, Bopfingen – John P. Langellier, Los Angeles – Eugène Lelièpvre, Montrouge – Eric I. Manders, North Syracuse – Mercedes Palau, Madrid – Barry Rich, Halifax – David Ross, Winnipeg – Jack L. Summers, Saskatoon –Ronald Volstad, Edmonton – David Webber, Charlottetown

as well as the following institutions, for their invaluable assistance:

Anne S. K. Brown Military Collection, Brown University, Providence – National Archives of Canada, Ottawa – Archives nationales du Québec, Quebec City – Army Museum, Halifax – Department of National Defence Library, Ottawa – National Library of Canada, Ottawa – Parks Canada Library, Ottawa – Smithsonian Institution, Washington – National Army Museum, London – Musée de l'Armée, Paris – Musée de l'Armée, Salon-de-Provence – Canadian War Museum, Ottawa – Musée du Château Ramezay, Montreal – David M. Stewart Museum, Montreal – McCord Museum of Canadian History, Montreal – Museo Naval, Madrid –Royal Canadian Military Institute, Toronto

as well as:

Serge Bernier
William Constable
Donald E. Graves
Department of National Defence of Canada
Directorate of History

Sandy Balcom
Derek Cook
Yvon Desloges
André Gousse
Yves Goyette
Renée Martel
Claudette Lacelle
Claude Lefèbvre
Carol Whitfield
Parks Canada

my assistant

Pierre Dufour

for their editorial work

Suzanne Bélanger
Hélène Ouvrard
and Jane Broderick

my wife

Luce Vermette

René Chartrand

TABLE OF CONTENTS

FOREWORD

From 1755 to 1871, Canada was a highly coveted land. Threats of invasion from all quarters created a climate of considerable instability. In 1755 New France encompassed most of the territories of North America, and its inhabitants, few in number but highly militarized, had up to then been able to fend off frequent incursions by the much more populous Anglo-American colonies.

After many epic battles, the Anglo-American armies were eventually able to conquer the French colony and take its territories. It was at this point that France confirmed its lack of interest in Canada by ceding New France to Great Britain. The Americans, who disputed British hegemony in North America, attempted on a number of occasions to take Canada, which caused the deployment of British reinforcements on a regular basis.

On the Pacific coast, meanwhile, the Spanish were giving way to the more recently arrived British and Canadian merchants. Canada's frontiers now extended north of the 49th parallel, from the Atlantic all the way to the Pacific. Worsening international relations quickly raised fears of an invasion once again and placed the issue of Canadian security back onto the agenda. Developments in weaponry and combat methods were also used as rationale for the construction of appropriate fortifications and for the building of canals to give strategic access to the interior of the continent. The defence of such a vast country thus became a key issue.

Canada's military institutions also underwent profound transformation, the major consequence of which was that much of the population was demobilized. With the defence of Canada thus assured by British officers and soldiers, fewer and fewer Canadians joined the regular forces. And the militia, which had been compulsory until that time, was replaced by corps of volunteers recruited from among some of the most affluent citizens of British North America. In Lower Canada, which was populated mainly by Francophones, the British authorities even denied the French-Canadian elite the right to raise their own units of volunteers in the 1820s.

This trend towards demilitarization of the population at large continued during the 1837 and 1838 rebellions, with British reinforcements once again lending a hand. There was, however, a renewed interest in military matters in 1855 with the creation of volunteer militias equipped, armed and paid by the government.

Towards 1860, with further threats of invasion on the horizon, the perception grew that all the colonies in British North America ought to be united to better defend themselves, and the end result was Canadian Confederation on July 1, 1867. Military matters became the responsibility of the federal government, in cooperation with the British authorities, who were already planning to remove their troops from the country while maintaining control over the Halifax and Esquimalt naval bases.

In 1871 the last British contingents to leave the Quebec Citadel were replaced by a tiny corps of regular Canadian troops and a volunteer militia under the command of Anglophile officers who imposed British traditions and insisted on the sole use of English.

But beyond this cultural and linguistic reality, Canadians of all origins were tired of military quarrels. In 1870 only one Canadian in 100 was volunteering to serve in the militia, whereas all men had been part of the militia in the eighteenth century.

With the return of peace, Canadians looked to the future and opted to build civilian infrastructures that would contribute to the development of their country. At the end of this turbulent era, Canada, undeniably demilitarized, could not deny that it had a rich and considerable military heritage.

Chapter 1

THE CONQUEST

At the beginning of 1755, two great European powers were about to clash in North America: France and Great Britain. The British colonies occupied a limited area along the Atlantic coast; there were more than a million colonists, essentially farmers and seamen. For its part, with just over 70,000 inhabitants, New France was in control of an immense land area from the St. Lawrence to the Mississippi, in addition to vast territories in the continental interior.

Following the War of Austrian Succession, the French saw the need to place a major garrison in New France to protect its strategic geographical position. In 1750, they therefore considerably added to the military personnel in their colony. In Louisiana the increase was from 850 to 2,000 soldiers, in Île Royale from 700 to 1,200, and in Canada from 812 to 1,500. These 4,700 soldiers were led by more than 300 officers. The total number of regular colonial troops

in New France thus totalled approximately 5,000 servicemen of all ranks. These were primarily infantrymen, most of whom belonged to the Compagnies franches de la Marine, in addition to which were about 100 artillerymen.[1]

Soldiers of the French regiments La Reine (left) and Languedoc (right), c. 1756. Reconstitution by Eugène Lelièpvre.
Parks Canada.

These troops were allocated as follows: the 1,200 soldiers defending the 7,000 inhabitants of Île Royale and Île Saint-Jean were nearly all posted at the fortress of Louisbourg. In Louisiana, with 2,000 soldiers to defend a population of approximately 6,000 colonists,[2] there were more than 1,000 soldiers in the city of New Orleans alone, about one third of its population; another 500 soldiers were stationed in Mobile, and 500 more were

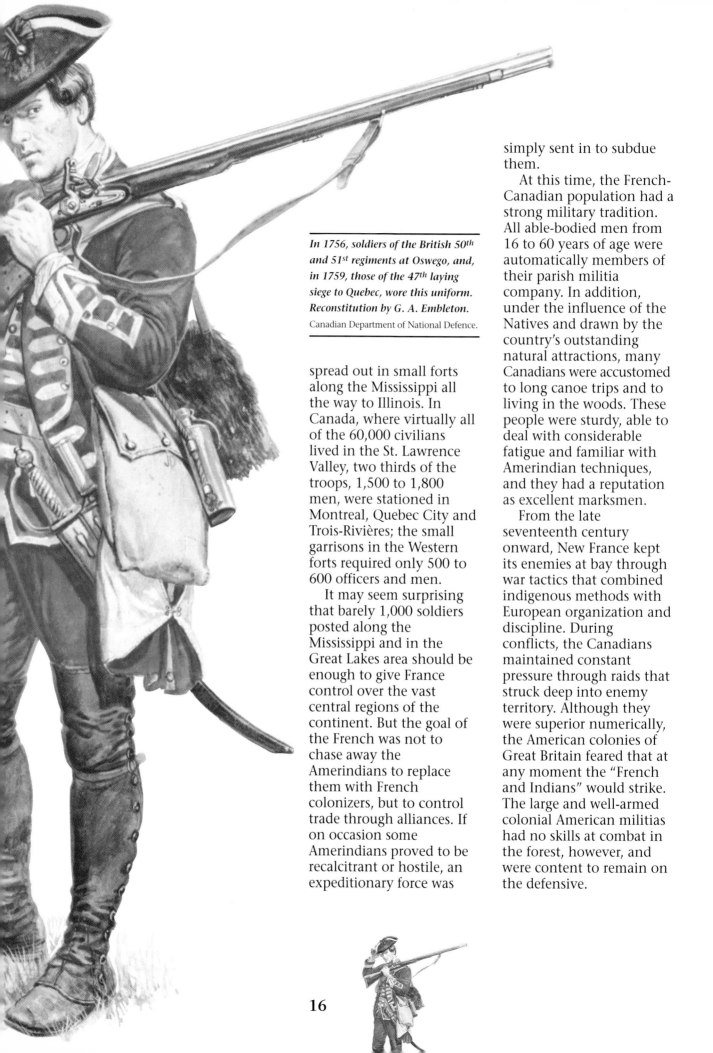

spread out in small forts along the Mississippi all the way to Illinois. In Canada, where virtually all of the 60,000 civilians lived in the St. Lawrence Valley, two thirds of the troops, 1,500 to 1,800 men, were stationed in Montreal, Quebec City and Trois-Rivières; the small garrisons in the Western forts required only 500 to 600 officers and men.

It may seem surprising that barely 1,000 soldiers posted along the Mississippi and in the Great Lakes area should be enough to give France control over the vast central regions of the continent. But the goal of the French was not to chase away the Amerindians to replace them with French colonizers, but to control trade through alliances. If on occasion some Amerindians proved to be recalcitrant or hostile, an expeditionary force was simply sent in to subdue them.

At this time, the French-Canadian population had a strong military tradition. All able-bodied men from 16 to 60 years of age were automatically members of their parish militia company. In addition, under the influence of the Natives and drawn by the country's outstanding natural attractions, many Canadians were accustomed to long canoe trips and to living in the woods. These people were sturdy, able to deal with considerable fatigue and familiar with Amerindian techniques, and they had a reputation as excellent marksmen.

From the late seventeenth century onward, New France kept its enemies at bay through war tactics that combined indigenous methods with European organization and discipline. During conflicts, the Canadians maintained constant pressure through raids that struck deep into enemy territory. Although they were superior numerically, the American colonies of Great Britain feared that at any moment the "French and Indians" would strike. The large and well-armed colonial American militias had no skills at combat in the forest, however, and were content to remain on the defensive.

Until the 1740s, the British colonies had few regular soldiers. The largest contingent, the 40th, was in Nova Scotia. Following the founding of Halifax in 1749, the city garrison grew by two additional regiments, the 45th and 47th, to a total of approximately 1,500 officers and men. The Thirteen Colonies of New England had barely 550 soldiers in British colonial independent companies posted to New York and South Carolina. Towards 1754, with the addition of a few artillery detachments and some 100 Rangers from Nova Scotia, there were about 2,300 men and officers of all ranks, representing too few professional soldiers given that their role was to defend a coastline that stretched from Nova Scotia all the way to Florida. With the exception of the Rangers, these troops also knew nothing about the art of bush-fighting.

Reinforcements from Europe

That, then, was the status of the forces when the Jumonville incident occurred in 1754 followed by the capture of Fort Necessity. The assassination of a Canadian officer on a parliamentary mission caused considerable indignation in France, and Great Britain was outraged to learn that French soldiers were chasing American subjects from the Ohio Valley. In the British colonies, exasperation reached a peak. When Virginia raised its own small army, North Carolina, New York, Connecticut and Massachusetts were preparing to follow its lead. American politicians unanimously demanded

Grenadier of the French Guyenne regiment (left) and a corporal from the Béarn regiment (right), c. 1756. Reconstitution by Eugène Lelièpvre. Parks Canada.

that many regular troops from the British army be sent to America to deal once and for all with the problem of New France.

Giving in to these pressures, the British government towards the end of 1754 authorized the funds for two regiments, the 50th and the 51st, each of which consisted of 1,000 men recruited in the North American colonies. The government also ordered that two regiments of 700 men each, the 44th and the 48th, both under the command of General

17

Edward Braddock, be sent to Virginia. These regiments, with field artillery, left Ireland in January 1755 and reached their destination in mid-March. The British strategy was to weaken New France by taking its outposts. With the help of the colonial troops, Braddock and his soldiers were to chase the French from the Ohio Valley. At the same time, the English troops stationed in Nova Scotia were to take the isthmus of Chignectou, with still others attacking Fort Saint-Frédéric on Lake Champlain and, if possible, Fort Niagara on Lake Ontario.

In France, reaction to the arrival of the British troops in Virginia was swift. To reinforce his North American garrisons, Louis XV decided in February 1755 to immediately send battalions detached from the metropolitan "army troops," because there was not enough time to recruit new troops in the colonies. The 2nd battalions of the La Reine, Languedoc, Guyenne, Béarn, Bourgogne and Artois regiments were chosen for this purpose, representing a total of 3,336 officers and men. The Bourgogne and Artois battalions were assigned the task of reinforcing the garrison at the fortress of Louisbourg, while the other four, under the command of General Jean-Armand Dieskau, were to serve in Canada. At the beginning of May, the six battalions left Brest for New France.

It's War!

When it learned that France was sending armed forces to America, the English government immediately ordered the Royal Navy to intercept any French ships with troops on board. Given that war had not yet been declared, this was a virulent response. On June 8, off the coast of Newfoundland, Admiral Edward Boscawen's squadron sighted three French ships separated from their own squadron by fog: these were the *Alcide*, the *Lys* and the *Dauphin royal*. With the English and French ships within hailing distance, the commander of the *Alcide* asked, "Are we at peace or at war?" "We can't hear," answered the HMS *Dunkirk*, the nearest of the English ships, before adding, "Peace, Peace!"[3] But after moving to within 100 metres of the *Alcide*, the *Dunkirk* opened fire. Some 80 French sailors were cut down and the ship lost its rudder. The broadside was a complete surprise. The French gunners did what they could to respond to the English fire, but the battle was already lost. The *Alcide* and the *Lys* had to lower their flags. Only the

Dauphin royal was able to escape and reach Louisbourg. Following this bloody incident, war was declared between France and England, even though hostilities would not be officially declared until a year later.

The Anglo-Americans Attack

The British decided to immediately take the offensive on land as well, and to attack the forts defending the isthmus of Chignectou. On June 3, 1755, a powerful contingent of Anglo-American troops, under the command of Lieutenant-Colonel Robert Monkton of the regular army, disembarked only a few kilometres from Fort Beauséjour. To face these 2,000 attackers, Commander Louis Du Pont Duchambon de Vergor had only 150 soldiers from the Compagnies franches de la Marine and a dozen canonniers-bombardiers. The fort was soon under siege, and the shelling lasted several days, as would any siege in Europe. On June 16, a large English bomb went through the roof of a casemate that was supposed to be bombproof and killed many of its occupants. Vergor laid down his weapons. The following day, Fort Gaspareau fell before it was even attacked. This defeat deprived the French of an

important foothold in Acadia, at the very doorstep of Nova Scotia, without, however, truly threatening the security of Canada.

Meanwhile, the British directed their main offensive against the Ohio Valley. The stakes for New France were considerable, because Ohio linked Louisiana to the Great Lakes and to Canada. A

The Battle of Monongahela, July 9, 1755. Reconstitution by E. W. Deming.
State Historical Society of Wisconsin, Madison.

and even a few seamen. The objective was Fort Duquesne, some 200 kilometres away over forests and swamps. The troops were to build a road along the way and erect bridges to transport equipment, for Braddock was conducting his campaign in the European fashion. The army advanced with considerable difficulty,

defeat could sound the death knell for the French alliances with the many Amerindian nations in the area. In May 1755, General Braddock's troops were mustered west of Virginia: this consisted of an army of 2,200 men, including the 44th and 48th regiments, a number of regular independent companies, the Virginia Regiment under the command of George Washington, militiamen, only a few kilometres a day, and had to leave heavy siege artillery behind, even though Braddock was hoping to be able to use it to shell Fort Duquesne. Despite its slow progress, the Anglo-

American army appeared to be unstoppable. In early July, it finally reached the Monongahela River, where the terrain was easier to cross, and it was just over 20 kilometres from Fort Duquesne. Finding no trace of the French, several of the British officers expected to hear a loud noise in the distance, that of the fort being blown up by the French before they evacuated the Ohio Valley.

General Braddock's Disaster

On July 9, Braddock's army advanced in ranks, with drums beating, when the forward party met the enemy and began to fire into the woods, where a corps of 105 officers and men of the Compagnies franches de la Marine, along with 146 Canadian militiamen and more than 600 Amerindians, waited in ambush. The troop was under the command of Liénard de Beaujeu until he was killed by the first English salvos, to be immediately replaced by Captain Jean-Daniel Dumas. Confusion soon reigned within the ranks of the Anglo-American army, decimated by the deadly fire of an adversary well hidden in the forest, from whence frightening Amerindian war cries were emanating; several officers were killed attempting to rally their men and then General Braddock himself finally fell, mortally wounded. The confusion was followed by panic and then flight. After four hours of combat, the routed Anglo-American army abandoned all its field artillery, baggage and approximately 25,000 pounds in silver on the battlefield. The English toll was 977 men, some 500 of whom were killed. It was a genuine disaster for the British forces. The French losses were only 23 dead – three officers, two men, three militiamen and 15 Amerindians – and 16 wounded, 12 of whom were Amerindians.

From the standpoint of the Canadian officers of the French colonial troops, the victory was undeniable proof that their tactics could win not only over the New England militiamen, but also over a strong contingent of regular troops from Europe. For the first time, a modest corps of skilfully camouflaged light infantry deploying quickly had shown that it could foil a powerful army by subjecting it to decisive losses with only muskets for weapons. Unfortunately for New France, the metropolitan officers did not learn from the tactical lesson they were given by the colonial officers in Canada.

General Dieskau's Defeat

Meanwhile, Baron de Dieskau arrived in New France with his troops. Except for the 350 men who were captured from the *Lys*, all the French battalions had finally reached their destination. General Dieskau was responsible for tactical decisions, but for matters of strategy he was required to take orders from Governor General Pierre de Rigaud de Vaudreuil. The latter's primary objective was to attack Fort Oswego (which the French called "Chouaguen") on the south shore of Lake Ontario. However, he cancelled this expedition when he learned that a 3,000-strong army of American militiamen was gathering south of Lake Champlain under the command of Colonel William Johnson to take Fort Saint-Frédéric. If this army made its way to the top of Lake Champlain and then the Richelieu, Montreal would indeed be at its mercy.

The La Reine and Languedoc battalions, as well as the Marine troops, militiamen and Amerindians, therefore assembled at Fort Saint-Frédéric under the command of Dieskau. With 1,500 men, the general decided to avoid the enemy army assembled at Lake George and to attack

Fort Edward further to the south to cut off its avenue of retreat. This daring plan failed. Dieskau had to abandon his plans near Fort Edward because the Mohawks who were allied to the French refused to join the battle. They said that they were ready to defend Canada, but not to attack the English on their own territory. The fact was that they did not want to fight their Mohawk brothers who were English allies. Dieskau thus decided to go northward once

again and to attack the camp where Johnson was with part of his army.

Johnson found himself in a difficult position, for Dieskau's movement had cut off his communications with Albany. More serious still, his army consisted solely of New England militiamen who had enlisted for the campaign. Johnson sent 1,000 men to

Camp of the British 43rd Regiment during the siege of Fort Beauséjour in 1755. Reconstitution by Lewis Parker.
Parks Canada.

meet Dieskau, who was waiting to ambush them. However, the Mohawks allied to the French warned those in the enemy camp of the ambush. The American militiamen got off with light losses and took refuge in the barricaded camp containing the rest of Johnson's troops on the current site of Lake George in New York State.

Although he had fewer men, Dieskau refused to listen to the warnings of the Canadians and the Amerindians, and decided to attack the fortified camp

and its artillery with a general assault in closed ranks, in the purest European style. Deeming this form of combat ridiculous, the Canadian militiamen threw themselves prone onto the ground and looked for some kind of shelter from which to return enemy fire. The French soldiers, who had got to within 50 metres of the barricades and point-blank range, hesitated to advance. Dieskau was then seriously wounded as he urged his men on. The French withdrew soon afterwards, since enemy reinforcements were arriving from the south. Dieskau, abandoned on the field of battle, was captured by Johnson's militiamen.

This first battle by the French metropolitan forces thus turned into a fiasco. In Canada, it was an unprecedented event: a general captured and troops beaten with heavy losses by militiamen from New England! Dieskau blamed his defeat on the fact that the Canadians had not marched in ranks.

The Acadian Tragedy

The year 1755, which had more than its share of military events, was also the year of a great tragedy: the deportation of the Acadians from Nova Scotia. In 1713, under the Treaty of Utrecht, France had ceded Acadia to England,

and it had become a British colony under the name of Nova Scotia. A few Acadians had afterwards taken up arms against the British, but most had remained neutral. Nonetheless, the presence of a prosperous, Catholic and French-speaking population within an English colony elicited considerable jealousy and rancour, particularly given that the approximately 9,000 Acadians occupied the best land. In the name of "security," it was finally deemed opportune to replace them with loyal subjects. In July 1755, therefore, Charles Lawrence, Governor of Nova Scotia, decreed that the people of Acadia be deported. During the operation, which today we would call "ethnic cleansing," the armed forces played a major role.

Responsibility for rounding up the Acadians was assigned to some of the British regular troops and to the Massachusetts regiments of lieutenant-colonels John Winslow and George Scott. The scenario ordered by Winslow at Grand Pré has entered the annals of history. All men were asked to go to the church for the reading of an important decree. As they listened, horrified, to the deportation order being read by Winslow and his officers, troops surrounded the church. Then soldiers went to

collect the women and children at their farms, which were then burnt. The scene was repeated throughout Acadia during the entire summer. Soon thousands of civilians of both sexes and all ages were rounded up in what we would today call "concentration camps" to wait for the ships that would take them away. After several weeks, the ships finally appeared, and on October 8 embarkation began. The military tried, to a degree, not to separate families, but this was not always possible and there were heart-rending scenes with wailing women, held back by soldiers on the shore, watching their husbands and sons sail into the unknown.

Some 2,000 Acadians were able to escape to Canada, while the others were deported to the English colonies. But this cruel policy of dispossession and deportation did not yield the desired results. The soldiers of Massachusetts – perhaps through remorse – refused to take the prosperous lands offered to them, and only a minority of the new colonists, of British allegiance, settled in Acadia. Moreover, the alleged security problem used to justify the operation was not solved. Many Acadians who took refuge in the forest began, with the help of the

Deportation of the Acadians from Île Saint-Jean (present-day Prince Edward Island) in 1758; the Acadians of Nova Scotia had undergone similar heart-rending scenes three years earlier. Reconstitution by Lewis Parker.
Parks Canada.

Amerindians, to use guerilla tactics until the end of the war, which required the British to maintain garrisons in western Nova Scotia. This cleansing operation was no accident of British policy: terrible scenes of deportation were reported again in 1758 at Île Royale (Cape Breton Island) and Île Saint-Jean (Prince Edward Island).

At the beginning of 1756, the military situation in North America was virtually unchanged from the year before. The British continued to pursue the objectives that they failed to meet the previous year: to occupy the Ohio Valley and to take Fort Saint-Frédéric on Lake Champlain and Fort Niagara on Lake Ontario. It was with this in mind that the colonies of

New England mobilized several thousand militiamen and asked for extra troops from England, which sent the 35th and 42nd regiments and created the 60th. With four battalions instead of only one, as most regiments had, the 60th consisted in part of American recruits, hence the name "Royal American." General Braddock's defeat

nevertheless caused the British staff serious doubts about what methods to employ to weaken New France.

The French recovered very quickly from the loss of General Dieskau. Governor General Vaudreuil knew that he had to earn the esteem of the Amerindian allies for the French armies by doing something dramatic, and he ordered a raid against Fort Bull, near Oswego. On March 27, 1756, Fort Bull was attacked and destroyed by a group of soldiers, militiamen and Amerindians under the command of Lieutenant Gaspard-Joseph Chaussegros de Léry, who at the same time found and drove away an American contingent that had come to the rescue of the fort. The traditional tactic of the Canadians once again proved its worth, and the Amerindians were reassured.

General Montcalm Takes Oswego

In Quebec, the great event of the year was the arrival in May of the

Soldier of the French La Sarre regiment in 1757.
© Photo: Musée de l'Armée, Paris.

second battalion of the La Sarre and Royal-Roussillon regiments, as well as the battalion of General Louis-Joseph de Montcalm replacing that of Baron de Dieskau. The Marquis de Montcalm, a Provençal nobleman, was a veteran of many campaigns since 1733. Vigorous and energetic, he was nevertheless quick-tempered and irascible, a characteristic that would compromise relations among senior officers and cause tensions among the staff.

Montcalm's first action was to prepare an attack against Oswego in accordance with the wishes of Governor General Vaudreuil. The area, sheltering a garrison of 1,800 men from the 50th and 51st regiments and the New Jersey regiment, one of the best corps thus far

raised by an American colony, was well defended by three forts that were generously provided for in terms of artillery. Montcalm, who arrived in Oswego on August 10 leading 3,000 men equipped with siege artillery, had Fort Ontario bombarded. It was evacuated quickly and the garrison took refuge at forts George and Oswego. These in turn were intensively bombarded by the French artillery. On the morning of August 14, the British commander, Colonel James Mercer, was decapitated by a cannonball, and one hour later the garrison surrendered. The French took 93 cannons and mortars and five regimental flags. This fine victory demonstrated that a European-style siege, with considerable logistics support, could take fortified locations well into the interior of the country.

Tensions Among the French Staff

In the fall of 1756, Montcalm, in a secret letter, complained to the Minister of War that Governor General Vaudreuil and his colonial officers knew nothing about warfare. Vaudreuil, for his part, responded to the Minister of the Navy that the French metropolitan officers showed contempt for the Canadians and that they

Worker, gunner and sapper of the French Royal-Artillerie regiment in 1757.
© Photo: Musée de l'Armée, Paris.

had a cavalier way of treating colonial officers. This animosity quickly spread, and soon two camps had emerged within the staff: the French officers around Montcalm, and the Canadian officers led by Vaudreuil.

Intendant François Bigot's dishonest management of Canadian finances did nothing but accentuate the tensions. Some goods went missing, and there was galloping inflation. The intendant and his acolytes authorized endless spending, some of the money lining the pockets of the Canadian officers responsible for supplying the troops. While speculation allowed

a few to a amass fortunes, others saw their salaries dwindle to almost nothing. Although several could rely on family connections and income from their seigneuries to counteract the shortfall, this was not the case for the officers in the regiments that had come from France, who found themselves considerably impoverished by the effects of inflation. Rumours that some Canadian officers were stealing with impunity only increased the bitterness. Following the lead of their general, the French showed profound contempt for their Canadian colleagues, considering them to be not true military men and to fight "like savages." The Canadian officers restricted their relations with them. This attitude hit home, because one of the metropolitan officers noted that he felt he was perceived to be an enemy in Canada.

The non-commissioned officers and soldiers, both colonial and French, were better protected against inflation, because they were accommodated, fed and clothed at the expense of the King. As the war continued and food became scarcer, beef was replaced by horsemeat and rations were cut.

In spite of the tensions that kept them apart, all the officers agreed on one point: the need for

reinforcements to defend New France. In Canada itself, Vaudreuil reorganized the troops to increase the number of men available to Montcalm. In May the artillery added a company of workers recruited from among the Canadians. In July a battalion of 500 men from the Compagnies franches de la Marine was

A soldier from the French Berry regiment in 1757.
© Photo: Musée de l'Armée, Paris.

established to support the metropolitan regiments. It was soon called the "Régiment de la Marine."[4] Nevertheless, it was felt that additional troops should be brought in from France. During the summer, the 2nd and 3rd battalions of the Régiment de Berry disembarked at Quebec City, and there were also several hundred recruits,[5] but the numbers were still inadequate. Seven "brigades" of

Canadian militiamen were therefore formed, with 150 men in each, 16 regular soldiers of the Compagnies franches de la Marine serving as their instructors.

The British Invasion Strategy

In reality, it was in England, and not in France or Quebec, that the fate of New France would be decided. In December 1756 the new government of William Pitt considerably changed the manner in which the war was being waged. The British Prime Minister was a talented, energetic and visionary man who was convinced that the wealth and glory of his country lay not in Europe but overseas. He therefore convinced King George II to launch a major war effort in North America, where, contrary to any logic, a few tens of thousands of French colonists and soldiers kept more than a million English inhabitants huddled along the Atlantic coast. Only one solution seemed possible to deal with New France: large-scale invasion.

This was of course not the first attempt at an invasion of Canada, but this time a strategy was formulated, considerable resources were made available and resolve was greatly strengthened. The commanding officer of the Anglo-American forces,

Soldier of the New York Provincial Regiment in 1757; the colour of the uniform was "drab." Reconstitution by Herbert Knötel.

Anne S. K. Brown Military Collection, Brown University, Providence.

John Campbell, Earl of Loudoun, was an excellent officer who had been the King's aide-de-camp. A clever diplomat, he began by instilling harmony in the often turbulent relations between British and American officers, because in New England, as

in New France, the British officers tended to show contempt for their colonial counterparts. Unlike Montcalm, Loudoun understood that such an attitude could only compromise success. He also recognized the value of the tactics used by the Canadians, and, to ensure that the British army would be able to appropriate them, was in favour of raising a light infantry corps and rangers.

Loudoun, a talented strategist, formulated an impressive plan to invade New France, which was approved by the new government of William Pitt. This involved first taking Quebec City, the gateway of the colony to Europe, followed by Montreal, the main military base in New France and key to the interior of the continent.

The first objective was to be met from the St. Lawrence River, by calling upon the formidable Royal Navy. But first it would be necessary to take the fortress of Louisbourg. The British could not allow such a large naval base to remain available to the French navy. This preliminary operation required mustering, in Halifax, an army of regular troops to embark on a powerful fleet. The plan was to lay siege first to Louisbourg, then to Quebec.

Soldier of a provincial Massachusetts regiment, between 1756 and 1763. Reconstitution by Herbert Knötel.

Anne S. K. Brown Military Collection, Brown University, Providence.

The second objective, to take Montreal, required the creation of two armies with a core of regular British troops supported by provincial American troops. The former, the larger of the two, would assemble at Albany, sail up Lake Champlain and then down the Richelieu River. The second would gather in Virginia and Pennsylvania and then move up the Ohio River, Lake Erie and Lake Ontario on their way to the St. Lawrence. The final phase of the operation would be set in motion only after the fall of Quebec, so that the three Anglo-American armies would join at Montreal. The plan could not be executed quickly.

Though the strategy was good and the forces mobilized considerable, 1757 was not an auspicious year for the Anglo-American forces.

The French Take Fort William Henry

The French did not remain idle. As soon as the 1756 campaign was over, Governor General Vaudreuil set himself the objective of taking Fort William Henry (Fort George, to the French), on Lake George. This would prevent an attack against forts Carillon (Ticonderoga for the English) and Saint-Frédéric.

In August 1757, Montcalm left Montreal to lay siege to Fort William Henry with a powerful corps of 6,000 soldiers and militiamen accompanied by 1,600 Amerindians, to place the British on the defensive. On August 6, after only three days of shelling, Lieutenant-Colonel George Monro, commander of the fort, surrendered. Montcalm granted the honours of war to the garrison of 2,500 men, allowing them to withdraw, with flags, guns and baggage, if they promised not to fight for 18 months. But this arrangement failed to give due regard to their Amerindian allies. Frustrated by their inability to obtain any booty or capture prisoners, they

Soldier of the Provincial New Jersey Regiment, between 1756 and 1763. Reconstitution by Herbert Knötel.

Anne S. K. Brown Military Collection, Brown University, Providence.

attacked the Anglo-American soldiers as they withdrew, killing several and taking approximately 600 captive. The French officers, including Montcalm, intervened and were able to free about 400 men. Vaudreuil was later to purchase a large number of them. But some were killed, others tortured, and a few of those killed even eaten. Outraged, the British staff refused to recognize the conditions of surrender and decided to no longer grant the honours of war to French troops. The surrender of Fort William Henry was nevertheless a harsh blow to the British, and it prevented them from effecting any operations south of

Montreal for the remainder of the year.

In Halifax, preparations for the siege of Louisbourg were already compromised by poor weather when Loudoun learned early in August that a French fleet had recently arrived there. Because he was no longer assured of naval superiority, and because he felt that it was too late in the year, he decided to cancel the whole operation. In England, public opinion showed impatience and Loudoun became the scapegoat for everything that went wrong during the year. Pitt recalled him to England for reasons more political than military.

At the end of 1757 the boundaries of New France remained unchanged. France's military position had declined considerably in Europe, however, requiring mobilization of its war effort on that side of the Atlantic, while England concentrated most of its efforts in North America.

Thus the year 1758 saw the British intensify their campaign preparations. Major General James Abercromby succeeded Loudoun as commander-in-chief of the Anglo-American troops, but Loudoun's strategy for the conquest of New France was retained. Louisbourg was to be attacked by General Jeffery Amherst and the Ohio Valley by General John Forbes, while Abercromby was to eliminate the French forts on Lake Champlain. The 15th, 28th, 58th and 62nd line infantry regiments joined the army already in place. In addition, a light infantry regiment, the 80th, was raised, bringing the regular British army in North America to approximately 23,000 men. France sent the 2nd battalions of the Cambis and Volontaires-Étrangers regiments to Louisbourg, but there was no support for Montcalm. In total, there were only some 7,000 French soldiers to defend Canada and Île Royale.

The British Lay Siege to Louisbourg

On June 2 an impressive British fleet of more than 150 vessels, transporting 27,000 men, 13,000 of whom were professional soldiers, arrived off the coast of Louisbourg. In spite of the French reinforcements, the forces of Governor Augustin de Boschenry de Drucour amounted to only a quarter those of the attackers, even taking seamen and militiamen into account. The French garrison knew that it had lost but was determined to hold on to the very end. The British disembarked on June 8, and quickly dug trenches and surrounded the fortress with their artillery, beginning on June 19 to methodically shell the city. The defenders resolutely returned fire. The wife of the governor herself willingly went up onto the ramparts every day to fire three cannon shots, an act that greatly encouraged the garrison and earned her the admiration of the enemy.[6]

After five weeks of intensive shelling the fortifications were breached in many places, and the artillery was virtually reduced to silence, with the few French warships anchored in the port sunk or burned; the city was reduced to ruins, the civilian population hiding in shelters. On July 26 Governor Drucour inquired about the conditions for surrender. The British refused to grant the honours of war to the French troops, in spite of the bravery they had shown. The French were therefore forced to turn over their arms and their flags. Outraged, most of the officers wanted to continue the battle. The administrative commissioner, Jacques Prévost de La Croix, argued in favour of safety for the civilians, holding that a general assault could degenerate into theft, murder and rape. These arguments were

Soldier of the Volontaires-Étrangers regiment, a German corps serving France in 1758, at Louisbourg. Reconstitution by Eugène Lelièpvre.
Canadian Department of National Defence.

convincing and the surrender was signed that very day.

When the news was announced, the soldiers in the Régiment de Cambis broke their muskets and burned their flags so that they would not have to surrender them, but the other corps met the terms of surrender.[7] The garrison was sent to Europe and the entire French population of Île Royale and Île Saint-Jean were deported in the autumn. The fall of the "sentinel of the Gulf of St. Lawrence" opened the way to the capital of New France. But the long and valiant defence by the garrison of Louisbourg required that the British delay their siege of Quebec until the following year.

French Victory at Ticonderoga

As Amherst was laying siege to Louisbourg, General Abercromby was gathering his troops to the south of Lake Champlain. This was the largest army ever in North America – approximately 15,000 men, with no fewer than 6,000 regular British infantrymen. In July the army boarded some 1,500 barges and launches and went up Lake George close to Fort Carillon.

As for the French, Montcalm decided to post his eight French battalions on a hill near Fort Carillon, in the shelter of a long barricade of tree trunks. The colonial troops, the militiamen and the allied Amerindians were spread throughout the adjacent woods. Abercromby could, of course, have circumvented this position and placed his artillery on the neighbouring hills, but this would have taken several weeks and what the Anglo-Americans wanted was a clear and rapid victory. Informed by the engineers that the French barricades could be taken in an assault, Abercromby decided on a general frontal attack set for July 8. The 3,000 French soldiers had dug in and placed their regimental flags on the barricades and remained at the ready.

At noon, they could see three columns of several thousand men slowly coming up the hillside towards them, but they opened fire only when the British were close to their position: a first terrible salvo decimated the enemy ranks. The British and American troops launched one assault after another, but were unable to make any headway in spite of their best efforts. At the end of the day some 2,000 dead and wounded covered the hillside, and the French continued to resist in spite of 527 dead and wounded.

Officer of the 2nd Provincial Connecticut Regiment, c. 1759. Reconstitution by Herbert Knötel.
Anne S. K. Brown Military Collection, Brown University, Providence.

Abercromby eventually had to beat a retreat, the British attack proving to be a disaster.

The French camp was ecstatic over the unexpected victory. Montcalm sent news of his triumph to France, crediting the French metropolitan officers and soldiers for the success of the operation. There was near revolt among the colonial troops "when they learned that Monsieur de Montcalm, instead of boasting of their efforts, attributed their success to the land troops,"[8] reported Governor General Vaudreuil. Participation by the colonial troops and the Canadian militiamen in the battle were indeed relatively modest, but comments like these could only poison the already tense relations between the colonials and the troops from the motherland. The fact remained, however, that the British invasion of Canada from the south had been repulsed for the moment!

The Invasion of the Ohio Valley

Meanwhile, a third Anglo-American army, under the command of General John Forbes, was slowly approaching Fort Duquesne in the Ohio Valley. Forbes had 400 men from the 60th Regiment, 1,400 men from the 77th Scottish Highlanders

Soldier of the Provincial Virginia Regiment, between 1755 and 1763. Reconstitution by Herbert Knötel.
Anne S. K. Brown Military Collection, Brown University, Providence.

Regiment and approximately 5,000 American militiamen. To avoid suffering the fate that Braddock had met three years earlier, Forbes had a new supply route built, with fortifications along the way as well as supply depots. His army advanced at a snail's pace, in small stages. At the end of August the Anglo-American advance guard reached Loyalhanna, where it built Fort Ligonier as well as a large fortified camp

only 70 kilometres from Fort Duquesne.

Persuaded that the bulk of the Anglo-American army would use the old Braddock route, the French commander in the Ohio, François-Marie Le Marchand de Lignery, was initially troubled by Forbes' deliberate pace. But when he discovered that Forbes had built a new route Lignery immediately adopted harassment tactics to further slow his progress. Soon Anglo-American soldiers who strayed from their camps fell at the hands of the allied Amerindians, who were constantly on the lookout at the edge of the forest. To boost the morale of the soldiers, who were losing their courage in the face of the terror, a raid was organized on Fort Duquesne. On September 14 Major James Grant, with a party from his 77th Highlanders Regiment and a group of American militiamen, some 800 men in all, reached the environs of the fort and decided to wait for nightfall to attack. But Lignery and his second in command, Captain Aubry, were not fooled. Grant and his men were quickly surrounded by approximately 500 soldiers from the Compagnies franches de la Marine, Canadian militiamen and Amerindians "letting out

cries like Savages." The battle was described as "heated and tenacious."[9] The Scots were virtually wiped out, with 300 men dead in the field and 100 prisoners, including Major Grant himself, not to mention the numbers who took flight. The French had only 16 dead and wounded.

On October 12, on the strength of this victory, Captain Aubry, leading 450 soldiers and militiamen and 100 Amerindians, organized a raid on Fort Ligonier. The British and Americans, who had to take refuge in the fort, were powerless to stop them, and for two days watched their camp being destroyed and pillaged. One month later, another raid by some 30 Canadian militiamen and approximately 140 Amerindians caused so much confusion that the Anglo-American regiments fought one another, each side believing the other to be the enemy!

These French victories could not, however, offset their serious weaknesses. Forbes, becoming increasingly ill – he was now being carried on a stretcher – understood this well. His troops were certainly unable to carry out raids, but with their numbers and the strength of their artillery they would be able to take Fort Duquesne. As the Amerindians, who could

sense a change in the wind, began to abandon him in growing numbers, Lignery was equally aware of this. On November 26, when Forbes' army was only a few kilometres away, he sent his garrison to the small forts of Machault and Massiac and blew up Fort Duquesne. The Anglo-Americans built another fort on that very site, called Fort Pitt or Pittsburgh, which was to become a major city in Pennsylvania.

The taking of Fort Frontenac (present-day Kingston, Ontario) by Lieutenant-Colonel John Bradstreet amounted to another French defeat. His 3,000 men, nearly all militiamen from the American colonies, crossed Lake Ontario in boats and assaulted the fort. The 110 men in the garrison held for three days before surrendering on August 28. Bradstreet withdrew after burning and demolishing the fort. In the short term, the strategic consequences of the destruction of Fort Frontenac were not serious, but for the first time French communications with Niagara, Detroit and the Ohio forts were seriously threatened.

The year 1758 thus ended with significant gains by the British: in

Soldier of the Pennsylvania Provincial Regiment, c. 1758. Reconstitution by Herbert Knötel.
Anne S. K. Brown Military Collection, Brown University, Providence.

spite of the Carillon French victory, they had taken part of the Ohio Valley and, most importantly, the fortress of Louisbourg, thus opening the way to Quebec. Vaudreuil and Montcalm were keenly aware of this, and in spite of their differences agreed to beg the French authorities to send a large number of reinforcements, the fate of New France more than ever in the balance. To plead the cause of the colonies, they sent Louis-Antoine de Bougainville to Versailles.

Soldier of the British 58th Regiment, between 1757 and 1762.
Reconstitution by G. A. Embleton.
Parks Canada.

This young and brilliant staff officer of Montcalm's, destined to become one of the great explorers of the Pacific, did everything in his power. But prospects for the French armies and fleets in Europe were dim indeed. The Minister of the Navy, Berryer, told him curtly, "When the house is on fire, you don't worry about the stables."[10]

A Change in Tactics

From the beginning of the war the Anglo-American armies continued to grow. In 1755, there were approximately 11,000 British soldiers and American militiamen, a number that was to exceed 44,000 in 1758, not to mention the thousands of sailors and allied Amerindians who took part in the war effort. The total number of men mobilized – between 60,000 and 70,000 – represented almost the whole population of New France. This numerical superiority enabled the British to use European strategies, and guerilla tactics could no longer hold off such numerous armies indefinitely.

However, unlike the officers from France in Canada, several members of the British staff understood the importance of such tactics, and even thought, quite rightly, that they could be integrated usefully with classic European strategy. In 1756 General Loudoun recruited American Rangers to serve as pathfinders for the regular army. In 1758 a whole regiment of regular light infantry, the 80th, was raised by Lieutenant-Colonel Thomas Gage. The men in this regiment were armed with light muskets. They wore caps rather than the traditional tricorne, which tended to get caught in tree branches, and short-skirted coats that were less restrictive. Most striking of all was the colour of their uniform, dark brown, with no lace, with dark brown lining and black buttons[11] for better camouflage, instead of the sacrosanct red coats faced with bright colours, multicoloured lace and buttons that shone in the sun. These soldiers were good pathfinders, trained to conceal themselves and to move quickly. In short, they were experienced in what were called "light" infantry tactics as opposed to the rigid methods and manoeuvres in ranks used by the line infantry.

All these innovations introduced in the British army were based on tactics

Light infantry soldier of the 48th Regiment in 1759-60.
Reconstitution by G. A. Embleton.
Parks Canada.

that had been used since the end of the seventeenth century by Canadians. Soon one out of the 10 companies in each British line infantry regiment in North America was converted to a "light company," whose men wore red uniforms cut short, with no lace, and felt caps made from old tricorne hats. The British light infantry corps and the Rangers could never quite match the French and Amerindians in this type of combat, but it was definite progress, and these troops won many battles. The changes did not go unnoticed among the Amerindians – the true masters of the forest – who decided as a result that the Anglo-Americans were "beginning to learn the art of war."[12]

General Mobilization in Canada

Louisbourg defeated, Fort Frontenac destroyed, Fort Duquesne replaced by Fort Pittsburgh... At the beginning of 1759 Vaudreuil and Montcalm were convinced of an imminent massive attack on all fronts that would converge simultaneously on Quebec and Montreal. And all that remained to them were 4,600 professional soldiers, in both French regiments and colonial troops, and they could not count on any reinforcements. In 1755,

The Cavalry Corps, the first mounted unit formed in Canada; it existed from May 1759 to September 1760. Reconstitution by Eugène Lelièpvre.
Canadian Department of National Defence.

the Compagnies franches de la Marine had been increased to 40 companies with an official total of 2,600 soldiers; at the beginning of 1759 this number had decreased by more than half. The only source of recruits was Canadian militiamen. In May 1759 approximately 600 of these were conscripted and placed in the battalions. Hundreds of others were assigned to Lake Champlain and the West. However, the authorities did not dare to include significant numbers of militiamen

among the troops. For two years in a row Canada had suffered a serious shortage of wheat and meat, and to prevent famine the Canadians had to devote themselves to sowing and harvesting. These men were nevertheless ready to join the army at any time in the event of an emergency.

In May 1759, with a view to a campaign to be conducted "in the European manner," a new type of corps was established in Quebec: the Corps de cavalerie, which consisted of 200 Canadian volunteers and five French officers. These cavalrymen wore a blue uniform with a red collar and cuffs. They performed excellent work, pursuing enemy patrols or acting as scouts or dispatch riders. It was the first

33

mounted corps established in Canada and is therefore considered the ancestor of the many cavalry units of the Canadian Armed Forces.

The Siege of Quebec

In the spring of 1759 three battalions of the La Reine and Berry regiments were sent to Carillon, while 150 soldiers from various regiments and 800 militiamen went to reinforce Fort Niagara. The French staff, although they hoped they were wrong, expected that Quebec would be the main target of the British. These sombre predictions were confirmed by mid-June. Every day, messengers were arriving from the capital with news of the presence in the Gulf of St. Lawrence of many sailing ships flying the British flag. The troops and militia were called to Quebec, where they combined their efforts to quickly prepare for the defence of the city. At the end of the month Montcalm had approximately 15,600 men, but only 3,000 or so of these were regular soldiers.

At the end of June a British fleet of more than 200 ships manned by some 13,000 sailors arrived within sight of Quebec. Approximately 50 of these were Royal Navy warships, including that of Vice-Admiral Charles Saunders,

Colour-officer of the British 15th Regiment between 1757 and 1767. Reconstitution by G. A. Embleton. Parks Canada.

the powerful HMS *Neptune*, with 90 cannon. The other ships transported the 15th, 28th, 35th, 43rd, 47th, 48th and 58th regiments, two battalions of the 60th, the 78th Highlanders, three artillery companies, three companies of Louisbourg Grenadiers[13] and six companies of Rangers – in other words, about 8,500 soldiers from the regular army. A marine infantry battalion of 600 men, in addition to marines on the various warships, were held in reserve. The British forces totalled some 23,000 sailors and soldiers.

This army was commanded by a 32-year-old officer who had already distinguished himself at the siege of Louisbourg, General James Wolfe. His appointment as leader of

the expedition caused jealousy among the staff officers, but the young general had the support of King George II. Although he was of fragile health, Wolfe was an excellent officer and a brave soldier. His mood swung from hot-tempered to cheerful, and he was often taciturn, finding it difficult to cooperate with the other army and navy officers. The men admired him, however, seeing him as "the soldier's friend."[14]

Unable to defend both banks of the St. Lawrence, the French concentrated their forces on the north shore. The south shore and Île d'Orléans were immediately occupied by the British troops, who installed a large siege artillery battery on Pointe de Lévy to fire on Quebec.

Wolfe also knew he would be unable to take the city, a natural fortress strengthened by many fortifications, with artillery alone: he had to find a way to breach the French lines. In spite of its cliffs, the Beauport shore soon struck him as the most appropriate place to carry out the manoeuvre. He therefore decided to launch an attack near Montmorency Falls. On July 31 scores of landing boats carrying hundreds of elite soldiers made for the beach. After landing, the troops met very little resistance and Wolfe immediately ordered them

to attack the entrenched positions on the heights. This proved to be a costly error. Instead of reforming ranks, the grenadiers, carried away by their enthusiasm, began to climb the escarpment in a very disorganized manner and quickly became an ideal target for the heavy fire of the French soldiers, militiamen and Amerindians, who were well sheltered behind their positions. The assault turned into a disaster. Having lost some 200 soldiers in this failed operation, Wolfe ordered a retreat.

This defeat caused concern in the camp of the frustrated British attackers. As the weeks went by, they could see failure on the horizon because they would have to lift the siege no later than October if they were to avoid winter. They nevertheless continued to shell Quebec, primarily in the hope of seriously damaging the fortifications, which had remained relatively untouched. Exasperated, Wolfe did something less than glorious, reminiscent of the terrible retribution he had meted out in Scotland 13 years earlier. He sent columns of soldiers to raze the Canadian countryside. At the end of August, they pillaged and burned approximately 1,100 houses, from Kamouraska to Lévis, sparing only the churches.

But none of the devastation changed the fact that the siege of Quebec was hobbling along lamentably.

The Battle of the Plains of Abraham

Time was short, and in September the generals on Wolfe's staff presented him with a final, desperate plan: attempt a night landing to the west of the city and climb the cliffs onto the heights and prepare to battle the French. Whether the attempt would be successful depended entirely upon the element of surprise.

The risk was great, to be sure, but Wolfe liked danger, and he agreed. During the night of September 13 fortune smiled on him at last. His men were able to elude the watchful French sentinels. By morning, some 4,500 British soldiers, equipped with a few field cannon, formed ranks on the Plains of Abraham with Wolfe leading them. Having avoided committing any tactical errors, the young English general was preparing for the battle with remarkable composure.

When he learned that the English had reached the Plains of Abraham, Montcalm gave in to his impulsiveness and acted too hastily. Instead of harassing the enemy with

hidden militiamen, while waiting for part of his army, posted further west, to attack the British from the rear, he decided to attack immediately. He had approximately 4,500 men: the five French battalions were placed in the centre, colonial militiamen and colonial troops on the flanks.

At approximately 10 a.m. Montcalm gave the signal to advance. His half-formed lines began to move. At about 120 metres from the British, too far to be effective, the French opened fire. Their ranks soon broke, but they continued to advance to within approximately 90 metres, when the British began to fire sporadically, platoon by platoon; Wolfe ordered them to wait until the enemy was within range to fire a general salvo. When only 30 metres separated the two armies, the British suddenly fired on the poorly aligned ranks of the French battalions. The manoeuvre was a success. The French soldiers panicked and ran for their lives. The British then charged with fixed bayonets, but succeeded in catching only a small number of runaways. Brandishing a broad sword in one hand and holding a dagger in the other, as was the custom when they were charging, the Scottish Highlanders of the 78th Regiment were the most

General Montcalm, mortally wounded on the Plains of Abraham, is taken back to Quebec. Bombled. Engraving.

La Nouvelle-France, Hachette, 1904.

how they run." "Who runs?" asked Wolfe. "The enemy, Sir." Wolfe added before expiring, "Now, God be praised, I will die in peace."[16]

Montcalm was injured in the lower belly while attempting to organize the retreat. Four soldiers, helping him to maintain his balance on his horse, took him back to Quebec, and the frightened populace learned of the defeat from the routed soldiers who were running in the streets. At the hospital it was determined that nothing could be done for the French general, for his injury was mortal. Vaudreuil, who was at Beauport and wanted to counterattack immediately, wrote to him for advice. Montcalm, feeling this would be too risky, recommended that the army retreat and the city surrender. Vaudreuil gave in and ordered the retreat during the night. Montcalm died at dawn on September 14 and Quebec surrendered three days later.[17]

determined pursuers. They soon came upon Canadian militiamen hidden in ambush, who inflicted heavy losses on the British troops as they covered the retreat of the French army.[15]

Quebec Surrenders

This decisive battle lasted only a half hour, but the losses were great on both sides: 658 British dead and wounded, approximately the same number of French. Both generals were mortally wounded. Wolfe was shot in the chest – probably by Canadian militia snipers – while leading his Louisbourg Grenadiers on a charge. He asked those close to him to support him when they took him away so the soldiers would not see him fall. Four men were stretching him out on the ground when one of them cried, "They run, see

Other Fronts

While Wolfe lay siege to Quebec, General Amherst was slowly moving up Lake Champlain at the head of an impressive Anglo-American army of 11,000 men. On July 23 he arrived at Fort Carillon, held by General François-Charles de Bourlamaque and

approximately 2,000 men. With the strength of the forces so unequal, the French blew up the fort three days later, after having evacuated it. Continuing northward, Amherst's army reached Fort Saint-Frédéric, which the French also blew up. By the time the Anglo-American forces reached the fort on August 4 nothing remained but ruins. Amherst immediately ordered another fort built at the same location, to be called Crown Point (today in the State of New York). Amherst's army then attempted to approach Île-aux-Noix, on the Richelieu, where Bourlamaque had dug in with his men, but four small French ships kept the army at bay. With winter coming, the Anglo-Americans eventually withdrew to Crown Point.

On the western front, the main objective of the British invasion of 1759 was Fort Niagara. Under the command of General John Prideaux, 5,500 British and American soldiers left from Albany, accompanied by 600 Iroquois warriors led by Sir William Johnson, reached the proximity of the French fort at the beginning of July. The garrison, under the command of Commander Pierre Pouchot, was barely 500 men.

In spite of the overwhelming superiority of the Anglo-American forces, Pouchot declined the offer to surrender, and on July 9 the siege began. The Anglo-Americans had to dig trenches to protect the siege cannon, because Niagara was not typical of the forts of western North America. Since 1755, the French had been building bastions and glacis like those used in the fortifications erected in Europe by Maréchal Vauban. Prideaux thought it was better to shell the fort with mortar fire while conducting siege operations in the European fashion with parallel sapping trenches. On July 17 the heavy British cannon, installed at last, were put into action. The French responded immediately. In the British camp, in a single day, July 20, two senior ranking officers, a lieutenant-colonel and a colonel, were mortally wounded. But the worst was yet to come: that very evening, General Prideaux was killed accidentally by one of his own mortars. Refusing to give up, Sir William Johnson took command of the army. Four days later, at La Belle Famille, a few kilometres to the south of the fort, he crushed the reinforcing troops from Illinois and Ohio, which consisted of approximately 800 soldiers and militiamen, supported by 600 Amerindians. The next day, giving up all hope of

further assistance, Pouchot surrendered.[18] French communications to the West were cut off from that moment on.

The War Continues in Canada

Brigadier François de Lévis, who succeeded Montcalm, had a great deal of experience in the French army. His personality was

The surrender of Fort Niagara: in 1759, the French troops finally capitulated to the British. Reconstitution by F. Ray.
Old Fort Niagara.

completely different from that of his predecessor; Lévis, who always spoke in measured terms, had a calm temperament and a pragmatic bent. He shared the opinion of the other French officers regarding how to conduct the war in

Canada, but he was careful not to denigrate the Canadian officers. Knowing that staff cannot be effective if there is tension, he maintained relatively good relations with the colonial officers and was no doubt careful to defuse tension caused by any incendiary remark made by his leader.

Lévis was in command of the troops in Montreal in the summer of 1759 when he learned the news of Montcalm's death and the fall of Quebec. When told what had happened, he said that Montcalm ought not to have gone into battle until the reinforcements had arrived, but then added immediately – words that are revealing of his personality – that it is easy to judge generals who are unlucky in war, because they are always wrong.

Lévis was faced with a dead-end situation. With the taking of Quebec, one of the three Anglo-American armies now held a key position. The other two armies were seriously threatening the borders, one to the north of Lake Champlain and the other south of Lake Ontario. In the spring of 1760 these three armies would inevitably converge on Montreal, the heart of the colony and the geographically strategic base to the interior of the continent.

Drummer of the Compagnies franches de la Marine in New France between 1755 and 1760. Reconstitution by Eugène Lelièpvre. Parks Canada.

Lévis was convinced that to avoid such a result he had to retake Quebec at all costs in the early spring, before the navigation routes were open, in the hope of receiving the reinforcements from France that would make it possible to put up a better fight against the other armies during the summer. Governor General Vaudreuil fully shared his views. During the winter in Montreal the army was thus prepared for this final effort. Lévis finally managed to assemble an army of 6,910 officers, soldiers and militiamen.[19]

The Battle of Sainte-Foy

The idea of laying siege to Quebec had its detractors, who did not hesitate to call the undertaking "Lévis's folly." But Lévis knew that his army, isolated and surrounded by enemy forces that were numerically superior by far, would become discouraged after their defeat on the Plains of Abraham if something daring were not suggested to them. The men had to be given a boost, to become galvanized to fight hard against the British. Lévis managed to do this, and in May 1760 the French army arrived at Quebec.

General James Murray was in command of the British garrison of approximately 7,300 officers and soldiers, all regulars. When informed that the French army had come to lay siege he began by evacuating the entire population of Quebec, Sainte-Foy and Lorette, and ordered that the suburbs of Saint-Roch and Sainte-Famille be razed so that the attackers could not hide behind houses to approach the fortifications. Part of the garrison was then assigned the task of building forward trenches to the west of the city near Sainte-Foy. On April 27, as the French army approached, there were a few skirmishes between the French cavalry and the

British detachments. The very next day, Murray decided to attack the French before they could entrench. The British line, 3,200 men strong, advanced on Lévis's troops. Field artillery nearby shelled the French positions. If Murray managed to break through the left side of the French line, Lévis's army would find itself cornered between English bayonets and the St. Lawrence River.

The battle was bitter. The hardest-fought engagements occurred at the site of the house of a man named Dumont, which was in a pivotal position. The Régiment de La Sarre and the 43rd and 60th British regiments engaged in hand-to-hand combat there, and the house changed sides several times. The Régiment de Berry came to support the Régiment de La Sarre, and charged the British artillery under a hail of grapeshot, taking the cannons. The line was shaken. Murray ordered a retreat and it was carried out in good order. The British lost 1,100 men, dead, wounded or taken prisoner, whereas Lévis's losses totalled 572 dead and wounded.[20]

General de Lévis at the Battle of Sainte-Foy in 1760. Bombled. Engraving.
La Nouvelle-France, Hachette, 1904.

The Arrival of Reinforcements

But the British still held Quebec. Lévis's troops surrounded the city, but they did not have any large-calibre guns and, more serious still, were short of ammunition. Lévis even had to limit the number of cannonballs per gun. Murray, on the other hand, had considerable artillery and plenty of ammunition. When the French artillery began to bombard Quebec on May 11, the response was "vigorous," to use Lévis's term. Each camp was counting on help from the mother country. On May 9 a single English frigate dropped anchor in Quebec Harbour. It was indeed the arrival of a fleet that would settle the issue. The eyes of both sides from then on fixed on the river, and on May 15 three sails could be seen on the horizon at last. Soon, sick at heart, the French recognized the British warships. The next day, early in the morning, Lévis began to withdraw to Montreal.

Hoping to block the small craft that accompanied the French army, the British ships attacked two frigates to the west of Quebec, the *Pomone* and the *Atalante*, which were under the command of Captain Jean Vauquelin. The French vessels sacrificed themselves to cover the army's retreat. With the *Pomone* sunk, the *Atalante*, commanded by Vauquelin, managed to hold the British ships for a time. With his ammunition gone and his ship full of holes from enemy shelling, Vauquelin nevertheless refused to lower the flag. Instead, he nailed it to the mast of his ship under incessant enemy fire before being taken prisoner along with his crew.

The arrival of the British ships caused the French camp to lose all hope of receiving help from France.

Battle between the Atalante *and the English fleet in 1760. Webber. Engraving.*
La Nouvelle-France, Hachette, 1904.

France did, however, send a small reinforcement to Canada. Four hundred soldiers of the Compagnies franches de la Marine embarked on five transport ships escorted by the frigate *Machault*. In spite of all its courage, this expeditionary force knew ahead of time that it was being sacrificed, because it was clearly inadequate. When it reached the Gulf of St. Lawrence, it was sighted by ships of the Royal Navy already there.

Pursued by the English, the French fleet took refuge in Baie des Chaleurs and engaged in a final battle at the mouth of the Restigouche River in July 1760.[21]

Within the French colony, the already difficult situation worsened from day to day. The army's coffers were empty and the soldiers were no longer receiving their wages. Food supplies of various kinds ran out and a real famine was feared. There was no

hope; everyone knew that New France was dying. In May 1760 the militiamen began to desert in large numbers to go and plant their fields. Even Lévis's threats to put them to death had no effect. Soon the professional soldiers followed their lead. But in spite of the desertions and shortages the French army continued to resist, and the Anglo-Americans had to make another major military effort to overcome it.

The Final Invasion

Hoping to give Lévis's small army its coup de grâce, three Anglo-American armies attempted to surround it at Montreal. Murray's army went up the St. Lawrence from Quebec, William Haviland's army went down the Richelieu from Crown Point, and the commanding general's army, that of Jeffery Amherst, went down the St. Lawrence from Oswego on Lake Ontario.

With its 11,000 men and 700 Amerindians, Amherst's army encountered particularly stiff resistance at Fort Lévis (near Prescott, Ontario). From August 20 to 25 it was held at bay by just over 300 soldiers, seamen and militiamen under Commander Pouchot. The French artillerymen even managed to damage two English ships and forced a third to lower its flag. When Pouchot finally surrendered the fort, it was no more than a heap of rubble, and the British had trouble believing that such fierce resistance could have been put up by such a small garrison.

In the south, Haviland's army of 3,500 men remained blocked at Île-aux-Noix for most of August by 1,400 French and Canadians. On August 28 the Anglo-Americans finally took the trenches abandoned the previous night by the French

Soldier of the Compagnies franches de la Marine of Canada between 1757 and 1760. Reconstitution by Eugène Lelièpvre.
Parks Canada.

soldiers and Canadian militiamen. Their commander, Louis-Antoine de Bougainville, decided to withdraw because he was afraid that his retreat to Montreal would be stopped by Murray's 3,500 men who had arrived in Sorel on August 27.

The Surrender

Amherst's army was approaching Montreal by boat when, following an inaccurate estimate of the strength of the rapids at Cascades, 55 boats were carried away, drowning 84 men. The rest of the large army was nevertheless able to reach Lac Saint-Louis without difficulty, and they disembarked on September 6 in Lachine, on Montreal Island, to the west of the city. The next

day, Vaudreuil and Lévis withdrew the French troops to within the Montreal city walls, while Murray's soldiers arrived to the east of the city and those of de Haviland appeared on the south shore of the St. Lawrence. The three British armies finally succeeded in joining up, and approximately 18,000 Anglo-American soldiers surrounded Montreal.

Any attempts at defence appeared hopeless. The city's fortifications – a simple stone wall that enemy artillery would be able to breach in a few hours – were not designed to withstand a European-style siege. Vaudreuil and Lévis had no choice but to capitulate. They delegated Bougainville to negotiate the terms of surrender with the British. Amherst was intractable: the regular French troops were to surrender without the honours of war and to hand over their weapons and flags, conditions particularly harsh for the period, and even unfair – for an army that had fought so doggedly and so bravely. Outraged, Lévis considered retrenching with the French regiments to Île Sainte-Hélène, near the city, for a final battle. Vaudreuil refused, probably because he was disheartened and wished to avoid an unnecessary bloodbath and to defend the civilians against any

41

consequent misdeeds by undisciplined soldiery during an assault.

Lévis therefore surrendered. But during the night of September 7-8 the French soldiers held a moving ceremony in which the standard-bearers of each battalion burned the regimental flags, sacred symbols that they were. The next day, September 8, 1760, Vaudreuil signed the terms of surrender. The British light infantry grenadiers went to the parade ground, where the French troops deposited their weapons. When the British demanded the flags, Lévis answered that, on his honour, they no longer existed at the time of surrender. Offended at being unable to get these trophies, Amherst suspected the French of having hidden them, which he considered "scandalous."[22] But he was forced to accept Lévis's word.

Amherst, though, had more pressing problems. The British had 3,116 French officers and soldiers held prisoner, 907 of whom were from colonial troops. Along with the women, children and servants who usually followed the army, the total number of persons in their care exceeded 4,000. Because a large number of French soldiers had married Canadian women during the war, it was made possible for many of them to leave the service and remain in Canada, which hundreds of men did.

The Fate of the Canadian Officers

Something surprising and revealing about this period has to do with the officers in the Compagnies franches de la Marine and the canonniers-bombardiers companies. Among the 63 officers in Montreal at the time of the surrender, 44 chose to return to France. Others were to leave the following year – some perishing in the wreck of the *Auguste*.

The basic difference between these officers and the other officers in the French regiments is that the Canadians were not "returning" to France – because they had never been there. Descended from gentry that had settled in New France in the seventeenth century, most had been born in Canada. Not only did these officers act as defenders of Canadian society, they were also its leaders; because of their family connections they also had a significant impact on the economy of the colony.

Under these conditions, one may well ask why they left their native land. The fact is simply that some of them found it impossible to live in Canada in anything other than military service. Others could not conceive of withdrawing to their family seigneuries to be governed by the British while awaiting peace between France and England. And, last but not least, these men were all soldiers in the service of their King, and wished to continue their careers in the armed forces and to fight for France – and war continued elsewhere.

The Military Regime

In September 1760, after the fall of Montreal, Amherst and his officers were faced with a new challenge, that of governing Canada. This was a major undertaking, because the country was in ruins, there was a threat of famine and many families were without shelter. It was also essential that public order be kept. But the British troops were unable to express themselves in the language of the country.

Amherst therefore called on the Canadian militia. On September 22, 1760, he decreed that the militia officers were to maintain order and act as the police[23] in the parishes and cities, as they had under the French regime, and that they were to serve as intermediaries between the government and the people. Under the terms of surrender, all Canadians were to be disarmed. But two weeks later the British authorities reversed their decision, authorizing

militia officers to keep their weapons and extending this permission to all militiamen who asked to keep them. In addition, militia officers were to serve as justices of the peace for minor cases, because the magistrates had returned to France, taking with them their knowledge of the laws and customs. This was what lay behind the creation of the "militia courts." Although the new judges were unfamiliar with jurisprudence, the militia court system was far preferable to the people to the British court-martial system. Having the Canadian militia take over some civilian government functions was a key event. The militia were a credible intermediary between a confused populace and a foreign army that could well have fallen into certain excesses during this troubled period.

The regular troops of the occupying army were instructed in proper behaviour. They showed moderation and there were few incidents between the Canadians and the British soldiers, who moreover kept their distance from one another. No one knew whether Canada would become a British colony or be returned to France at the end of the war.

England Wins the War

Of France's former colonies, there remained only Guyana, Louisiana and Haiti, then called Saint-Domingue. It therefore agreed to a final effort to reinforce these colonies by sending 5,000 soldiers, escorted by a few of the warships remaining. At the same time, peace talks had begun. Probably in the hope of creating a diversion and retaking territory located close to the rich fisheries at the mouth of the St. Lawrence, a French fleet with 650 soldiers on board took St. John's, Newfoundland, in June 1762, to the great surprise of the British, who organized an expedition that enabled them to retake it in September. France thus lost the base it wanted near the fisheries. Meanwhile, its reinforcements arrived in its other colonies, which would remain French until the end of hostilities. Spain's entry into the war on the side of the French in 1762 did nothing to change the situation. The British and their allies had become too powerful. Their army and their naval forces were triumphant everywhere, and they eventually won the Seven Years' War.

Soldier of the British 45th Regiment, c. 1763. Reconstitution by Charles Stadden.
Parks Canada.

The Treaty of Paris

But military victories alone did not determine the fate of the territories. This prerogative also rested with the diplomats who eventually had to sort out the gains and losses of the generals, and the fate of New France was no exception. During these months British and French emissaries negotiated for the return of Canada to France and for the ceding of Guadeloupe to England!

Now, exchanging a small island for virtually half the North American continent was not necessarily a bargain: New France was expensive and brought nothing into the Royal Treasury, whereas Guadeloupe cost almost nothing and was very profitable. All indications were that the State coffers were empty. On both sides, business people and intellectuals of all stripes took a stand. To retake control of New France, France would have to make huge investments to contain the Anglo-

Soldiers of the 1st and 77th Scottish regiments mounting their assault on Signal Hill in St. John's, Newfoundland, in 1762. Reconstitution by Douglas Anderson. Parks Canada.

American pressure on its borders; these same pressures were, moreover, what had lost them the war. Back in France, public opinion, tired of Canada, no longer wanted to fight for "a few acres of snow," to use the famous description by the philosopher Voltaire. In the end, the Duke of Choiseul decided that France would keep Guadeloupe and abandon Canada.

New France ceased to exist from that time on. Canada, Île Royale and Île Saint-Jean, as well as that part of Louisiana located to the east of the Mississippi River, were ceded to Great Britain. The other part of Louisiana, including the city of New Orleans, went to Spain, France's ally.[24] France received Martinique and Guadeloupe in exchange for a few small islands in the West Indies, as well as a few seaports in India, including Pondicherry. Because it remained interested in the lucrative fisheries of Newfoundland, France was even able to obtain the small islands of Saint-Pierre and Miquelon to serve as a base for its fishermen, with a right to maintain a modest garrison there. All in all, France did reasonably well for itself, but the Canadians were sacrificed.

For the Canadian officers still living on French soil, the time had come for major decisions. A few returned to Canada, but most remained in France, some retiring there, others pursuing their military careers in the French overseas forces. The Treaty of Paris thus confirmed the loss of most of the Canadian social and military elite. For the former Canadian officers who had become seigneurs on their lands, as for the rest of the Canadian population, France had become part of the past. It was the beginning of a new era, full of uncertainty and likely requiring new battles to be fought.

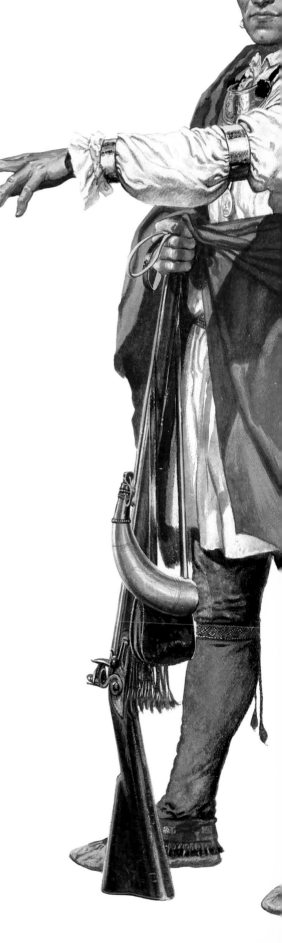

Chapter 2

THE REVOLT OF PONTIAC AND THE AMERICAN INVASION

The news of the signing of the Treaty of Paris on February 10, 1763, reached Canada as the spring navigation routes were opening up. No sooner had Canadians learned that their country was to remain under the British flag than information that was more worrisome in the short term reached Quebec from the West and the Ohio Valley. The forts there, which had been evacuated by the French and were now occupied by British garrisons, were being attacked by the Amerindians. Indeed the presence of the British in these areas did not please many of the Native nations, who preferred the cordial diplomacy and gifts of the French era. More serious still, the Americans were behaving as if they were in a conquered land and considered the Amerindian hunting grounds land to be colonized. This caused resentment among the warriors. Why, they asked themselves, should battles between white people in remote places have anything to do with their fate and that of their land? Chief Pontiac,[25] an exceptional man, was able to rally several Amerindian nations. His plan was very simple: get rid of the British and the Americans.

During May and June there were whirlwind attacks on forts Sandusky, St. Joseph, Presqu'île, Miami, Venango and Michilimackinac, as well as on several smaller posts, which were literally stormed. The many skilful subterfuges of the Amerindians enabled them to take most of the forts. At Michilimackinac, for example, the Ojibwa warriors were playing lacrosse outside the palisades. At one point the ball landed near the door, where a few officers and soldiers were watching the game. The players ran towards the ball, followed closely by their women; in a flash, the women handed them the weapons they had hidden under their blankets and the men rushed inside, killing everyone in the garrison. Only forts Pitt (Pittsburgh), Ligonier and Detroit were able to stand up to Pontiac, even though Fort Pitt was attacked twice and the Detroit garrison, galvanized by Major Henry Gladwin, had to withstand a long siege. Pontiac and his men spared only Fort

Iroquois chief between 1760 and 1790. Reconstitution by G. A. Embleton.

Parks Canada.

Niagara, deeming it – correctly – to be too strongly fortified.

The Canadians had never seen anything like it. Amerindians attacking fortified positions defended by regular garrisons, and taking them! This was certainly not in keeping with their customs. The British military and the American colonists were concerned. The whole West was about to fall, and along with it much of the fur trade. The Canadians – who were newly minted British subjects – were perplexed if not worried. In New York, General Amherst, supreme commander in British North America, was at first taken aback by the vigour of Pontiac's attacks; but he eventually decided that a strong contingent of regular troops, supported by volunteer American militiamen, should go as quickly as possible to the Ohio Valley to rescue the forts under attack. A second contingent, made up of British troops assisted by their implacable former enemies – the Canadian militiamen – would leave later from Montreal to retake the small forts located further west.

In July 1763 the contingent of Colonel Henry Bouquet, a Swiss officer in the British service, went as quickly as possible to the Ohio Valley. Bouquet's small army of 600 men, consisting of the 42nd Scots Regiment, part of the 60th and the American Rangers, went towards Fort Pitt. On

The lacrosse game at Fort Michilimackinac a few seconds before the surprise attack by the Amerindians. Reconstitution by Robert Thom.

Michigan Bell Telephone Company.

46

August 5, at Bushy Run (Pennsylvania), the Amerindians opened fire on the rearguard. The troop was surrounded fairly quickly, and Amerindian war cries came from all sides. But Bouquet was an admirer of the Amerindian tactics that had been used in the past against Braddock so successfully by the Canadians. The cunning tactician arranged his men in a circle and let the Amerindians attack the following day. After a while, he feigned defeat, ordering some of his soldiers to retreat. Believing themselves victorious and hoping to take some scalps, the Amerindians then charged into the breach, rushing headlong into the trap. Their flanks were immediately fired upon by soldiers waiting in ambush for them. They then charged the Amerindians with their bayonets, routing Pontiac's warriors. This disaster was the turning point of the campaign, Bouquet succeeding in beating the Amerindians at their own game. By combining their tactics with the discipline and fire-power of his troops, he showed that British soldiers could keep the Amerindians at bay, as had their predecessors, the French.

Following this defeat, the Amerindians raised their sieges of Fort Ligonier, Fort Pitt and Fort Detroit. In the spring of 1764 Bouquet's army, reinforced by hundreds of volunteers from Virginia and Pennsylvania, moved to the very heart of Amerindian territory without encountering much resistance.

1764: The Canadian Volunteers Battalion

As these events were taking place in the Ohio Valley, instructions from Amherst about the formation of a contingent of troops in Canada reached General Murray. At the beginning of March 1764 Murray ordered the formation of five companies of Canadians, 60 men each commanded by Canadian officers. Murray asked the militia captains to assemble "young people from their parishes and to ask for volunteers."[26] Montreal and Quebec were to supply two companies each, Trois-Rivières one.

The conditions offered to the Canadians were new to them, however, accustomed as they were to serving for no remuneration under the French regime. They were to be paid six sous per day while serving, in addition to being supplied with clothing, equipment and weapons. Militiamen in the other British colonies received the same benefits, but the offer elicited the Canadians' mistrust of "the English." The rumour spread throughout the parishes that the young people, because they were being paid, would be signing up in the British army "for life."[27] At the end of March recruiting was moving slowly indeed. The British governors were finally able to reassure the Canadians, explaining as well that their officers and non-commissioned officers would not be British.

The Amerindians return captured children to Colonel Bouquet at the end of battle. Engraving from a drawing by Benjamin West.
Private collection.

*Grenadier of the 60th Regiment
between 1768 and 1772.
Reconstitution by P. W. Reynolds.*
Canadian Department of National
Defence Library.

Command was indeed given to Canadians, several of whom were, moreover, former officers of the Compagnies franches de la Marine, including Battalion Major Jean-Baptiste-Marie Blaise Des Bergères de Rigauville. Confidence returned little by little, and by mid-April the five companies were complete. The Canadian uniform was different from that of the regular soldiers: woollen cap, capote, leggings and moccasins;

the colours appear to have been red and green. The Battalion of Canadian Volunteers[28] left for the West in May, accompanying the British soldiers first to Fort Oswego, and then Niagara, Detroit and finally Fort Sandusky. However, the hostilities were already coming to an end. Pontiac's Amerindians surrendered in the summer of 1764 and made peace.[29] The Canadians were therefore not involved in any battles, but the news of their presence alongside the British worried the Amerindians because they were thoroughly familiar with their bushfighting skills. Once the campaign was over, in the fall, the Canadian companies returned to their respective districts, as agreed, and were eventually dissolved in early December. This battalion was thus a link between on the one hand the former troops of New France, and the militia companies that had existed in the parishes since 1760, and on the other hand the troops of the British regime. Although the Canadians were abandoned by France, they continued their military tradition.

The British Garrison

With the Seven Years' War won and the Amerindians under control, England now had to consider providing its new colony with a

sufficiently large garrison of regular soldiers. It was felt that two or three regiments, some of which would be dispatched to the forts of the Great Lakes, would be adequate. The most westerly fort to receive a garrison was Michilimackinac, because it was considered useless to maintain such forces in the small Prairie forts. One or two regiments were also posted to Nova Scotia and Newfoundland.

Nor did Great Britain intend to neglect the naval aspect, which was always considered very important. A fleet of small ships was kept on the Great Lakes, with several officers and seamen of the Provincial Marine – a kind of small navy assigned to the lakes. The military shipyard used to build warships under the French regime was abandoned, and Quebec would become a port for warships, although it was not the largest British naval base: this remained Halifax, a city admirably located, with its large harbour, to play the role of sentinel of the North Atlantic.

Military and Civilian Organization

From a military standpoint, the position of Great Britain, an island nation, was different from that of other Western European countries. Without land borders to

48

defend, it did not need to maintain large armies or build imposing fortresses. Its army was therefore numerically much smaller than those of the other great European powers. It totalled approximately 40,000 men in peacetime, whereas other countries had to keep armies of between 200,000 and 300,000. Moreover, much of the British army did not serve in Great Britain itself, but in the various overseas territories under the British flag. Other than the Indian troops maintained by the English East India Company, England did not have distinct colonial troops as did France and Spain. It was the British army itself that manned the colonial garrisons.

In each British colony, a rotation system provided a permanent military presence. One regiment relieved another, and each one, after a few years spent in England, would leave in its turn for other horizons. There was nothing immutable about the process and some regiments remained in a colony for a decade, others for less than two years.

The system was a great novelty for the people of former New France, and it led to major social changes. Because of this form of organization, the officers were no longer recruited from among the colonial gentlemen, which deprived the Canadian

elite of its main source of employment, income and influence. The soldiers were also affected. After their term of service was over, many soldiers of the French Compagnies franches de la Marine had settled in Canada. This became less and less feasible under the new system, because the regular army was, rather than an integral part of society, a group of foreigners isolated in the very midst of the colonial population.

The Military Reputation of Canadians

Many British officers had admired the fighting qualities of Canadians for some time and wished to recruit corps of colonial troops from among them. "The Canadians are a hardy race of people & have been accustomed to arms from their infancy...those people are certainly the properest kind of troops to be employed in an Indian War.... The moment the Indians see a body of Canadians in arms against them, they will be persuaded that America has but one master...,"[30] wrote one officer. General Amherst himself used similar words, adding that the British government should make use of the outstanding talents of the former officers of the French colonial troops living in Canada.

Amherst also considered the Canadians, owing to their skill and discipline, superior to the American Rangers. Various corps of Rangers had taken part in the Seven Years' War, and the most highly rated by the British high command appear to have been those of Colonel Joseph Goreham. "Rogers' Rangers," as Major Robert Rogers' Rangers were called, had done battle on many occasions but had been unable to beat the Canadians, particularly in one forest battle that took place in 1758, and to Amherst were nothing but adventurers. Even as he encouraged the authorities in London to approve the raising of a colonial corps of Canadians, he was applauding the fact that the Rangers were being let go, "for I have a very low opinion of them...."[31] The establishment of a Canadian regiment was thus an excellent idea from the military standpoint. Unfortunately, it proved to be impossible politically. At that very moment, as it happened, the British government was attempting to economize by reducing its regular infantry from 124 to 70 regiments. Under such conditions, English public opinion would have been very much opposed to dropping tens of thousands of officers and soldiers of British origin, to be replaced by recently

recruited enemies who were not only Catholic, but of French descent!

Soon after his arrival, Guy Carleton, who succeeded Murray as Governor of Canada in 1766, also recommended the raising of one or two regiments of Canadians. He even used statistics to support his case, noting the large number of officers of various ranks who were suitable to serve, from among the "French Noblesse in the Province of Quebec"[32] – i.e., 51, of whom 10 were captains. To rally the gentlemen of the colony for England, Carleton maintained that these men ought to be given officers' commissions in a new regular colonial regiment, and even be given a few commissions in the British army.

London refused again, claiming this time that there was an insurmountable problem, both legal and political. Under English law, Catholics could not hold official positions in the kingdom. It was therefore impossible to commission Canadian officers in the regular armed forces. There was a risk that the situation could degenerate at any time, although the Canadians, still weakened and ruined by the invasion of their country, did not for the moment show open hostility to the British. But what would happen in the future if their discontent

British soldier in winter dress, between 1765 and 1783. Reconstitution by G. A. Embleton. Parks Canada.

were to grow? Of the 18,000 Canadians able to bear arms, most had already fought and were more familiar with guerilla tactics than the regular soldiers were; in addition, they were outstanding shots and excellent militiamen. A population as militarized as this was unprecedented, in both Europe and the other colonies. If a serious conflict were to arise with

the Canadians, it would require not two British regiments in garrison in the St. Lawrence Valley, but a dozen!

The Quebec Act

Although Canada became a British colony in 1763, another latent political problem was ready at any moment to degenerate into confrontation. On August 10, 1764, a civilian government replaced the military regime, but because of the British royal proclamations and laws the governors were faced with virtually insoluble contradictions. Thus on the one hand a small group of American and English adventurers and merchants who had recently settled in Canada vigorously demanded a legislative assembly – this would give them the right to act as lords in a conquered land, because only "former subjects" of the Protestant faith could sit in the assembly. On the other hand the "new subjects" demanded to be governed in accordance with the provisions of the Treaty of Paris, which guaranteed them free exercise of religion and the continuance of their civil laws. Not least, the militia, which had been indispensable in managing the colony, represented an extremely thorny problem because, in principle, only Protestant British subjects

could be officers – a ridiculous rule that the Canadians, who had always been very proud of belonging to the militia, felt was demeaning. At the end of November 1765 the militia was even abolished and the captains replaced by "bailiffs" in each parish. But the bailiffs were asked to discharge their civil duties only, the matter of their military obligations left pending. Years of confusion and administrative disputes were to follow. While Governor Murray was able to handle both camps tactfully, his successor, Sir Guy Carleton, knew that he would soon have to act on the situation, all the more so in view of the worsening political tensions between England and its Thirteen American Colonies in New England.

For Carleton, and for the members of the British government, a massive emigration from Great Britain to Canada seemed unlikely. They were convinced that the "Province of Quebec" would remain a largely French-speaking and Catholic population. Only 2,000 British and Americans lived there – most in Quebec and Montreal – and it was unlikely that their number would increase significantly, for even attempts to populate the province with the military proved fruitless.[33]

The only way to assure security, peace and prosperity for the colony was to rally Canadians to the British cause. To accomplish this, the British Parliament eventually, in 1774, passed the Quebec Act. The Act established the continuance of French civil law and freedom of religion; it also made it possible for Catholic Canadians to enter public office, but within the colony only. Native-born gentlemen were still excluded from military careers in the regular army.

The militia was restored the following year, with seigneurs as officers. Influenced by the clergy and the nobility, who sought to consolidate their social position, Carleton concluded that the colony would benefit from a kind of feudal system of government in which seigneurs, members of the clergy and great merchants would advise the governor. Canadians, who were accustomed to an autocratic system, understood nothing, according to Carleton, of legislative assembly, and would be happier obeying their seigneurs and their priests. It was a fundamental error, indicative of a poor understanding of the government of the French regime.

The American Revolution

The Thirteen Colonies established in the seventeenth century in North America prospered and were proud of their local independence. They were governed by legislatures elected through a form of restricted suffrage, and a governor appointed by the King represented British authority. Such authority was not always welcome. During the Seven Years' War, considerable tension between the officers and soldiers of the British army and those of the American provincial regiments had been noted.

Once peace had returned, the British government, in the name of the supremacy of the imperial Parliament and the royal will, took very unpopular measures. It began by levying a variety of taxes, prior to the 1765 vote in favour of the Quartering Act, which required Americans to accommodate British soldiers in their homes, a situation that was widely practised in Canada but which they found intolerable. The rallying cry for the Americans became "No taxation without representation!" Intellectuals such as the inventor, philosopher and journalist Benjamin Franklin put forward the idea of political

An American rifleman from Colonel Morgan's Regiment, c. 1775-76. Reconstitution by G. A. Embleton.
Parks Canada.

independence as a solution. With the situation degenerating, England decided to strengthen its garrison in Boston.

It was in this explosive context that the Americans learned of the Quebec Act. They interpreted it as an attempt by the British to appease Canadians with a view to eventually using them against Americans, which was indeed the case. Given such a scenario, the Americans would have to expect new raids by Canadians and Amerindians, who would, on behalf of the British, ravage the border areas of the recalcitrant colonies!

American indignation reached a peak on the day that 19 British regiments disembarked in Boston to stifle by force any signs of protest. The first Continental Congress, attended by all the American colonies, was held in Philadelphia in October 1774; it was declared that the English laws, including the Quebec Act, infringed upon American rights. On May 10, 1775, Congress decreed that a standing army be created under the supreme command of George Washington.

The Invasion of Canada

While a first American army would encircle Boston under the command of George Washington, a second would assemble in Albany, under the command of General Richard Montgomery, to invade Canada. There was even a third army, commanded by Benedict Arnold, which would enter Quebec through the woods along the Kennebec River further east. Montgomery's army was to take the forts along Lake Champlain and the Richelieu River, and then capture Montreal before joining up with Arnold's troops to lay siege to Quebec. It was a daring invasion.

In May, Fort Ticonderoga and Fort Crown Point were taken by small groups of Americans without resistance. These defeats augured poorly for Canada. That very month, Carleton ordered mobilization of the Montreal militia, but encountered considerable resistance from English merchants, some of whom were on the side of the Americans, as well as within several Canadian parishes located near the city. On May 22 Monseigneur Briand announced that the Americans would be repulsed, and on June 9 Carleton instituted martial law.

At the time, there were only two regiments in garrison, the 7th and the 26th. The appeal to the militia, the main force to defend the province, was only moderately successful, because many Canadians were afraid the English authorities would involve them in a conflict that did not concern them. Nonetheless, the Canadian bourgeoisie formed a company of volunteers to guard the Montreal residence of the governor. At the beginning of July the English merchants formed their own company, but it was infiltrated by American sympathizers – as shown by the sabotage of muskets one night in the guardhouse. When the approach of Montgomery's

army was announced, 120 Montrealers, "all Canadians under the command of Monsieur de Longueuil," volunteered and went to reinforce the fort's British garrison.[34]

Montgomery's 2,000 men soon surrounded Fort Saint-Jean, and the siege began on September 18. On the 25th an American advance party of 200 men, under the command of Ethan Allen, was repulsed at Longue-Pointe near Montreal by 200 Canadian volunteers supported by approximately 30 British soldiers and as many English volunteers. Allen was taken prisoner and sent to England.

Montreal: An American City

On the strength of this victory, the British were able to counterattack immediately by harassing the Americans who were laying siege to Fort Saint-Jean. This was recommended by the Canadian militiamen gathered in Montreal, who were accustomed to these kinds of tactics. But they were faced with a vacillating governor. According to a report of the time, the militiamen "complained – as did the citizens of the city of Montreal – when they said that General [Carleton] was determined not to cross to the south shore to repulse the enemy." Rather than be "bored doing nothing," they soon began to think about returning home. Worse still, more and more of them began to think that the inaction meant "that the government did not have any confidence in the Canadians."[35] With their wounded pride, many even asked themselves why they should be loyal and fight for the British when their English fellow citizens – who treated them like a conquered people – often refused to do so. After all, had the Americans not been Britain's allies against Canada until 1760? The situation began to look like a dispute between Englishmen, with both sides attempting to bring the Canadians into their camp. Faced with such contradictions, and left to their own devices by Carleton, most Canadians opted for neutrality.

In October there were a number of skirmishes at Longueuil, on the south shore of the river, which a number of American detachments had reached. Once again, the Canadians, powerless, were discouraged to see Carleton "unwilling to cross to the south shore to repulse approximately 40 men in Fort Longueuil."[36] On October 18 Fort Chambly

---

American infantry officer, c. 1775-76. Reconstitution by G. A. Embleton.
Parks Canada.

fell to the Americans, after weak resistance by its garrison. Encouraged by these victories, the invaders redoubled their efforts at Fort Saint-Jean, which, with no hope of rescue, fell on November 2 after 45 days of siege. This was the final obstacle before Montreal. Carleton could do nothing but flee for Quebec. The English residents were increasingly unhappy with the defections as the American army approached, so much so that on November 13 Montgomery entered Montreal without firing a single shot.

Some Montrealers, including James Livingston, Moses Hazen and Jeremiah Dugan, then joined the Americans, who assigned

City of Quebec militiaman, c. 1775-76. Reconstitution by G. A. Embleton.
Canadian Department of National Defence.

them the task of raising Canadian troops for their army. The recruiting effort did not, however, yield the desired results, and few Canadians took up arms for the American cause.

The Americans Lay Siege to Quebec

Meanwhile, in London, the authorities were hoping to profit from the positive effects of the Quebec Act. In July the Secretary of State to the American colonies, Lord Dartmouth, asked Carleton to mobilize a light infantry corps of 6,000 Canadians to serve on a standing basis against the Americans. Light cannon made of brass, weapons, ammunition and uniforms were sent hastily to equip the new army.[37]

But when these instructions and the required equipment reached Quebec it was already too late. It was no longer a matter of recruiting 6,000 Canadians, but simply of saving what could still be saved. The fall of Montreal was all the more serious because communications with the Western forts were interrupted. To restore matters it was absolutely essential that the city of Quebec be held until the spring of 1776, when the reinforcements were to arrive from Great Britain; but in the immediate future the Americans were coming. On November 14 the inhabitants of Quebec saw, coming from south of the city, the first members of the small army of 1,100 men commanded by Benedict Arnold. At the beginning of December Montgomery's army joined up with Arnold's, and on the 6th the Americans began the siege of Quebec City.

Fortunately for the British, Carleton regained control of the situation and finally displayed his leadership qualities. In Quebec, all that remained of the regular troops were a few staff officers, approximately 60 soldiers from the 7th Regiment, 37 naval infantry soldiers and six artillerymen. Carleton also had the assistance of 200 recruits who had just arrived from Newfoundland and who belonged to a new colonial regiment called the Royal Highland Emigrants, as well as sailors taken from the ships in the port and approximately 80 artificers and workmen. Finally, he had some 900 men from the city militia, divided into eight "Canadian Militia" companies and six "British Militia" companies.[38]

Carleton began by expelling from the city anyone who supported American ideas. He took measures to strengthen the fortifications and assembled a good supply of rations and ammunition. He then reorganized his incongruous garrison and equipped it with the supplies recently received from England. With the regular soldiers and Scottish recruits, he established an elite reserve corps; he integrated the sailors and artificers into the artillery and into engineering, and assigned

the bulk of the defence effort to the two militia corps. He distributed green uniforms to everyone, and, in anticipation of winter, fur hats, capotes, mittens and other appropriate clothing. Not least, Carleton was able to rouse his men. Suitably fed, armed and sheltered within the walls of the city, they resolutely awaited the Americans.

For the attackers, on the other hand, life became increasingly difficult as the temperature dropped. They had nothing but tents and huts, which were ineffective against the icy winds; they had also failed to gather enough firewood, and they sometimes lacked rations. Their uniforms barely protected them against the rigours of the climate. And Montgomery did not have any true siege artillery, which meant that he could not cause the defenders much harm. In short, the only solution was to attack the city! There was another reason for this decision as well: the Americans were convinced that many Canadian militiamen secretly supported their cause and that they would lay down their arms as soon as Lower Town had been taken.

American soldiers laying siege to Quebec in the winter of 1775-76 suffered greatly from the harsh climate. Reconstitution by G. A. Embleton.
Parks Canada.

The Attack on Quebec

The American staff chose the night of December 31 to launch three simultaneous attacks against the city. That evening, a snowstorm helped them by preventing the defenders from seeing and hearing them arrive. Towards 4 a.m., flares went up from the American lines: this was the agreed upon signal! The attack began with cannon fire on the Saint-Jean Gate. In the city, drums and church bells sounded the alarm. But this initial attack was only a feint, during which Montgomery, leading four New York regiments, moved unnoticed below Cap-aux-Diamants and came up a narrow street (today Rue Petit-Champlain) leading to Place Royale.

Soon afterwards, Montgomery and his men were able to make out a house through the storm. "Forward, men. Quebec is ours!" shouted the general, running forward, sword in hand. A moment later, there was a terrible explosion. It came from the first defence post in Lower Town, held by some 30 Canadian militiamen and a few British seamen. Montgomery and everyone with him fell bleeding in the snow. The only survivor, aide-de-camp Aaron Burr, who would become an American vice-president, remained standing, completely stunned. There were further cannon shots and ripples of gunfire. The New Yorkers beat a hasty retreat!

Meanwhile, Arnold and some 700 men were detected close to the Palais Gate. They went on the attack in Lower Town, believing that Montgomery's column was already there. Arnold, who was injured in the assault on the first barricade in

55

Canadian militiamen and British soldiers repulse the American assault at Sault-au-Matelot (in Quebec City's Lower Town) during the night of December 31, 1775. Reconstitution by Allan Daniel.

Rue du Sault-au-Matelot, was replaced by Colonel Daniel Morgan, who took command and reached the second barricade. Behind it waited a detachment of the 7th Regiment, in battle ranks, as well as Canadian militiamen hidden in some houses. When the Americans reached the top of the barricade, they were met by a heavy fusillade. Carleton then decided that the moment had come to cut off their avenue of retreat. He sent a large detachment of Scots and sailors through the Palais Gate to take Morgan's men as they retreated. The Americans, knowing that all was lost, lay down their arms. When the day dawned, approximately 100 of them lay dead, including General Montgomery; 300 others were taken prisoner, including Colonel Morgan.[39] The Quebec garrison had only five dead and one wounded. Thus ended the last recorded assault on city of Quebec.

The American Tyranny

The defeat did not put an end to American ambitions, however. For several months still they continued to lay siege to the city. In fact, it was more of a blockade than a true siege, because their artillery was not a serious threat. From December 1775 to May 1776 some 780 cannonballs and 180 bombs were fired on Quebec, injuring two seamen and killing a child. The defenders returned their fire a hundredfold, sending 10,466 cannonballs and 996 bombs onto their lines! The American soldiers were also decimated by smallpox, which broke out in their camp, causing many deaths.

Livingston and Hazen, in spite of repeated attempts, were having

difficulty recruiting Canadians for the American army. Of those who enlisted, "most were French soldiers who had remained in Canada after the Conquest,"[40] according to a contemporary. The Canadians were all the more mistrustful of the Americans because they were acting increasingly like tyrants, so much so that some Canadians outside the city even agreed to take up arms to fight them. One such was Louis Liénard de Beaujeu de Villemonde, Seigneur of Île-aux-Grues, who at Carleton's request was able to recruit Canadian volunteers to attempt to break the American blockade of Quebec. His plan was exposed, though, and the Americans drove back his volunteers on March 25, 1776, at Saint-Pierre-de-la-Rivière-du-Sud, near Beaumont. The skirmish nevertheless did not augur well for the Americans.

In fact relations between Americans and Canadians were worsening, particularly in Montreal. At the suggestion of English merchants who had rallied to the American cause, General David Wooster, the commander, had a dozen distinguished Canadians arrested on the grounds that they were suspected of having remained loyal to the British. Following a protest movement they were released, but

Wooster's soldiers then took hostages, disarmed some of the Canadians and caused all sorts of oppression. A "political prison" was even set up in Fort Chambly. Goods were seized without compensation, and some merchants were paid in worthless paper money. A Canadian doctor was derided and humiliated when he submitted his bill after caring for American soldiers. As a fervent Protestant commanding in a Catholic country, Wooster pushed his arrogance so far as to have the churches closed to prevent the people from attending Midnight Mass. It was not long before secret pamphlets began to

circulate in Montreal decrying "the most cruel tyranny."[41]

Reinforcements from Britain

In early May 1776 several ships flying the English flag appeared on the St. Lawrence making their way towards Quebec. This was the relief so eagerly awaited. The news spread like wildfire throughout the land. On May 6 the frigate HMS *Surprise* dropped anchor in the port of Quebec, followed soon afterwards by other ships. As soon as the reinforcements had disembarked, Carleton organized a sortie outside the city, with his troops and his militiamen, to attack the Americans. But they had already left their positions and were fleeing to Montreal. Carleton followed them as far as Trois-Rivières. On June 8 American General John Sullivan considered counterattacking the British immediately, but the arrival of English warships prevented him from doing so. A battle that followed nevertheless ended in an American

An officer of the British 42nd Regiment; officers of the Royal Highland Emigrant Regiment, raised in Canada, also wore this uniform from 1776 onward. Reconstitution by G. A. Embleton.
Parks Canada.

defeat by the elite soldiers of the 9th, 20th and 62nd regiments.

During the American invasion, the forts located to the west of Montreal, whose garrisons consisted partly of soldiers from the 8th Regiment, remained in the hands of the British. In May 1776 Captain George Forster, with 36 soldiers, supported by Claude-Nicolas-Guillaume de Lorimier leading 11 Canadian volunteers and approximately 160 Iroquois, reached Les Cèdres, on the western end of Montreal Island, where 390 American soldiers were holding a fort. Other Canadian volunteers joined Forster and quickly surrounded the fort. With no cannon, the attackers harassed the Americans with gunfire, hoping to intimidate them with the war cries of the Amerindians. It was a complete success! Terrified by the prospect of being scalped, the occupants surrendered to Forster on May 19. Two days later in Vaudreuil, a detachment of reinforcements, consisting of 150 American soldiers, fell in an ambush set for them by de Lorimier in command of a group of Canadians and Amerindians. This time, almost 100 Americans surrendered.

It was becoming increasingly difficult for the Americans to maintain their positions. On June 15

General Arnold and his soldiers suddenly evacuated Montreal, but not without committing a final perfidious act: attempting to burn the city. The Montrealers were nevertheless able to put out the flames, and the Canadian militia was mobilized to maintain order. Two days later the British troops arrived. The Americans then abandoned forts Chambly and Saint-Jean, after burning them, and regrouped at Crown Point. Thus ended the first American invasion of Canada.

A Poorly Defended Colony

After the Seven Years' War, Nova Scotia developed and its population increased steadily. In October 1758 the colony established an elected legislative assembly, the first in Canada, and the militia was organized on the basis of the counties into which the province had been divided. Halifax had a British garrison because of its importance as a naval base. Over the years, its commercial harbour became a hub of naval transportation and its shipyards were to become the largest builders of merchant vessels north of Boston. In addition to its militia regiment, Halifax had an independent militia company for the shipyard, no doubt recruited from

among the workers, and a company of "cadets,"[42] which probably included members of the bourgeoisie.

When the American Revolution erupted in 1775, the British garrison was extremely weak throughout the Maritime colonies. There were only three companies of the 65th Regiment in Halifax and one in Newfoundland. Charlottetown, a small town on Île Saint-Jean (Prince Edward Island) with neither a garrison nor a militia, was sacked by American privateers. In Nova Scotia, rumours of dissent were rampant, particularly in the western part of the province – the former Acadia – where American families had gone to settle after the Seven Years' War, and in Halifax itself.

The Governor of Nova Scotia, Francis Legge, therefore asked in vain for reinforcements from General Thomas Gage, commander-in-chief of British forces in North America. In July, after American sympathizers attempted to burn down the army storehouses in Halifax, he mobilized militiamen to patrol the city. In the autumn, in the eastern part of the province, where the population was more dependable, Legge organized a few light infantry companies of volunteer militiamen. In

the west, ironically enough, it was the Acadians, after returning from exile, who took up arms to defend the British Crown, raising two militia companies in Annapolis and two in Chignectou. But unless regular troops were to be sent to support the people who had remained loyal to the British, there was every likelihood that the province would fall into the American camp.

The Invasion of Nova Scotia

In view of the gravity of the situation, Gage sent two companies of the 14th Regiment and 100 recruits from a new colonial corps, the Royal Fencible Americans, under the command of one of the great names in Nova Scotia military history, Joseph Goreham – the very Goreham who had earlier commanded a corps of Rangers. Governor Legge was authorized to raise another colonial regiment from among loyal members of the population, the Loyal Nova Scotia Volunteers. In December additional regular troops from England reached Halifax. Legge could finally breathe easier and prepare the province to defend itself. In early summer 1776, Colonel Goreham and his Royal Fencible Americans mounted guard at Fort

Cumberland – formerly Fort Beauséjour – to defend the isthmus of Chignectou against an American incursion.

The dreaded attack came in November, when approximately 500 Americans attacked Fort Cumberland, held by a garrison of 200 soldiers and Loyalist families who had taken refuge there. The garrison had done what it could to prepare the fort, which had been abandoned since the 1760s, and to restore it to a viable condition, even using old French bayonets to make stakes. They did not have the provisions needed, and rations were equally low. The soldiers, who had not been given uniforms, were in rags. Goreham allowed them "to

wear the Barrack Rugs and Blankets[,] otherwise they must suffer greatly if not entirely perish."[43]

The Americans, without any artillery, launched an assault the night of December 13, but they were turned back. On the 22nd and 23rd they attempted to burn down the fort and managed to destroy several buildings, including the hospital, but Goreham held his ground. On December 28 the warship HMS *Vulture* appeared, carrying soldiers of the Royal Highland Emigrants and marines,

When the Americans approached in November 1776 the loyal inhabitants took refuge at Fort Beauséjour. Reconstitution by Lewis Parker.
Parks Canada.

Standard-bearer of the Prinz Ludwig of Brunswick Dragoons Regiment, between 1776 and 1783. Reconstitution by G. A. Embleton. Parks Canada.

taking of Liverpool by American privateers in September 1778. Generally, though, the Maritime colonies were no longer being bothered by the Americans, most of the people having chosen the British camp.

John Burgoyne's Army in Canada

Throughout the summer of 1776, British reinforcements continued to arrive. Dozens of ships reached the docks of Quebec to unload tons of provisions, dozens of brass field cannon and thousands of soldiers from Europe. The 9th, 20th, 21st, 24th, 47th, 53rd and 62nd regiments arrived, as well as the grenadiers of the 29th, 31st and 34th, accompanied by approximately 500 artillerymen. But no doubt most surprising of all for the Canadians was the arrival of infantrymen in blue or green uniforms, the grenadiers, wearing a kind of tall mitre of brilliant metal and performing perfect drill.

German soldiers!

The English government had decided to "hire" from German princes the services of their small armies to reinforce its own. At the time, Germany, except for Prussia, Bavaria and Saxony, was divided into hundreds of small

autonomous states. Thus, beginning in 1776, thousands of German soldiers crossed the Atlantic to fight alongside the British.

These British and German troops together totalled 8,000 men, approximately 5,000 of whom came from Brunswick and Hesse-Hanau. All were under the supreme command of General John Burgoyne, supported by General Friedrich Adolphus von Riedesel of Brunswick. Burgoyne's primary task was to rid Canada of the Americans, which he accomplished easily in 1776. The next year he was to go with his army to Albany in New York State to join up with the forces of General William Howe. This would cut into two the United States of America – the American colonies had declared their independence on July 4, 1776 – and thus make it easier to neutralize them.

Raising Troops in Canada

In Canada, the arrival of this army signalled demobilization of the militias. The Canadians had seen everything by now! Although concerned about defending their land, they preferred to remain neutral, leaving the English to fight among themselves, particularly as the British could now rely on

who, when they joined the soldiers of the garrison, were able finally to chase away the attackers.

Garrisons were later posted in Annapolis and other strategic points in Nova Scotia and Prince Edward Island. A few skirmishes occurred, the most serious being the

Drum major of the British 7th Regiment, c. 1793.

Anne S. K. Brown Military Collection, Brown University, Providence.

Black kettledrum player of the British 7th Regiment, c. 1793.

Anne S. K. Brown Military Collection, Brown University, Providence.

Military Bands

It was most likely the British army which introduced true military bands to Canada. In the beginning, these bands consisted of small groups of 10 or even fewer musicians, such as the band of the 46th Regiment, which in 1765 had only six musicians. But the bands grew in size over the years, and at the beginning of the eighteenth century often had around 20 musicians.

The band music heard by our ancestors was certainly different from contemporary bands, as attested to by the following list of instruments for the band of the 49th Regiment, formed in 1813: 14 clarinets, 2 bassoons, 10 flutes, 2 horns, 1 trumpet, 1 serpent, kettledrums and a pair of triangles. Several also had a "jingling Johnnie," an instrument consisting of a cymbal or crescent-shaped crossbars made of copper, all hung with small bells and attached to a wooden pole. It was fashionable for a regimental band to have Black kettledrum players. They dressed in the Turkish style with turbans and embroidered vests, and usually wore a silver collar and bracelets.

Army musicians often played as orchestras at balls and concerts, for which they were generally paid by means of an admission charge. There were also many benefit concerts. In 1820 the bands of the two regiments in garrison in Quebec gave a concert to raise money for needy immigrants. Theatre actors also depended on military bands for some of their financing. A public band concert was a rare opportunity for ordinary people to hear orchestra music free of charge.

excellent German soldiers. Also, when Burgoyne decided to raise 300 Canadians to serve with his army, he encountered considerable difficulty, finding few volunteers. The captains of the three companies were indeed seigneurs, but "the impopularity of their Seigneurs"[44] caused the Canadians to be reluctant to join, and in any case the Canadians were afraid of being forced to enlist in the British army. Finally, in May 1777 Governor Carleton had to fall back on the Militia Act to enlist young bachelors. To prevent any attempts at resistance, he even threatened to "take two married men for each boy...who deserts," with the result that "the three companies were soon complete."[45] The governor nevertheless had to promise the men they would be back with their families in November. On the strength of these assurances, the Canadians marched off, two companies leaving with Burgoyne's army and the third with the auxiliary corps of Lieutenant-Colonel Barrimore Matthew St. Leger.

After the withdrawal of the American troops, refugees were arriving in growing numbers in Canada, primarily from New York State. They were called "Loyalists," Americans who had not espoused the cause of the majority in favour of independence and who preferred to remain loyal to the British Crown. Those who wished to remain British subjects were being persecuted. Many had been able to reach the English lines and, armed by the British, formed Loyalist regiments. Several Loyalist military corps had also been established in Canada itself.

The first significant group of refugees, approximately 200 persons, arrived in Montreal in May 1776. The group was led by Sir John Johnson, to whom Carleton had granted permission to form a regiment of Loyalists "to furnish people so circumstanced with the means of defending themselves."[46] Called the King's Royal Regiment of New York, it served along the Canadian border. In early 1777 the Jessup brothers arrived from Albany with several refugees to form the King's Loyal Americans. The Queen's Loyal Rangers was established from a group of other refugees at around the same time. The first battalion of the Royal Highland Emigrants was also recruited from among the Loyalists. These new troops were mostly stationed in the Montreal area.

Burgoyne's Expedition

As the Loyalists were forming these various regiments, Burgoyne was planning the British campaign against the northern United States. The troops would advance along two routes. The main army, under his own command, would go to the south of Lake Champlain by boat and then march all the way to Albany. A second expeditionary corps, under the command of Lieutenant-Colonel St. Leger, was also to move towards Albany, but through the Mohawk Valley, taking Fort Stanwix (at Rome, New York) along the way before rejoining the main army.

In 1777, at the beginning of June, 7,000 soldiers, 3,000 of whom were German, reached the southern end of Lake Champlain without difficulty; but once this stage was completed, many problems began to afflict the expedition. Burgoyne lost valuable weeks assembling baggage and equipment and building a road and bridges.

The slow British advance gave the Americans the time they needed to mobilize an army of some 12,000 men, consisting largely of militiamen under the command of General Horatio Gates. The British army soon became the target of deadly fire from snipers hidden in the

woods. General Simon Fraser, the second in command, was killed by their fire – and his loss was deeply felt. The Americans managed to surround Burgoyne's army near Saratoga. After a desperate and futile attempt to break through enemy lines, Burgoyne surrendered on October 17. His defeat was one of the worst disasters in the annals of the British army. The repercussions of the American victory were enormous, giving dazzling military credibility to the Americans throughout all of Europe. The fact was, how could the Americans still be considered farmers barely able to hold on to their pitchforks after they had defeated the British and German troops, regarded at the time as the best in the world? The Americans kept the regular soldiers prisoner, but released the Canadians and Loyalists because they did not consider them professional soldiers.

Meanwhile, St. Leger arrived at Fort Stanwix with his troops, consisting of Johnson's Loyalists, approximately 200 soldiers from the 8th British Regiment, a company of Canadian militiamen and some 800 Amerindians. But the Americans were well entrenched and able to fend them off. At the end of August, unable to take the fort, St. Leger had to call off the attack and return to Canada. The

Americans were thus completely victorious in warding off the British offensive. The victory was somewhat attributable to General Howe: rather than send troops to rescue Burgoyne in the north, Howe had left New York with his army and proceeded southward.

The Militia and Fatigue Duties

This disastrous defeat called into doubt the defensibility of Canada in the event of another invasion. In the spring of 1777 Governor Carleton had proclaimed a Militia Act, the first since the French regime had ended. Generally speaking, the Act maintained the provisions that had been in force since 1669. All men aged 16 to 60 able to bear arms were to join the militia. Grouped into parish companies, they were required to take part in drill and civilian duties, including fatigue duties. Something new, however, was that English residents were now subject to the Act, though their obligations were in fact not entirely the same. The Canadians, moreover, complained that "the English residents and craftsmen, who are numerous enough in Canada,"[47] were never called upon for the difficult construction and maintenance duties.

In March 1778 an incident in Mascouche aggravated this uneasiness: many militiamen "refused to obey their captain," who was described as "a drunk." Although it appeared relatively harmless on the surface, the matter grew in importance when the Montreal commander sent to the village a detachment of soldiers, "who pillaged nearly all the houses and raped several girls and women...a terrible punishment that even barbarians do not practise among themselves." The news spread quickly throughout the countryside. Carleton did not intervene to punish those responsible, and many believed that he tacitly approved of such

conduct. This event, added to the injustice of the fatigue duties, led to the Canadians becoming even more neutral. One of them noted, "How can they expect Canadians, after such harsh treatment, to take up arms on their behalf?"[48]

The German Presence

In such a context, the inclusion of many Germans in the garrison of regular troops at the time may be considered to have been providential. The German soldiers got along well with the French-Canadian population and most of their officers understood French better than English. Their administrative correspondence was usually written in French or German. One of them wrote that the Canadians were "very good people, serious, attractive and very upright. Once won over, their friendship was boundless.... No nation could support so much effort, work and fatigue with such patience."[49] The Canadians, for their part, appreciated the order and discipline of the German troops. At Kamouraska, for example, the excellent deportment of a detachment of the Anhalt-Zerbst Regiment won the full approval of the militia captains.

Most of the German troops were stationed at

Sapper of the Brunswick von Riedesel Regiment, 1776-83. The sappers were tough, elite soldiers whose task was to clear obstacles laid by the enemy. They wore the mitre, the emblem of elite German soldiers, and their uniform was protected by a leather apron; they were equipped with an axe and a saw. Reconstitution by G. A. Embleton.

Parks Canada.

Sorel. They consisted primarily of Brunswick regiments and battalions under the command of General von Riedesel, part of which remained in garrison during the 1777 campaign. The following year, the German soldiers captured by the Americans were exchanged and returned to Canada. With the exception of the Prinz Friedrich Regiment, all infantrymen, dragoons and light infantrymen were

incorporated into the Ehrenbrook Battalion and the von Barner Regiment in the fall of 1778, for a total of 2,000 men, excluding the approximately 800 Hesse-Hanau infantrymen, light infantrymen and artillerymen. In addition, the 600- to 700-strong Anhalt-Zerbst Regiment arrived in May 1778 to be assigned the task of guarding Quebec and its surroundings. Standing guard on the ramparts, they must have evoked in many Canadians memories of the French, because, instead of the usual blue of German soldiers, these wore an attractive white uniform with scarlet lapels, cuffs and collar. The German regiments totalled 3,200 men at the time, half the regular troops in garrison in the St. Lawrence Valley.

In the years that followed, the British increased this German presence. In May 1780 the number of German soldiers went from 3,600 to 4,300 with the arrival of troops from Hesse-Cassel, and at the end of 1782 their number reached approximately 5,000. The reinforcements from Brunswick made it possible to re-establish the dragoons and grenadiers, and to increase the number of infantry regiments to five. When peace was restored, the troops

returned home, but many German soldiers chose to settle in Canada. The German names that many Quebeckers bear today go back to these ancestors. The Wilhelmys, for example, are descendants of a soldier in the Hesse-Hanau Chasseurs. In addition, many hard-to-pronounce German names were gallicized: Maher became Maheu, Beyer became Payeur, and Schumpff became Jomphre.

These German soldiers introduced to Canada a beautiful tradition: the Christmas tree. At Christmas 1781 Baroness von Riedesel, the wife of the General, gave a party at their Sorel residence, and the guests were pleasantly surprised to see a magnificent fir tree bearing candles and decorated with a variety of fruits. People liked the idea and it caught on. We therefore owe this custom to the German soldiers who came to defend this country more than two centuries ago.

Guerilla Warfare Along the American Border

Maintaining a garrison sufficiently strong to ensure Canada's security was not enough, however. It was equally important from then on to keep the Americans on the defensive, to discourage any attempts at a new invasion.

Soldiers of the German Anhalt-Zerbst Regiment in garrison in Quebec from 1778 to 1783. Reconstitution by Herbert Knötel.
Anne S. K. Brown Military Collection, Brown University, Providence.

The solution was to follow the earlier methods of New France: launch surprise attacks by sending groups of soldiers and Amerindians to sow confusion and disarray along the American borders. But this time, instead of Canadians it was the Loyalist refugees who carried out these raids, supported by those Iroquois who had also remained loyal to the British. Like most Amerindians, the Iroquois were not fond of the Americans. Even before the

---

Colour-bearer of the Brunswick Prinz Friedrich Regiment, from 1776 to 1783. Reconstitution by Herbert Knötel.
Anne S. K. Brown Military Collection, Brown University, Providence.

hostilities began, a great deal of pressure had been placed on them by the Americans; in the Susquehanna Valley many colonists had even moved into their traditional territories. From the very beginning of this new phase in the conflict, the British easily rallied the Iroquois to their cause, especially since a remarkable chief whose allegiance was clear had been emerging as leader within their nation: Thayendanegea, better known under the name of Joseph Brant.

At Niagara in the fall of 1777, the Loyalist Major John Butler, with the help of his son, Walter, recruited

the eight companies of Butler's Rangers, a new colonial light infantry corps consisting of refugees primarily from areas bordering western New York State and Pennsylvania. These men wanted revenge against the neighbours who had chased them from their native provinces. At the end of summer 1778, the Wyoming, Scholarie and Susquehanna valleys were virtually devastated by their many raids, which the American troops had been unable to stop. In November, Butler's Rangers and a group of Iroquois successfully attacked Cherry Valley, even though there was an American regiment there. It suffered heavy losses and was forced to take refuge in the small forts, unable to fend off the attackers.

These large-scale raids, combined with many smaller expeditions, shook the Americans. George Washington ordered General John Sullivan to counterattack. In 1779, Sullivan, in command of some 3,500 soldiers, destroyed the Iroquois villages, causing considerable damage. More than 2,600 Iroquois were forced to take refuge at Fort Niagara. In spite of this, the Americans were unable to neutralize the British and Iroquois forces. There were many skirmishes, with the Americans generally on the losing

A soldier of Butler's Rangers, between 1778 and 1783. Reconstitution by G. A. Embleton. Parks Canada.

end, and Sullivan did not dare to attack either Oswego or Fort Niagara, where Butler and Brant were headquartered. In spite of the destruction of the Iroquois villages, the raids began even more intensely the following year, not only from Niagara, but also from Crown Point, by detachments of Sir John Johnson's Loyalist Regiment. Fort Stanwix was placed under such heavy harassment by Butler and Brant that the Americans abandoned it in May 1781. In 1781 and 1782 a detachment of Butler's Rangers left Detroit to fight as far away as Kentucky. Meanwhile, in 1781 several small corps of

Loyalists were formed into a battalion of Loyal Rangers in Montreal; with the support of another Loyalist corps, the King's Rangers, it carried out a few reconnaissance expeditions in Vermont. Throughout the conflict, the guerilla tactics forced the Americans to be on the defensive from Lake Champlain to Detroit.

France and Spain Enter the War

From a military standpoint, the British were forcing the Americans to fight on their own terrain rather than in Canada. Diplomatically speaking, however, England's situation was becoming precarious. It had little sympathy within the forum of nations, and found even fewer allies to support it against its rebel colonies. France had been eagerly awaiting an opportunity to avenge itself for the humiliations suffered in the Seven Years' War. Its army, which had been reorganized, modernized and strengthened, had become one of the most powerful in Europe. Its fleet, which had been virtually wiped out 20 years earlier, had added several modern warships and it was now the second most powerful navy in the world.

In July 1778 hostilities between France and England broke out openly,

and the French were immediately successful in the West Indies and on the high seas. In 1779 Spain too joined the war against Great Britain, and the following year Holland joined as well. The conflicts became worldwide, and the British, overwhelmed, were attacked at Minorca and Gibraltar in the Mediterranean, and in Florida, India and the West Indies, all at a time when they saw a powerful French corps join the American army. In October 1781 General Charles Cornwallis, driven back to Yorktown in Virginia, had to surrender, putting an end to the hostilities along the Atlantic coast. That same year, the Spanish army forced the fall of Pensacola in western Florida, thus putting an end to the British presence in the Gulf of Mexico.

At Halifax, the prospect of a French fleet in the vicinity of the Gulf of St. Lawrence did nothing to inspire confidence. As soon as France entered the war, the British organized an expedition against the small French islands of Saint-Pierre and Miquelon to neutralize them as a potential naval base. The island garrison, with only 50 soldiers of the Compagnie franche de Saint-Pierre-et-Miquelon, surrendered in exchange for the honours of war.

Several corps of Loyalists, including Jessup's King's Loyal Americans, in 1776, and the Loyal Nova Scotia Volunteers, c. 1783, wore the red, green-faced, uniform.
Reconstitution by G. A. Embleton.
Parks Canada.

In spite of this victory, the British remained on the alert – and not without reason, because the following year they intercepted American dispatches suggesting a French attack against Newfoundland. The alarmed inhabitants of the island raised a colonial regiment to help the small garrison of regular troops stand guard. In 1780 the 350 men of the Newfoundland Regiment were posted to St. John's and Placentia.

The fear of naval raids proved to be well founded when French vessels attacked British convoys en route to North America. At

Quebec, Governor Frederick Haldimand was also worried about the consequences of France's entry into the conflict. A declaration by the King of France addressed to Canadians was also circulating covertly; how would they react if a corps of French troops were to land on the shores of the St. Lawrence? As it happened, Haldimand had nothing to fear and the Canadians nothing to hope for from their former motherland, for France had secretly promised the Americans that it would not retake Canada, neither militarily nor by treaty.

Lapérouse at Hudson Bay

On the other hand, French raids on distant territories were still possible. On August 8, 1782, the employees of the Hudson's Bay Company occupying Fort Prince of Wales saw three sails on the horizon. As the ships approached, the employees realized, to their great surprise and distress, that they were not the usual merchant ships arriving from England to collect furs, but a 74-gun warship, the *Sceptre*, accompanied by two 36-gun frigates. And they were flying the French flag! Not only were there several hundred seamen on board, but 250 soldiers of the Armagnac and Auxerrois regiments, a

Officer of the French Armagnac Regiment at Hudson Bay in 1782. Reconstitution by G. A. Embleton. Parks Canada.

colonial artillery detachment with field guns as well as marines and naval artillery. All were under the command of Jean-François de Galaup, Comte de Lapérouse, a daring navigator who was to become one of the great explorers of the Pacific. His expedition had left from Cap Haïtien with the intent of pillaging the lucrative English Hudson's Bay establishments.

The reason for the French arriving in such strength is that Fort Prince of Wales, their objective, was well protected to discourage any attempts to take it. Following the raids

made by Iberville at the end of the seventeenth century, the Hudson's Bay Company had begun in 1717 to build a large bastioned fort on an island near what is today the city of Churchill, Manitoba. Called Fort Prince of Wales, it was made of stone and armed with an impressive amount of artillery.

This remarkable structure, the only large stone fort overlooking the Arctic Ocean, took some 60 years to build. Hudson's Bay Company employees were responsible for guarding it, and they held weekly weapons drills. Decades of peaceful isolation, however, convinced them that such military measures were now unnecessary – the French would never dare attack again! So when Lapérouse arrived at the fort Governor Samuel Hearne – who is also known for his explorations of the Canadian North – had only about 80 men, Amerindians included, to operate his 42 pieces of artillery. The next morning the French troops disembarked "unimpeded." When asked to capitulate, "the governor and his garrison surrendered unconditionally."[50] The scenario was repeated at York Factory and Severn. After loading furs and blowing up the forts, the French left Hudson Bay at the beginning of September.

The entry of Spain into the war in July 1779 also caused concern among the British, with respect to their being able to keep the West. The Spanish already occupied much of the territory west of the Mississippi. In addition, in 1778-79, General George Rogers Clark's Americans, helped by some inhabitants of French descent, had already taken the British forts of Vincennes, Cahokia and Kaskaskia. There was thus a risk that the British territory south of the Great Lakes could fall into Spanish and American hands. To prevent this, the British at Michilimackinac decided to attack St. Louis, the capital of Spanish Illinois. This small city had only 29 soldiers of the Fijo de Luisiana Colonial Regiment and 281 militiamen, virtually all of French descent. In July 1780 they were nevertheless able to repulse the attack of a group of approximately 750 Amerindians, Canadian volunteers and a few British soldiers. At Cahokia, the Americans also fended off a British attack. The following year, the Spanish went on the offensive: 65 St. Louis militiamen, accompanied by approximately 60 Amerindians, took Fort St. Joseph. An attack on Michilimackinac, a key post for the fur trade in the Great Lakes area, was

feared. Its garrison was transferred to a new fort built on Mackinac Island, which was nearby and felt to be safer. As it happens, neither the Spanish nor the Americans wished to get involved in such an attack, and they both remained in their positions until the end of the hostilities.

The British Lose the War

At the end of 1782 the British armies in North America remained in only a few places to the south of Canada: New York, Charleston, South Carolina, and eastern Florida. The Americans and Spanish held the rest of the territory east of the Mississippi. Elsewhere in the world, the British position was far from enviable. With little hope of being able to improve their military position, they began peace talks. On January 20, 1783, an armistice was proclaimed following the signing of preliminary agreements which were to be formally ratified by the Treaty of Versailles the following September 3. Outside of North America, there were no geographical changes except for ceding a few British islands in the West Indies to the French and Minorca to the Spanish. In North America, however, there were major changes. England recognized the independence of its

Drummer of the French Auxerrois Regiment at Hudson Bay in 1782. Reconstitution by G. A. Embleton. Parks Canada.

Thirteen former colonies, which became the United States of America. The Spanish took Florida and kept all the land taken from the British on the Gulf of Mexico. Even the islands of Saint-Pierre and Miquelon became French once again. Great Britain thus lost all of its North American empire to the south of Canada.

The Arrival of the Loyalists

For Canadians of French descent who still had hoped that Canada, with the exception of the Maritime colonies, would be returned to France, the Treaty of Versailles put an end to any such illusions. England, in its turn, was humiliated, but Canada remained a British colony.

There was also a serious human problem: the thousands of American Loyalists who had fought alongside the British in their former colonies. These men and their families could not remain in the United States without exposing themselves to reprisals. They had to be evacuated. Thus in 1783-84 approximately 40,000 Loyalists – men, women and children – took refuge in Canada. Most came from regiments of disbanded Loyalist volunteers, and they settled in a new province created for them, New Brunswick. Many others went to Nova Scotia and Prince Edward Island. The Loyalist regiments established in Canada during the war were also disbanded. The men of the King's Royal Regiment of New York and the Loyal Rangers settled with their families in eastern Ontario, while the 469 soldiers of Butler's Rangers, with their 111 women and 257 children, were offered land on the Niagara Peninsula.

For the immediate future, these thousands of Loyalist veterans provided an excellent source of defence against possible aggression from the United States. But in the longer term they were to radically alter the composition of the country's population. Ten years earlier, when the Quebec Act was passed,

such a demographic influx would have been impossible to predict. The Maritime colonies were sparsely populated, and the St. Lawrence Valley was overwhelmingly French. With the arrival of these tens of thousands of English-speaking Americans, who were Protestant and fiercely attached to their British values, everything was to change.

Tensions could be expected between the Loyalists and the Canadians of French descent. And indeed such tensions appeared from the very outset – and they persist to the present day. The British governors attempted to play down the mutual prejudices, and in this were somewhat successful. After all, the two groups, although they had their differences, had certain affinities. The Loyalists had suffered a terrible defeat that forced them to flee their homeland, and the French Canadians had been turned over to the British following a similar defeat. Both groups had a strong military tradition, because they consisted largely of veterans – militiamen or soldiers. Above all, each group in its own way suspected the Americans of harbouring plans to invade Canada.

Each group mistrusted the Americans for different reasons. For the English Canadians of Loyalist descent, it was their distaste for a republican political system and their collective painful memory of their former fellow citizens. The French Canadians were neither seduced by British royalty nor very hostile to the Americans; their principal interest lay in keeping their

---

Men of the King's Royal Regiment of New York settling in Johnstown in 1784. James Peachy. Watercolour.
National Archives of Canada, C2001.

language, their religion and their laws, which the British guaranteed them. Thus beyond prejudice and rivalries, each group knew that they had to work together to help the British troops repel American invasion attempts.

Lastly, the Loyalists were not all of British descent; among them were Iroquois left at the mercy of the Americans at the end of the war because their traditional territory had been in New York State. Chief Joseph Brant convinced Governor Haldimand to cede to them the Grand River Valley (near Brantford, Ontario), and in 1784 approximately 400 Mohawk left their ancestral lands to settle there. Others moved to eastern Ontario and the Montreal area. They too had their reasons to mistrust the Americans.

Chapter 3

THE COVETED PACIFIC COAST

As the wars were fought between the French and the British, and then the British and the Americans, the territories to the west of the Prairies remained uncharted. No one had yet crossed the continent, neither by land across the Rocky Mountains – which were deemed impenetrable – nor by ship through the enigmatic Northwest Passage. In the eighteenth century, however, a series of events would propel the northwestern part of the North American continent onto the world scene. The great powers almost went to war to maintain their geostrategic interests in this part of the globe, which in the end would become the Canadian Pacific coast.

Until the eighteenth century, the Pacific Ocean was virtually unknown, few explorers having dared to venture there. In the sixteenth century, the Spanish established colonies on the Pacific coast of America, as well as in the Philippines, in the Far East. They thus inaugurated the first regular trans-Pacific link with their famous "Manila galleons," which shuttled between Manila in the Philippines and Acapulco, Mexico. Little by little, the Spanish began to consider the Pacific their own domain, because they controlled the whole western coast of America from Cape Horn in Chile to northern Mexico. The Spanish settlements dotting this immense coastline were never threatened, except perhaps by a few pirates or particularly daring buccaneers, and there were no other European colonies along the coast.

This situation changed after 1725. Peter I, Czar of Russia, from his capital, St. Petersburg, sent Vitus Jonassen Bering, a captain in the Imperial Russian Navy, to find a passage to America via Siberia. In 1741 Bering and Captain Alexis Chirikov reached Alaska. In the decades that followed, Russian traders in search of furs travelled the coastline to the north of what is now British Columbia. In the 1760s the Spanish embassy in St. Petersburg reported alarming news: the Russians intended to settle on the Pacific coast to the north of Mexico, thereby compromising the security of New Spain. That colony at the time occupied a vast territory rich in silver mines, and included

Central America, Mexico and the southwestern United States. When informed of Russia's ambitions, the Marquis de Croix, Viceroy of New Spain, took firm steps: he ordered the construction of a naval base at San Blas in northwestern Mexico and further ordered that Alta California (now the state of California) be explored with a view to colonization.

Early Explorations of the Northwest Coast

Prior to these events, the Spanish had not really explored the west coast at Canada's current latitude, making no more than a few reconnaissance trips. They thus had no accurate map of the area. Viceroy Antonio Maria Bucareli y Ursua, who succeeded the Marquis de Croix, therefore assigned the navy the task of exploring the coastline to the north of California, not only to locate the position of the Russians, but also to take accurate map readings. In January 1774 Ensign Juan Josef Pérez Hernandez, commandant of the frigate *Santiago*, left San Blas to sail northward. In addition to his second in command,

Estebán José Martinez, a chaplain and surgeon, his crew consisted of 84 seamen, one of whom was a gunner. There were no soldiers on board, but a dozen sailors had been trained in weapons drill and could fight if required. The Viceroy ordered them to avoid fighting with the Natives.

On July 18, 1774, the lookout of the *Santiago* signalled land on the horizon: the north of what is today the Queen Charlotte Archipelago in British Columbia. Without knowing it, Pérez and his men were the first Europeans to reach this part of northwestern North America and to meet the Haida. The Haida came out to greet them in large

Estebán José Martinez, c. 1785, in the full dress uniform worn by lieutenants in the Spanish navy.
Museo Naval, Madrid.

canoes, one of which carried as many as 22 paddlers and a drum. Impressed by the advanced civilization of these Amerindians, the Spanish deemed it wise not to go ashore, but they did trade goods. After continuing northward for a few days, Pérez headed south. On August 7 he reached the proximity of Nootka on Vancouver Island. As had the Haida, the Nootka Amerindians approached the *Santiago* in canoes. Relations were very cordial; the Spanish and the Nootka traded, the Spanish offering a variety of goods, including silver spoons, and received in exchange skins, finely braided hats decorated with scenes of whale-hunting, and various other items. This time Pérez wanted to go ashore but was prevented from doing so by bad weather. Finally, the *Santiago* turned southward and returned to Mexico.[51]

"The Vikings of the North Pacific"

During the era of these first European explorations, the west coast was inhabited by a large number of small Amerindian nations who spoke various languages. To the north, in what is now Alaska, were the Tlingit. The Queen Charlotte Islands belonged to the Haida, whereas along the coast of the mainland, at the same latitude, were the Tsimshian. The land of the Nootka (also called

---

During their expeditions the Spanish sometimes had to use their muskets and cannons to keep the Natives at bay. José Cardéro. Drawing.
Museo Naval, Madrid.

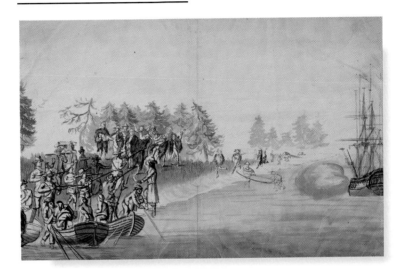

Wakashan) extended to the south of Vancouver Island, and the Salish area included the eastern part of the island as well as some of the mainland along the coast. These peoples were both sedentary and navigators, and they lived in an area where nature was generous. Fish were plentiful and the coastline was covered in magnificent cedars, which the Natives used to great advantage, building houses out of planks and making canoes to hunt whale – for these were outstanding sailors and fishermen. Their art was indicative of a high level of cultural refinement.

These people also proved to be formidable fighters and, like the other North American Native nations, they assigned a prime role to war. They were not familiar with firearms and their discipline was more that of warriors than that of soldiers. As far as we can determine today, their tactics were based on mass attacks rather than surprise raids. One of their awe-inspiring ruses was to feign friendship and then attack by surprise. Armed with bows and arrows, javelins, clubs and daggers (with blades carved out of bone), these warriors fought either naked or protected

by armour made of strips of wood or braided cord. Some wore magnificent wooden helmets sculpted and painted to depict animal heads.

The coastal nations, which consisted essentially of navigators, often attacked enemy villages or forts in flotillas of canoes. These large, richly decorated vessels could be 20 metres long. They were especially fast and effective when propelled by many paddlers: when the paddlers maintained a rapid pace, the canoes could travel at a speed of more than seven knots, which was faster than a European frigate. These people were also familiar with the use of the sail. Their sailing raids were used primarily to take prisoners, who were then kept as slaves. In villages accustomed to successful expeditions, up to one third of the population could be slaves. Unlike the Natives in the east and centre of the continent, those on the Pacific coast did not practise ritual torture and did not take scalps, but they did cut off the heads of the enemies they killed to keep as trophies. For both their bravery and their navigating skills, they were sometimes called "the Vikings of the North Pacific."

Apart from their impressive villages, these people built coastal forts using tall cedar trunks. They also erected such forts on the summits of hills and along the rivers to control and tax maritime traffic on the waterways running through their land. Recent archaeological digs revealed Fort Kitwanga, built on a promontory of this type located upstream on the Skeena River; there were many others used as toll stations. Occasional disputes concerning right of way may have led to sieges during which the attackers would attempt to set fire to the fort, with the defenders throwing tree trunks onto them from the top of the palisades.

The military art of the people of the American northwest was therefore relatively well developed, and they were potentially formidable adversaries for the Europeans. Indeed, when the first contacts occurred, they showed no fear of the white newcomers arriving in great sailing ships.

New Spanish Explorations

Following the first Spanish expedition by Pérez in 1774 came the second in 1775 under the command of Lieutenant Bruno de Hezeta. There were two ships: the *Santiago*, commanded by Hezeta himself, and the schooner *Sonora*, commanded by his second in command, Lieutenant Juan Francisco de la Bodega y Quadra. Viceroy Bucareli realized that the main error of the preceding expedition, to send only a single ship, had obliged Pérez to be excessively careful in his explorations and in his meetings with the Amerindians. This time, the Viceroy was keen for the explorers to go ashore so that the newly discovered territories would be recognized as Spanish lands. Most important for him was the identification of Russian settlements.

During their voyage north the two ships experienced many storms, and illness hit the crew. In July 1775 they reached the vicinity of Point Grenville, in what is today Washington State. With the Amerindians showing signs of friendship, a detachment of seven sailors was sent ashore to obtain drinking water and firewood. No sooner had they reached the beach than they were massacred in just a few moments by approximately 300 Amerindians surging from the woods, under the horrified gaze of their companions who had

remained on board the ships. Bodega had them open fire, but his ship was too far away.

Shaken by this disaster, Hezeta decided to return to Mexico, but Bodega refused to follow him without having completed the essential mission, which was to locate the Russians. He continued northward on the *Sonora* and got as far as the 58th parallel in Alaska. In a large bay, which he called Bucareli, Bodega went ashore with his crew to take possession formally in the name of Carlos III, King of Spain and the Indies, as ordered by the Viceroy. Having failed to find any Russians, Bodega returned southward, taking bearings as he went along the coast. This expedition made it clear to the Spanish that the Russians were not a serious threat. Some even asked whether it was worth continuing to explore the coast since there was no intention of establishing settlements there.

Enter Cook and the British

Meanwhle, other countries began to take an interest in the Pacific. Louis-Antoine de Bougainville, a member of Montcalm's staff in Canada, had explored the South Pacific in the 1760s, as had another participant

Juan Francisco de la Bodega y Quadra, in the full dress uniform worn by captains, c. 1785.
Museo Naval, Madrid.

in the siege of Quebec, Captain James Cook of the Royal Navy. It was to this seasoned explorer, who had already circumnavigated the globe twice, that the British government assigned the mission of exploring the northwest coast of North America. Cook's assignment was to find a possible Northwest Passage, a maritime passage that would join the Pacific to the Atlantic, by going around the continent.

Russian maps published in 1774 showed Alaska to be an island, a large strait separating it from the rest of the continent. In 1771 the explorer Samuel Hearne of the Hudson's Bay Company had reached the mouth of the Coppermine River in the Northwest Territories by a land route, and had seen the Arctic coast. This information led him to believe in the existence of

James Cook, in the full dress uniform of a Royal Navy captain. John Webber. Oil. 1776.
Museum of New Zealand Te Papa Tongarewa, Wellington.

a Northwest Passage, something of immense strategic importance for Canada; if it did exist, Great Britain would have to control it.

On July 12, 1776, the HMS *Discovery* left Plymouth with 12 cannon and 22 officers, 71 sailors and 20 marines, along with the HMS *Resolution*, carrying 81 officers and sailors. Cook was instructed not to oppose any of the Spanish or Russian territorial claims, but rather to take possession of any useful lands in the name of the King, with the agreement of the Natives.

In March 1778 Cook reached the northwest coast of America and undertook to sail along it. On March 29 his two ships dropped anchor in Nootka Sound, opposite the village of Yuquot. Europeans had already approached the village, but Cook and his men were the first to disembark. They were received amicably by the chief, Muquinna. Relations were excellent at first, and there were exchanges that were deemed very productive for both parties. The English noted that the Amerindians had a number of steel tools and two silver spoons, proof that there had already been contact, whether direct or otherwise, with Europeans.

These good relations did not last, however, since some members of the expedition accused the Amerindians of theft. Cook then had a temporary observatory built. He ordered his men to work armed, but the Amerindians explained that they were rarely armed and did not want to attack. To show the Amerindians what they might expect if they were to become hostile, Lieutenant James Williamson gave them a shooting demonstration, firing on an otter-skin coat from 20 metres away and making several small holes in it. The power of the musket had the desired effect, for "the Indians gazed at one another for some time with fright & silent astonishment."[52] Cook carried out accurate surveys of his position. On April 28, after having repaired his ships and refreshed his men, he took to the sea again, sailing northward.

Ships of Cook's expedition at Nootka in 1778. Engraving after a drawing by John Webber.
Parks Canada.

Bad weather forced Cook to remain offshore, and he did not see land again until Alaska. Here he went along the coast to Bering Strait, but soon came up against a veritable wall of ice, which caused him to turn back without having found the entrance to the Northwest Passage. He was eventually killed at the beginning of the following year by Natives in the Hawaiian Islands but the other members of his expedition were able to return to England. After this extraordinary reconnaissance of the Pacific, the existence of a Northwest Passage between Nootka and Alaska was seriously challenged. Unlike the Russians and the Spanish, who kept the findings of their explorations secret, the British, in 1784, published an account as well as excellent maps of Cook's voyage. They understood that making their discoveries public gave

them a considerable advantage in the event of any future dispute.

This openness was, moreover, part of a new trend that had appeared in the Age of Reason and was to reach its apogee with the Pacific explorations: recognition of the principle by which the security of ships and their occupants transcended issues of national boundaries. A nation that disseminated its scientific and cartographical knowledge for the benefit of others increased its prestige considerably.

Spanish Reaction

In Madrid, however, the Spanish authorities feared the consequences of Cook's expedition. Viceroy Bucareli was instructed to oppose Cook if he were to reach California, but he responded that any such orders were diplomatically risky, as well as unachievable given the means available to him. Bucareli even delayed until 1779 the departure of a new expedition northward.

On February 11 of that same year, the frigates *Princesa* and *Favorita*, under the command of Lieutenant Ignacio de Arteaga and his second in command, Lieutenant Bodega, left San Blas. Their mission was to explore the northwest coast, and not to intervene against the English navigators: merely crossing their path would be enough to confirm Spanish presence in the area. Such an encounter did not occur, however. Cook had already left some time before the Spanish frigates reached Nootka in July 1779 after sailing along the coast of Alaska. Arteaga and Bodega carried out detailed surveys, which were consigned to the archives along with those of the earlier expeditions, for Spain was now at war with England and its navy had been mobilized for combat.

After peace was made in 1783, the Spanish did not immediately resume expeditions to the north, now considering them useless. In 1786 the arrival in California of a French expedition led by Lapérouse made them change their minds. It confirmed to the Spanish not only that there were Russian posts in Alaska, but also that on the northwest coast there were English merchant ships that had begun to trade with the Amerindians. Cook's voyages had shown that extraordinary profits could be made by selling furs from the Pacific northwest coast in China.

Thus in January 1787 King Carlos III ordered that the Spanish resume expeditions. The following year, the *Princesa* and the *San Carlos* moved up the coast to Kodiak Island in Alaska. Along the way, the ship's ensign, Estebán José Martinez, who was commanding them, saw several English and American merchant ships plying the area. Back in Mexico, he strongly recommended that a fort be established at Nootka to protect Spanish rights.

Russian, British and Spanish Plans

In spite of all the fears elicited by the Russians, their presence in Alaska was much more limited than had been thought. They had only a few small trading posts and a tiny population, and maintained neither troops in garrison nor warships from their navy. But the English, Spanish and French explorations eventually worried the imperial authorities, and in December 1786 Czarina Catherine II ordered the Imperial Navy to organize an expedition to the Alaskan coast. Foreign merchants were to be expelled and Russia's sovereignty proclaimed over the whole of the territory north of the 55th

parallel (north of the Queen Charlotte Islands) by means of markers, officially taking possession, and warship patrols. Detailed scientific and cartographical surveys were also to be carried out. The Russian admiralty assigned four warships and a supply ship to the expedition, with a total of 34 officers, 639 sailors and soldiers, and some scientists on board. Command was assigned to Captain Gregorii Ivanovich Mulovskii, a talented officer who was only 29 years old. The expedition was to leave in 1789 and return in 1791, but at the end of the summer of 1787 war broke out between Russia, Turkey and Sweden and the Empress cancelled the operation.

Alejandro Malaspina in a captain's dress uniform, c. 1795.
Museo Naval, Madrid.

The Russians were not the only people to harbour imperial ambitions in the Pacific. The British had taken action in Australia when they founded Port Jackson in January 1788, and they also planned to settle on the northwest coast of North America, not only so that they would have a home port for English merchant ships, but also because they had major geostrategic designs: to create British hegemony over the whole of northern North America from the Atlantic to the Pacific!

In 1789 the British government prepared an impressive expedition to found a colony at Nootka. The exploration vessel HMS *Discovery* was to go to the Pacific escorted by the HMS *Gorgon*, a large, 44-gun frigate. In Hawaii, they would meet up with HMS *Sirius*, a 28-gun frigate. From there, the three ships would sail together all the way to Vancouver Island where they would establish a small naval base in the spring of 1791. At the same time, the Governor General of Canada was to organize an overland expedition to the Pacific coast from Montreal – something that had never yet been done – to establish a transcontinental link with the expedition that had left from England. However, this ambitious British project was to be short-lived.

As early as 1788, Spain was preparing an expedition to the Pacific with both a scientific and a political aim. It was to be commanded by one of Spain's foremost scientists, Captain Alejandro Malaspina. Although these scientific and political objectives were important, the military aspect of the expedition was important as well. In fact, after receiving his instructions Malaspina had to identify those harbours that would be suitable as bases for Spanish warships, to evaluate the security and defence of colonial maritime trade, and to determine how advanced were the European establishments in the Pacific, in particular those of the British in Australia. One portion of his route would also include a detailed exploration of the northwest coast of North America, along what is now British Columbia. Two corvettes, the *Descubierta* and the *Atrevida*, equipped with the most advanced scientific instruments and each carrying 24 guns, were built for the project, and Malaspina's expedition left Cadiz for the Pacific as planned on July 30, 1789.

The Nootka Incident

In Mexico, Viceroy Manuel Antonio Flórez approved Martinez' suggestion that Nootka be occupied. In February 1789 the *Princesa* and the *San Carlos* sailed towards Nootka where they planned to build a temporary post large enough to guarantee Spanish sovereignty. In addition to their crew, the two ships had 31 soldiers on board. Martinez, who commanded the expedition, had to ensure that foreign ships recognized Spanish authority, without the need to resort to force. But when he arrived in Nootka on May 5 he was surprised to find three merchant ships anchored there. Two were American, which was not a problem because the Americans were not considered a threat to Spanish claims. But the third ship, the *Efigenia Nubiana*, was Portuguese in flag and captain only, as all the crew were English. Martinez concluded that it was a British ship sailing under a flag of convenience. He also learned from the Natives that an English trade expedition under the command of John Meares, a former lieutenant in the Royal Navy, had not only stopped at Nootka the previous year to trade, but had also erected temporary shelters and even built a small ship, the *North West America*.

To strengthen Spanish control in the region, Martinez immediately began to erect an artillery platform and a few buildings. The work was well under-way when, on July 2, a British ship, the *Argonaut*, commanded by Captain James Colnett, arrived from China bearing 28 Chinese workers and considerable equipment in addition to the sailing crew. To top it off, Colnett told Martinez that he had been ordered by his king to build a settlement at Nootka!

This was all Martinez needed to conclude that there was an English plot to invade the northwest coast and to oust Spain. Colnett also refused to submit to Spanish authority. In the course of the discussion, the two commanders, each of whom was hot-tempered, got angry and Colnett put his hand to his sword. Martinez used this gesture as a pretext to arrest Colnett and take his ship. Soon afterward, on July 12, another British ship, the *Princess Royal*, arrived at Nootka from China. Martinez decided to settle the problem once and for all. Going beyond his orders, he seized all the English ships and sent them to the San Blas naval base in Mexico.

Until this point the Amerindians had stayed out of these disputes between whites. But the Spanish seizures prevented them from trading with the British, which royally displeased them! Unhappy and irritated, one of their chiefs, Callicum, went to meet Commander Martinez, and his cries from his dugout canoe were interpreted as insults. Giving in to his impulsive nature, Martinez fired a shot in the air to intimidate him. Then, one of the sailors in the crew, believing that his commander had missed his target, took aim, fired, and killed Callicum! The British propagandists later would not fail to make use of this disastrous mistake. Martinez remained at Nootka with his men until the fall, and was then given orders to return to San Blas to explain to the authorities why he had seized the English ships in peacetime.

In spite of these incidents, the Spanish decided to make permanent their military post at Nootka Bay. On April 3, 1790, three ships under the command of Lieutenant Francisco de Eliza y Reventa dropped anchor, and the construction work immediately began. Soon a battery of cannon defended the entrance to the port, while barracks were built for the soldiers,

a villa for the officers. Close to 80 soldiers wearing blue uniforms faced with the yellow of the first company of the Voluntarios de Cataluña, under the command of Lieutenant-Colonel Pedro de Alberni, moved in. These volunteers were Catalan in name only, however; they were in fact a corps of the regular army of New Spain, and most of the men had been recruited in Mexico.

This presidio, as the Spanish called their frontier forts, was the northernmost post of their whole empire. This military and naval base was also the first European settlement on the Canadian west coast.

The Nootka Crisis

No one in America had anticipated the diplomatic storm that would blow into the courts of Europe because of the seizure of the British vessels. As soon as rumours of the operation reached England, public opinion was shocked by the event, which had flouted the principle of freedom of the seas. The British were outraged: the British flag and the honour of the country had been sullied by the Spanish military. In April 1790 the arrival of John Meares, one of James Colnett's associates, confirmed the rumours and fanned the flames of anti-Spanish sentiment. In May the issue was debated in the House of Commons. The Admiralty cancelled the expedition that was to leave for the northwest coast of North America and

ordered the Royal Navy to prepare for hostilities.

In Madrid, King Carlos IV also ordered a mobilization of his navy, but to avoid being dragged into a hellish chain of events in spite of himself he informed the European governments that he would not be the first to declare war. In England, on the other hand, the winds of war were blowing! In July Admiral Howe was cruising off the European coast at the head of a powerful Royal Navy squadron consisting of 29 large warships to impress the Spanish with something resembling "gunboat diplomacy." The strategy backfired when the British Cabinet learned, to their great consternation, that an equally powerful Spanish squadron had left Cadiz to sail northward! What would happen when these two powerful fleets met on the high seas? Would they plunge Western Europe into a war over the possession of Nootka, which was located at the far end of the known world?

Fortunately, the two squadrons did not meet, but war, had it been declared, would have involved the navies of three countries. First the British navy, with approximately 400 ships of all sizes, but only partly in condition to do battle immediately. Then the Spanish navy, the third largest in the world after the English and French fleets but formidable chiefly because of its many large vessels – 64 out of 110 ships, including the largest warship in the world, the *Santísima Trinidad*, with its 130 guns. Lastly, because of the Franco-Spanish alliance, the French navy, with approximately 150 ships, could also have become involved. The Royal Navy was faced with a considerable challenge.

France's stand on the Nootka crisis was the key. The French Revolution had broken out in July 1789, but in the summer of 1790 the most serious consequences of this event were yet to come. The armed forces were still relatively intact and King Louis XVI was still on the throne, even though true power rested increasingly with the National Assembly. As a precautionary measure, France mobilized its navy before considering the main issue, whether to respect its alliances and to support Spain in its claims regarding Nootka, that faraway piece of land in its colonial empire. At the end of August, believing that public opinion would never agree to its becoming involved in such a dispute, the National Assembly declared that France would not go to war against freedom and the rights of man. This clearly meant that it would withdraw from the alliance.

Without France's support, the Spanish position was untenable. Fortunately for Spain, the British anger had subsided as the weeks went by, and it became possible to negotiate. On October 28, 1790, in Madrid, Spain and Great Britain signed the Nootka Bay Agreement. The threat of war was over. Under the terms of the treaty, each of the two colonial powers recognized that the other had rights on the northwest coast, to the north of California, and that each would have access to the other's settlements. Commissioners were to be appointed by each nation to work out the details of the agreement.

The agreement has often been interpreted as a commitment on the part of the Spanish to withdraw from the northwest coast. In fact, nothing required them to leave Nootka. On the contrary, they improved the land fortifications and build a floating battery in the port. What the Nootka Bay

Agreement changed was the idea that the Pacific coast belonged solely to the Spanish from Chile to Alaska. Great Britain would henceforth have rights to this coast to the north of California, rights which remained to be defined by the commissioners of the two nations.

Garrison Life at Nootka

While these events were taking place in Europe, life in Nootka was relatively peaceful, although difficult. The garrison, accustomed to the Mexican climate, was suffering greatly because of cold and illness, even though it was provided with warm clothing and medication. Several soldiers died, a few deserted, and others were sent to California for treatment. The garrison had between 73 and 76 soldiers in 1791, between 64 and 73 in 1792, and only 59 by 1793.

Pedro de Alberni, commander of the Nootka garrison, did everything possible to regain the friendship of the Amerindians after their withdrawal following the death of Callicum. They responded to the Spanish overtures and returned to Nootka. Alberni, a diplomat, even wrote a poem in their language, which his soldiers sang as a choir in honour of their chief, Muquinna: "Muquinna, Muquinna, Muquinna is a great prince, our friend; Spain, Spain, Spain is the friend of Muquinna and Nootka."[53] The chief was delighted and an era of harmony between the Spanish garrison and the Natives ensued. The very industrious Alberni studied botany, had gardens planted and raised cattle and poultry in this remote presidio to see to the needs of the garrison soldiers and seamen who stayed there during the summer. Alberni also compiled a Nootka vocabulary with the equivalent words in Spanish. In addition, he studied meteorology, and his detailed reports for the years 1790 and 1791 are the first to have been effected systematically on the northwest coast. Alberni left Nootka in 1792, but the Amerindians remembered him for a long time. The name of this talented Catalan volunteer officer is immortalized in Port Alberni, British Columbia.

In 1791-92, Nootka served as a small naval base for Spanish naval explorations, and several of the garrison soldiers were assigned to ships to serve as marines. These expeditions were sometimes perilous. For example, in 1791 near the town now called Esquimalt warriors in canoes forced Commander Francisco de Eliza's men to turn back. The following year a Spanish navy pilot was assassinated by Amerindians when he was hunting in what is today Neah Bay (Washington). This led his commander, Salvador Fidalgo, to open fire on two canoes of peaceful Amerindians,

killing several of them. It is worth noting that Fidalgo was reprimanded by his superiors in Mexico and Spain alike for this impetuous act. To the north, several men of the *Aranzazu* barely escaped the Haida of the Queen Charlotte Islands. In the vicinity of Vancouver Island the members of the crew of the small ships *Sutil* and *Mexicana*, on loan from the Malaspina expedition under the command of Dionisio Alcalá-Galiano and Cayetano Valdés y Flores Bazan, had more peaceful experiences.

Vancouver and Bodega y Quadra

To settle the details of the Nootka Bay Agreement, Great Britain appointed George Vancouver, a captain of the Royal Navy and a former companion of the explorer James Cook, to the position of commissioner; Bodega, a captain of the Spanish navy and a veteran explorer of the northwest coast, was his counterpart for Spain. Vancouver and Bodega met at Nootka in August 1792. They maintained good relations

Drummer of the first company of Voluntarios de Cataluña at Nootka between 1790 and 1794. Reconstitution by David Rickman. Parks Canada.

but were unable to agree on the details to be covered by the agreement. They therefore mutually decided to submit their problem to their respective governments so as not to risk another diplomatic incident.

Vancouver continued to explore the coast and he became the first European to circumnavigate the island that today bears his name. He also continued Cook's work by attempting to determine the existence of a Northwest Passage; for three summers he meticulously studied the whole coastline between the 30th and 60th parallels. He returned to England only in September 1795. Three years later he published an exhaustive and excellent account of his voyage. He asserted

without the slightest hesitation that the entrance to the Northwest Passage that was so eagerly sought after did not exist within the limits of the territory he had explored, which is correct.

The Evacuation of Nootka

In Europe, meanwhile, interest in Nootka diminished considerably. In February 1793 Great Britain and Spain had become allies in a war against France! The problems of the northwest coast already seemed far away, and the two allies signed an agreement on January 11, 1794, in which they agreed to abandon the region. That same year the Catalan volunteers in garrison at Nootka were relieved by some 20 soldiers of the Compañía fija de San Blas, which mounted the guard until March 23, 1795. On that day, following an official farewell ceremony attended by marine lieutenant Thomas Pierce, representing England, the Nootka presidio was dismantled. The artillery and the garrison were loaded onto the *Activa*,

Spanish naval officer Dionisio Alcalá-Galiano commanding the schooner Sutil *in 1792.*
Museo Naval, Madrid.

which sailed southward. Thus ended the reign of Spain on the northwest coast.

Throughout this first episode of exploration along the Canadian Pacific coast by European nations – exploration that came about because of the Spanish fears of a Russian invasion – the armed forces played an overriding role. These events are also indicative of the extent to which the soldiers of the maritime nations of the eighteenth century were interested in the progress being made in science and geography, as well as in the art of war. These men spearheaded the explorations and they were found everywhere within the known world, compiling geographical,

hydrographic, astronomic, meteorological and ethnographic data.

From Sea to Sea

At the end of the eighteenth century, the British Admiralty, even after several attempts, was still unable to discover the famous Northwest Passage joining the Atlantic and the Pacific. Others, meanwhile, attempted to make the link by land, including fur traders working for rival companies, the North West Company and the Hudson's Bay Company. One such trader, a partner of the North West Company, reached the Pacific at last. Alexander Mackenzie left Montreal, crossed the Rockies and reached the Pacific coast by the Bella Coola River on July 22, 1793.

Over the following decades other fur traders built trading posts all the way to the Pacific. These men from the east, often of French-Canadian or Scottish descent, could if necessary turn themselves into militiamen to defend the British flag flying over

their small posts. Thus at the beginning of the nineteenth century, soon after the departure of the Spanish from the northwest coast, the main beacons for the immense territory of British North America were in place from the Atlantic to the Pacific. One day, a country would emerge: Canada.

British marine infantry officer, c. 1795.
Anne S. K. Brown Military Collection, Brown University, Providence.

Chapter 4

THE NAPOLEONIC WARS AND THE WAR OF 1812

The decade following the end of the War of American Independence was relatively peaceful. The new republic of the United States no longer represented a threat, at least for the immediate future. Its powerful army was nearly completely demobilized in 1783 and it had no more than a few companies to guard its arsenals. Its modest navy had also been eliminated. Only the militias of the various states could, if required, raise a considerable number of troops. But their mandate was more defensive than offensive, because they were legally required to serve only within their boundaries. The British colonies to the north of the United States thus had nothing further to fear.

The last war had also exhausted the British army, and it took several years to recover. That is why, following the demobilization of the American army, Great Britain decided to keep only a small number

of regular troops in North America. The Royal Navy remained very powerful, however, keeping its position as the largest fleet in the world. The naval protection of Canada was provided by its North Atlantic Squadron based in Halifax and by the small ships of the Provincial Marine plying the Great Lakes.

The Militias of the New Provinces

In Canada this period of peace was accompanied by rapid growth, with tens of thousands of Loyalist war refugees establishing towns, clearing the land or becoming shipowners and sailors. Militias were also raised from among these newcomers. In New Brunswick, for example, the first militia act was passed in 1787, requiring all able-bodied men from 16 to 50 years of age to purchase weapons and equipment and to enrol in their local company. Each such company had 50 men, commanded by a captain assisted by a lieutenant and a sub-lieutenant, all of whom were attached to the county regiment. The county regiment had a small staff: a colonel, a lieutenant-colonel and a major.

In peacetime each company was required to muster twice a year for

inspection and training, and once a year – traditionally on June 4, the King's birthday – all the militia companies from a county took part in a general regimental parade. Militiamen who did not attend the various parades were fined and the money so collected was used to purchase regimental drums and flags. Officers were selected from among prominent citizens and appointed by the governor. Such positions were not paid, but they did carry some social status. On occasion the position could even be quite costly. For example, in Fredericton, one Stephen Jarvis, a prosperous man, "was invited to take command of a militia company" and he provided the company with a uniform at his "own considerable expense."[54] His purpose was to make a good impression when the Duke of Kent visited in June 1794, because, generally speaking, few officers would undertake such expenditures. The regimental colonel was usually some important figure in the county recognized for his loyalty to the Crown.

By and large, the organization was based on the militia system in Great Britain, whereby militias were organized into county regiments. Because the same type of territorial division into counties had been adopted for the new English colonies, it was also the model followed for the militia in Nova Scotia, New Brunswick and Prince Edward Island. The maximum age of service was, however, set at 60 years in Nova Scotia and Prince Edward Island but at 50 in New Brunswick.

The French Revolution

Whereas calm had returned to North America, major upheavals were on the horizon in Europe. On July 14, 1789, the people of Paris took the Bastille, the despised symbol of monarchical corruption. Revolution then spread throughout France. The Canadian press closely followed these events as they unfolded.

Because of the new ideas propagated by the French Revolution, and by the colonists arriving from the United States, there was increasing pressure across the country for elected assemblies. The British Parliament was so informed and, after heated debate, passed the Constitutional Act at the end of 1791. The Act divided Canada into two provinces: Upper Canada, with an English-speaking majority (present-day

Ontario), and Lower Canada, with a French-speaking majority (present-day Quebec). This new regime, with its elected parliaments, was introduced in 1792 and was welcomed as representing "true liberty...all the way to Hudson Bay."

From a military standpoint, the division of Canada into two provinces did not lead to many changes, but a regular colonial corps was created to augment the Upper Canada garrison. Commanded by the first lieutenant-governor of the new province, Colonel John Graves Simcoe, it took the name of the Queen's Rangers. It was a small regiment with an authorized 432 officers and soldiers. In fact, however, it consisted of only two companies, and these would never be complete, the corps never attaining a strength of more than approximately 350 men. Even though, apart from its guard duty, it was used mainly to build roads and fortifications, it was decided that the men should wear the green light infantry uniform. Some of the Queen's Rangers, including several officers, were recruited from among Loyalist veterans, and others still were recruited from England. In 1792 the regiment moved to Newark (present-day Niagara-on-

Soldier of the Queen's Rangers, c. 1800. Charles Hamilton Smith. Watercolour.
Houghton Library, Harvard University, Cambridge.

the-Lake, Ontario) and it stayed there until the seat of government for the new province moved to York (Toronto) three years later. Detachments of the Queen's Rangers had already been there since 1793 and they built the artery that would become the most famous in the Queen City: Yonge Street.

Canada at War with France

The situation in France was causing great concern. The execution of Louis XVI shocked many European countries. On February 1, 1793, Great Britain, together with several other countries, declared war on the French Republic, dragging along all of its colonies in its wake. Canada was thus by force

of circumstance at war with France.

The news of the King's death reached Quebec in the spring of 1793. It caused much grief among French Canadians, who, noted Philippe Aubert de Gaspé in his *Mémoires*, "for a long time after the Conquest kept affectionate memories of their French princes." "From that day on," he added, "I understood the horrors of the French Revolution. Upon learning the news, a feeling of deep sadness affected all the kind souls...and the sorrow was widespread."[55] Some French citizens who had fled to Canada confirmed the horrors committed in France. These new rumours, added to those already circulating about

John Nairne, Colonel of the Baie Saint-Paul Militia, c. 1795. Sir Henry Raeburn. Oil.
Private collection.

invading Republicans with their guillotines, were hardly reassuring.

For the moment, however, it was the activities of one Edmond-Charles Genêt that were of the greatest interest to the British authorities in North America. This French ambassador to the United States was the author of an appeal to Canadians entitled *Les Français libres à leurs frères du Canada* [From the free French to their brothers in Canada], inviting them to "awaken from their slumber," to take up arms, to call their "Indian friends" to the rescue and to "rely on the support of their cousins, the Americans and the French,"[56] to fight the British. This appeal secretly made the rounds of the towns and villages during the second half of 1793. In spite of the attractions it may have had, in terms of fine promises from the mother country, experience had taught the French Canadians not to place too much stock in illusions. The appeal was not the success that had been hoped for.

On the other hand, the British colonies along the Atlantic coast took the French threat very seriously, for they were vulnerable in the event of attack by warships from Saint-Pierre and Miquelon as a supply base. To

Soldier of the Royal Canadian Volunteers, c. 1798. Reconstitution by Charles Stadden.
Parks Canada.

counter this eventuality, the British decided to take preemptive action by attacking this small French territory, which the Revolution had impinged upon in spite of the distance: the previous year, hundreds of inhabitants of the archipelago took refuge on Cape Breton Island and the Magdalen Islands. As a result, on May 14, 1793, several British warships arrived at Saint-Pierre. Any resistance was useless, and the 120 men of the Compagnie franche de Saint-Pierre-et-Miquelon in garrison surrendered without a fight. During this time a portion of the regular

troops and the British ships posted to North America left for the West Indies, where furious battles were already under-way. To replace them, the authorities decided immediately to raise "provincial" (i.e., colonial) troops. They began recruiting for the Royal Nova Scotia Regiment, the King's New Brunswick Regiment, the Royal Newfoundland Regiment and two companies of the Volunteers of the Island of St. John.

Soon afterwards news reached Halifax, causing the sounding of a general alert. In July 1793 a large French squadron reached New York, carrying a contingent of troops under the command of General Galbaud. Ambassador Genêt saw this as the ideal instrument to attack Canada by sea and had even begun to recruit American volunteers to join the French. With this new fleet, according to reports from British spies, a corps of troops could disembark in Nova Scotia before the Royal Navy had time to reinforce its North Atlantic Squadron. In the Maritimes there was general consternation: the provincial troops were organized in record time – suitable weapons were found for them; but in Nova Scotia and New Brunswick there was a

temporary shortage of regulation red uniforms and the new soldiers had to parade in blue jackets with red collars and cuffs.

The militias were also placed on a war footing, particularly in Nova Scotia, where there was a serious threat of a French attack. In July the city of Halifax militia regiment had some 630 men training twice a week. In addition, a legion of 1,000 militiamen, broken down into infantry, cavalry and artillery companies, was ready to move quickly in the event of a coastal raid. The 400 Acadians who volunteered to join the militia led Governor Sir John Wentworth to report that the old wounds of the deportation had healed and that the Acadians were ready to help the British defend their province.

In the Maritimes the French were awaited. To everyone's surprise, it was in Montreal, in October 1793, that General Galbaud put in an appearance in person, without his troops! The General had abandoned his army, torn as it was by political dissension, to take refuge in Canada and to give himself up as a prisoner to the British. The French fleet returned to France, its men deeply divided by discord and political passions, all discipline lost. Thus ended the threat of a French invasion of the east coast.

These events confirmed in the minds of the French-Canadian population just how little they could count on support from France.[57] They eventually took a neutral stance vis-à-vis the former motherland, while at the same time condemning the excesses of the Revolution. Moreover, the authorities were already preoccupied with more pressing problems.

Tensions with the United States

Immediately following the American War of Independence the British continued to keep a military presence in several strategic points south of the Great Lakes, including Detroit, Mackinac and Niagara. In the early 1790s tensions between the United States and England over the issue of borders with Canada were becoming increasingly passionate.

Most of the Amerindian nations were hostile to the Americans and the settlers moving westward had to face guerilla warfare. In 1790 and 1791 the American government sent troops to quell the Amerindian hostilities, but they were wiped out by the alliance of several nations formed by the Iroquois chief, Joseph Brant. Some Loyalists and French Canadians who detested the "Yankees" helped the

Amerindians and sometimes fought alongside them, which did nothing to improve diplomatic relations between Canada and the United States.

Outraged by the hostility of the Amerindians and by what they considered a British plot to take the West away from them, the Americans took action in 1792. They passed a national militia act, established arsenals and, most importantly, recruited a regular army of 5,000 men under the command of General Anthony Wayne. This dynamic and talented officer galvanized the enthusiasm of his soldiers. On August 30, 1794, he crushed the Amerindians at Fallen Timbers (near Toledo, Ohio). Shortly afterwards, the British signed Jay's Treaty, under which they definitively recognized that the south shore of the Great Lakes belonged to the Americans. The American troops immediately moved in to take over the forts that had until then been occupied by the British. They may have given over these forts, but they moved into new forts built nearby on the Canadian side of the border. Thus the Mackinac garrison moved into Fort St. Joseph (on St. Joseph Island in Ontario), the Detroit garrison into Fort Malden (at Amherstburg,

89

François Mailhot, Captain of the 2nd Battalion of the Royal Canadian Volunteers. Christian de Heer, the painter, arrived in Canada as a soldier with the German troops and remained after the American War of Independence, working as a portrait artist. Oil, c. 1797.

Musée du Québec.

Ontario) and the Niagara garrison into Fort George (at Niagara-on-the-Lake, Ontario).

The Royal Canadian Volunteers

To guard against tensions with the United States, the British decided to raise in Canada a regiment of two battalions to serve only in North America. Recruited in 1794-95, this was the Royal Canadian Volunteers, which is the name that appears on the flags and insignia, although in French they are called the Volontaires royaux canadiens. The complement authorized for each battalion was 750 officers and soldiers, divided into 10 companies. Pay and allowances were identical to those of the metropolitan army. Officers' commissions were granted only to gentlemen living in Lower and Upper Canada. In addition, seasoned officers were chosen to command each battalion. For example, the commander of the first, Francophone, battalion was Lieutenant-Colonel Joseph-Dominique-Emmanuel Le Moyne de Longueuil, who had begun his military career as an officer in the Compagnies franches de la Marine in 1750 and who had been in many battles during the Seven Years' War and the American War of Independence. The commander of the second, Anglophone, battalion was Lieutenant-Colonel John Macdonell, an officer of Scottish descent who had emigrated to Upper Canada; he was a veteran of Butler's Rangers, a friend of the Iroquois and chief of the Scottish Macdonell Clan.[58]

The most unusual thing about this regiment was its enlistment of French Canadians for regular service, a first in the country's military annals. Even under the French regime, the authorities had had no success whatsoever in their attempts to incorporate Canadians as regular soldiers in the navy troops. On this occasion, the recruiting of the first battalion for the Royal Canadian Volunteers went off without a hitch, some French Canadians even enlisting in the second battalion. It is difficult to explain this change of heart, but it is clear at least that French Canadians no longer identified with revolutionary France. The regiment was raised without regard to the maximum authorized force, each battalion actually having approximately 450 officers and soldiers. Apart from a few details, the red uniforms of the soldiers resembled those of the British army regiments, and the equipment and weapons were similar to those of the British infantry.[59]

The Royal Canadian Volunteers were sent to forts in both Upper and Lower Canada. The first battalion's headquarters was in Quebec City, with detachments in Montreal, Trois-Rivières, Lachine, Côteau-du-Lac and Saint-Jean; the second set up headquarters at Fort George with detachments in Kingston and forts Erie, Malden and St. Joseph. The second battalion was

placed on alert for the winter of 1796-97, when a Spanish invasion from Louisiana was feared. Through a change in alliances in 1796, Spain had become France's ally against England. Rumours of mobilization of the Spanish in Louisiana quickly grew into fears that Canada would be invaded. The state of alert was eventually lifted when English spies learned that the Spanish had mobilized their troops along the Mississippi because they feared a British attack from Upper Canada!

Newfoundland Threatened

It was in the Maritimes, in 1796, that the most serious threat occurred, when a French fleet of seven vessels and a few frigates, under the command of Admiral Joseph de Richery, appeared off the coast of Newfoundland, almost creating a state of panic. There were soon rumours from every quarter that they would disembark on the island and attack St. John's. The British authorities remained sceptical, however, feeling that the French fleet would not dare to attack military objectives. In fact, it appears that Richery had come only with the intention of interfering with the fisheries, which he did. After lurking in the

Louis Fromenteau, Captain of the 1st Battalion of the Royal Canadian Volunteers. Oil, attributed to François Baillargé, c. 1796.
Musée du Québec.

vicinity for a few weeks, the Admiral returned to France, knowing full well that the Royal Navy would end up catching him if he were to stay longer. The only true landing in Newfoundland was at Bay Bulls, where the French sailors destroyed a few houses and warehouses.

Although worrisome, these raids were not a serious threat. The British therefore did not change their naval strategy and continued to assign a limited number of warships to guard the St. Lawrence and the Newfoundland fisheries. Even if some of the enemy fleet broke through the British blockade of the European coasts, as Richery did, they would be unable to stay in the vicinity of

North America too long without risking encounters with powerful pursuers. At any rate, the French and Spanish fleets were suffering defeat after defeat at the hands of the British, and towards the end of the 1790s England was virtually the undisputed ruler of the seas.

The 1802 Peace

In Europe, however, events were moving at a fast pace. Against all expectations, the armies of the Republic repulsed the Prussian and Austrian invasion attempts. The French then occupied Holland, part of Germany and northern Italy. In mid-1801 only Great Britain was still at war with France. It triumphed on the seas and in the colonies, whereas France won victories in Western Europe, leading to an impasse. The belligerents proclaimed an armistice on October 12, 1801, and signed a peace treaty at Amiens on March 25, 1802.

In Canada the news was received with considerable relief. In the summer and fall of 1802 all the colonial regiments raised in the Maritimes in 1793 were disbanded, along with the Queen's Rangers and the two battalions of Royal Canadian Volunteers.

Peace did not last long. Misunderstandings and incidents were rife, and on

Soldier of the British 6th Infantry Regiment in winter uniform in Canada, c. 1806.

Anne S. K. Brown Military Collection, Brown University, Providence.

May 16, 1803, hostilities between France and Great Britain were declared. The situation led to British North America preparing for action, but before the colonial legislatures had even had time to order the raising of local troops London decreed the establishment of four regiments of "Fencibles." Subject to the same laws, regulations and conditions of service as the other corps of the British army, the fencible infantry regiments were different in one respect: they were to serve only in North America. The British Treasury paid all of their costs, they appeared on the *Army List* – the official register of the regular army – and their officers were officially an integral part of the regular army.[60]

In the Maritimes, the Royal Newfoundland, Nova Scotia and New Brunswick regiments were recruited. In Upper and Lower Canada, it was decided to begin by raising part of the Canadian Fencibles Regiment in Scotland. The operation began badly and recruits mutinied in Edinburgh in 1804. Eventually most of the soldiers in the regiment were recruited in Lower Canada, but appointments of colonial gentlemen, Anglophone or Francophone, were few and far between, the officers of these regiments being mostly British.

In the eighteenth century, Great Britain obtained nearly all the wood it required for its navy and its merchant marine from states on the Baltic Sea. This situation changed radically in 1806, when Napoleon decreed a continental blockade in response to the Royal Navy's blockade of French ports. France thus prevented other European countries from trading with England, by threatening to send in the imperial army – Napoleon having proclaimed himself Emperor on May 18, 1804 – to invade any recalcitrant states.

England therefore turned towards Canada for its wood supplies. During the Napoleonic wars exports of Canadian oak and pine to Great Britain became so great that it may be said they supported the Royal Navy throughout its lengthy conflict with the French Empire. In 1811, for example, England imported 3,300 masts from Russia and Prussia and 23,000 from British North America –19,000 from Lower Canada alone! These figures are indicative of Canada's importance to Great Britain at this critical period in its history. To keep the flow of traffic moving, however, the Royal Navy had to protect the sea routes to England, and new threats appeared on the horizon.

The Battle of Trafalgar

The short peace of Amiens had made it possible for the French fleet to rebuild its strength. Together with its Spanish ally, it now constituted a serious threat. The invasion of England by an

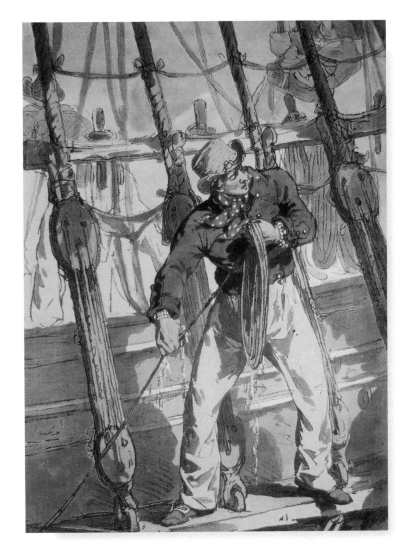

Seaman of the Royal Navy in 1807.
J. Atkinson. Engraving.
Anne S. K. Brown Military Collection,
Brown University, Providence.

army crossing the Channel was possible if the Franco-Spanish fleet were able to control this stretch of sea for a few days. Napoleon had clearly understood this strategic move and during the summer of 1805 found himself at Boulogne leading the Grande Armée, waiting for the Franco-Spanish fleet of Admiral Pierre-Charles de Villeneuve.

The future of England and its empire was directly at stake. The British fleet of Admiral Horatio Nelson, in attempting to cut off the French-Spanish fleet, intercepted it off Cape Trafalgar on October 21, 1805. By coincidence, war had grouped together, on the Spanish side, several officers who had explored the Canadian Pacific coast in their youth, including Dionisio Alcalá-Galiano, who was killed on board the *Bahama*, and Cayetano Valdés, who was injured on the *Neptuno*. A fierce battle ensued between Villeneuve's 33 vessels, 15 of which were Spanish, and the 27 British ships. Nelson was mortally wounded but the Franco-Spanish fleet was virtually wiped out. Admiral

Nelson's victory gave the British navy unquestioned supremacy over all the seas of the globe for almost a century.

In Canada the news of the victory at Trafalgar was greeted with immense relief. Any serious naval threats had been eliminated and communications with Great Britain were assured. Wood exports could continue in safety. Montreal merchants were

so happy that they erected a monument in Nelson's honour even before the people of London did!

New Tensions in America

Naval security was, however, not the only matter of concern to Canadians. New events required their attention. Right after the peace of 1802 had been declard, Napoleon announced that

France was retaking Louisiana. This would mean that western Canada would immediately find itself neighbouring an immense French territory! Nothing good could come of this, particularly when it was learned that a French prefect had arrived at New Orleans in March 1803 with a few officers, and an army of 3,700 men would soon be joining them to replace the Spanish. The joy of the people of Louisiana, who were almost entirely of French descent, did not last. When war against England resumed, Napoleon believed that Louisiana was impossible to defend and he sold it to the United States. On December 20, 1803, the Stars and Stripes replaced the French flag at New Orleans. This was the best geostrategic card Napoleon could have played, because Louisiana thus became part of a neutral nation, with no particular allegiance to the British.

As a consequence, the Americans, who had been confined to the east of the Mississippi, saw their western border disappear. Vast lands, most of which had been unexplored, were now open to them. Some,

including President Thomas Jefferson, began to dream of continental hegemony for their country, a dream that was later to be called "Manifest Destiny"; it was obvious to them that the United States was destined to dominate all of North America, including Canada and part of Mexico. In 1805 an expedition led by two officers of the regular American army, Meriwether Lewis and William Clark, reached the Pacific at the level of Oregon, thus establishing a transcontinental link to the south of Canada.

Relations between England and the United States gradually worsened. The Royal Navy prevented American merchant ships,

which were neutral, from entering European ports. Worse still, they searched ships flying the Stars and Stripes for British sailors who had deserted. The American navy at the time had only a few frigates and gunboats, but the men did not lack the courage to oppose the English cruisers. In 1807 and 1811 there were even a few isolated battles between ships of the Royal Navy and the U.S. Navy.

Eventually, diplomatic relations deteriorated to the point where in early 1812 it was decided to recruit another regiment of Fencibles in Upper Canada. The Glengarry Light Infantry was raised, partly of Scottish colonists in the eastern part of what is now the province of Ontario.

Mobilization in Lower Canada

At the same time, the political situation in Lower Canada worsened under the administration of Governor James Henry Craig, an effective soldier but a clumsy politician. In 1810, with the intent of frustrating the Opposition, he shut down the newspaper *Le Canadien* and imprisoned its publisher. Following close on the heels of the cancellation of the militia officers' commissions for several members of the Opposition sitting in the House of Assembly, this

plunged Lower Canada into political crisis – because the Opposition consisted essentially of French Canadians, while most of Craig's supporters were Anglophones. The rivalry between the two ethnic groups threatened to degenerate into a confrontation.

In 1811 London recalled Craig and replaced him with a Swiss officer who spoke French, Sir George Prevost. Politically astute and an excellent administrator, Prevost was to clean up the mess and prepare for an imminent conflict with the United States. Thanks to his conciliatory manner, Prevost soon rallied the Opposition. He realized that both French and English Canadians feared an American invasion more than anything. Indeed talk in Washington was far from reassuring: the War Hawks group, which had the approval of President James Madison and held the high ground, wanted to mobilize 50,000 militiamen to invade Canada, something they said would be easy to accomplish. The acquisition of Canada "will be a mere matter of marching,"[61] stated former President Thomas Jefferson, convinced that the people would be unable to fend off soldiers bearing the star-spangled banner of freedom.

Faced with this prospect, Lower Canada decided to raise its own small army. In March and April 1812 the Assembly approved the creation of a light infantry regiment of volunteers and four line infantry battalions to be conscripted from the militia owing to a shortage of volunteers. Some 2,000 officers and soldiers were thus mobilized and divided among the four battalions of the Lower Canada Select Embodied Militia in the spring and early summer. They had to be between the ages of 18 and 30 and serve for three months, but "in time of war" they could "be required to serve for two years."[62] They were posted primarily south of Montreal.

They would be clothed and equipped similarly to regular infantry soldiers – that is, in red. Traditionally, French-Canadian militiamen preferred blue. Lieutenant-Colonel Jean-Baptiste-Melchior Hertel de Rouville, commander of the 2nd elite militia battalion, confided to the Adjutant-General of the militia: "I am convinced, based on the prejudices that I am aware of among the inhabitants, that the red uniform is not the most appropriate at this time if the proper effect is to result."[63] In spite of his opinion, the Select Embodied militiamen of 1812 wore the red uniform,

as would many other militiamen when Governor General Prevost pointed out that otherwise they could be confused with the enemy American infantry, which also wore a blue uniform!

The light infantry regiment of volunteers was called the Canadian Voltigeurs, a name which, like that of its commander, Charles-Michel d'Irumberry de Salaberry, was to become famous in our military heritage. The Canadian Voltigeurs consisted of six companies recruited by the regiment's officers. They spread out through the towns and countryside to convince men between the ages of 17 and 35 to wear the grey and black uniform of the Voltigeurs. They were so successful that recruiting had to be stopped in June because the province was close to bankruptcy due to its military expenditures.

The British and Canadian Forces

In 1812 the British army in garrison in North America totalled 9,000 men, comparable to the complement of the regular American army. Of this number, 4,400 were posted to Lower Canada, 1,200 to Upper Canada and the rest to the Maritimes. The British colonial militias, on the other hand, had far fewer than the Americans. The total population of the

Sergeant and gunners (in the background) of the Royal Artillery, between 1806 and 1812. Reconstitution by Charles Stadden. Parks Canada.

British colonies in North America was barely half a million, three fifths of whom lived in Lower Canada. The vast majority of the 60,000 militiamen from this province were French Canadians. There were approximately 11,000 militiamen in Upper Canada, the same number in Nova Scotia and 4,000 in New Brunswick. By adding the militias of Prince Edward Island and Newfoundland, as well as the Amerindians, whose precise numbers are not known, the total was about 90,000 men.

The militia of Lower Canada was the only force capable of protecting the country, both numerically and geographically.

Without its cooperation it is doubtful that the British army would have been able to stave off the Americans indefinitely. In addition to the members of the Canadian Voltigeurs and the four battalions of the Embodied Militia, all men capable of bearing arms were recruited into what was called the Sedentary Militia. As before, militiamen were spread throughout parish companies. However, these were combined into numerous "districts," equivalent to regiments, commanded by a colonel and his staff. The Sedentary Militia was called up for active service only in emergencies.

The Upper Canada militia, though, was a source of considerable worry. Governor General Prevost reported to Lord Liverpool, Secretary of State for War and the Colonies, that "it would perhaps not be prudent"[64] to arm more than 4,000 of the 11,000 militiamen in the province in the event of war! This mistrust was the result of the fact that more than half the population was of American origin. In addition, the conduct of the Legislative Assembly was making the political situation unstable. In March 1812 General Isaac Brock, both "President" and administrator of Upper Canada, was nevertheless able to convince the

politicians to approve a significant defensive measure. Each militia regiment in Upper Canada would include two Flank companies of volunteers who would train six days per month. In emergencies, they would immediately be mobilized and serve for up to six months.

The War of 1812

On June 24, 1812, a courier from New York reached Montreal bearing the dreaded news: the United States had declared war on Great Britain seven days earlier.

The Americans' initial ambition was to invade and conquer Canada. To do so, however, they would need a strong regular army supported by dependable militias. With a population of some seven and a half million, they had enormous potential. In January 1812 they augmented their regular army by 10 infantry regiments and two artillery regiments. At the end of June this total grew again when Congress voted to maintain a regular army of 35,735 officers and soldiers. The states had at least 600,000 young men capable of bearing arms, and could therefore mobilize tens of thousands of militiamen for active duty to support the regular army.

This military force existed only in theory,

Officer of the New York State Militia, in 1812-13.
Reconstitution by H. C. McBarron.
Parks Canada.

however; the reality was something else again. In June 1812 the regular army had only 11,000 men, 5,000 of whom were new recruits who barely knew how to handle a gun. Apart from the artillery and the engineers, the officer corps was rather mediocre. An influx of inexperienced officers, many of whom had obtained their commissions through political favours, did nothing to improve things. And the militias were very uneven in quality. At this

Soldier of the 4th American Infantry Regiment, c. 1811-12.
Reconstitution by Don Troiani.
Parks Canada.

time, the militias from the various states were not subject to federal authority, which led to a lack of consistency – for example, a militia general could demand to be placed in command of regular troops! Worse still, a state could refuse to mobilize its militia even in wartime; that in fact was what the New England states did, because they were opposed to the declaration of war.

Soldier of the Glengarry Light Infantry, between 1812 and 1816. Reconstitution by G. A. Embleton. Parks Canada.

Finally, there was no real army staff to carry out the strategic and tactical planning required. The task was assigned to a politician, the Secretary of State for War, with varying degrees of support from the generals.

From a strategic standpoint, the Americans wanted to exploit Canada's main weakness: its relatively sparse population dispersed along a narrow strip bordering the United States, from present-day Windsor, Ontario, to the mouth of the St. Lawrence. If they were able to cut off this strip permanently, west of Montreal or in Upper Canada, everything to the west would be isolated. To do so, they would launch four simultaneous attacks. The most powerful army, consisting primarily of regular troops, would attack Montreal, while the three other armies, which were more modest in size and consisted essentially of militiamen, would invade Upper Canada. The idea was certainly a good one, but nobody appears to have realized that it would require proper organization to succeed.

Canada's Defence Strategy

From the outset, it appeared obvious that the Americans were very poorly prepared, both politically and militarily, to carry out the grand designs of the War Hawks. In Canada, on the other hand, they were awaited with considerable resolve. In Quebec the staff formed a centre of strategic and tactical planning for specialist officers supervised by the Governor General, himself a senior officer in the regular army. The soldiers may have been few in number, but, unlike the Americans, they were very well trained and disciplined in the severe manner typical of the British army.

The British strategy was simple. In Upper Canada, the troops commanded by General Isaac Brock were to slow down the Americans for as long as possible. In Lower Canada, most of the troops were to be posted south of Montreal. As Montreal was pivotal to the interior of the whole country, the British staff expected it to be the first target. If, through misfortune, both Upper Canada and Montreal were to fall into the hands of the enemy, the remaining troops would take refuge in the fortress city of Quebec, warding off a siege until English reinforcements arrived.

To everyone's surprise, instead of the expected attack on Montreal, the first American offensive occurred at the other end of the country. On July 12, 1812, General William Hull, Governor of Michigan, led his troops from Detroit to the village of Sandwich, Ontario, which did not have a garrison. He announced officially that he would be arriving to liberate all the inhabitants from tyranny, and to those who did not wish to be freed, "the horrors and calamities of war will stalk before you."[65] He commanded an army of 1,200 men, including 400 regular soldiers of the 4th Infantry Regiment, as well as militiamen from Ohio and Michigan. Although not very dependable, they could be moved to action by a good general.

However, Hull was indecisive and ultimately did nothing.

American Fiascos

While Hull hesitated, news of the war reached the commander of Fort St. Joseph, Captain Charles Roberts, who immediately decided to attack the American fort at Mackinac Island. On July 17, leading 45 soldiers of the 10th Royal Veterans Battalion, some 180 voyageurs and fur traders and approximately 400 Amerindians, he reached the fort. The surprise attack fooled everyone. Captain Porter Hanks and the 61 soldiers of the 1st American Artillery Regiment, which was the garrison, did not even know that war had been declared. With only muscle power, the Canadians managed to install a cannon on a neighbouring hillside. Roberts then asked Hanks to surrender, which he immediately did. From that point on, the British controlled the fur route all the way to lakes Michigan and Superior. This victory earned them prestige in the eyes of the Amerindians, who had been indecisive up to that time. Also, they were able, without firing a single shot, to take an essential strategic point. Immediately afterwards, the Americans were forced to abandon Fort Dearborn (present-day Chicago).

Soldier of the 10th Royal Veterans Battalion, c. 1812. Reconstitution by Charles Stadden.
Parks Canada.

Further south, British, Canadian and Amerindian troops were preparing to attack Hull and the troops stationed in Detroit. On August 13 General Brock went to Fort Malden with a party of the 41st Regiment, as well as militiamen and Amerindians, to meet the Great Chief Tecumseh. These two men, who were both very tall, immediately had great respect for one another. According to legend, Tecumseh turned to his braves and said, "This is a man," which is to say a true leader, like himself.

Brock then decided that the time had come to lay siege to Detroit. Leading 300 soldiers of the 41st Regiment and the Royal Newfoundland Fencibles,

400 militiamen and approximately 600 Amerindians, he arrived at Detroit on August 16. When the Americans saw the troops arrive, they almost panicked because of their fear of what the Amerindians might do. They also assumed that the British regular army was much larger than it really was, thanks to Brock's ploy of providing old uniforms of the 41st Regiment to his militiamen. When the British artillery opened fire, many frightened American militiamen deserted. General Hull, completely overwhelmed by events, capitulated. With the invasion of Canada from the west rebuffed, Michigan was in turn overrun!

At Niagara, another American army was slowly forming. After a number of delays owing to conflicts between the generals of the regular army and the militia of New York State, some 7,000 men were gathered together at the beginning of October. On the Canadian side, General Brock's army was much smaller in number: there were four Americans for each British or Canadian soldier! On October 13 General Solomon Van Renssalaer crossed the Niagara River with his men and dug in on a hillside at Queenston. Brock attacked immediately so as not to give the Americans time to settle in and allow the rest

99

of their army to cross. The 41st, the 49th, the Niagara militias, the Toronto volunteers and the Amerindians attacked. The American position was shaken, but Brock died from a gunshot wound to the chest. General Roger Hale Sheaffe took over, and sent the Americans scrambling.

This defeat exposed the major shortcoming of the Americans: the inconsistent quality of their armies. In this instance, the New York militia panicked and appealed to its constitutional right to serve only within the limits of the state of New York, refusing to cross the river! Thousands of these militiamen thus stood by and watched their compatriots calling to them for help as they fell to enemy fire or were taken prisoner.

Elsewhere, the planned attacks did not take place, and this is how the great invasion of 1812 ended. The Americans were routed everywhere and Michigan fell to the Anglo-Canadians. But in adversity the Americans were not quick to throw down the gauntlet; on the contrary.

Officer, Glengarry Light Infantry, between 1812 and 1816.
Reconstitution by R. M. Marrion.
Canadian War Museum, Ottawa.

New Invasions in the West

In 1813 the Americans would regroup, reorganize and augment their regular army, as well as strengthen their militias while pursuing their offensive against Canada. Their priority was to retake Detroit. At the end of 1812 a new army of approximately 7,000 men, many of whom were militiamen from Kentucky and Ohio, marched towards Michigan under the command of General William Henry Harrison. In January 1813 part of this army, under the command of General James Winchester, took Frenchtown (in Monroe, Michigan) on the Raisin River south of Detroit. The British commander in the region, Colonel Henry Procter, was, however, able

to secretly surround Frenchtown. On January 22 he attacked Winchester's 1,000 men with 200 British soldiers, 300 Essex County militiamen and French-Canadian sailors, and 450 Amerindians. The 17th Regular Infantry Regiment and three regiments of the Kentucky militia were wiped out. The Amerindian warriors took cruel vengeance on these men, who had burned their dwellings and their crops not long before. The American losses totalled 958 men, 397 of whom were killed; only 33 soldiers were able to escape. Following this disaster, the Americans returned to the defensive.

Procter retook the offensive at the end of April and attacked Fort Meigs (near Perrysburg, Ohio) with approximately 1,000 soldiers and Canadian militiamen and 1,500 Amerindians led by Tecumseh. General Harrison held the fort with 1,100 men. On May 5 reinforcements of 1,200 Kentucky militiamen attacked the English lines. Procter's men deliberately yielded to the first wave to attract the enemy into an ambush. The ploy succeeded and the Kentucky militiamen chased after them. Tecumseh's Amerindians attacked their flank and less than 200 men escaped. Despite this victory, Procter

had to withdraw a few days later after Tecumseh's warriors refused to continue the siege.

In July, Procter launched a second unproductive offensive against Fort Meigs, and then attempted to take Fort Stephenson, which was held by some 2,000 men under the command of Major George Croghan. The British assault went badly and Procter lost nearly a third of his regular soldiers, with 96 men dead or wounded. At the same time, thousands of Americans were arriving as reinforcements. Unable to contain them, Procter withdrew from Ohio.

The Americans Attack Upper Canada

The naval forces then came into play. Since February 1813, the Americans had been preparing a fleet at Erie, Pennsylvania, under the command of Commodore Oliver Hazard Perry. Their objective was naval supremacy over Lake Erie, to make the British position untenable. Under the command of Captain Robert Heriot Barclay, the small British squadron on Lake Erie was less powerful than Perry's. There was a fierce naval combat on September 10, and the Americans were victorious.

This setback put Procter in an awkward position by depriving him of his main

channel of communication with the rest of the British forces and his sources of supply. In addition, the Americans were now in a position to land an army on the north shore of Lake Erie, to cut off his retreat. With only some 900 men, Procter was forced to abandon the western part of Upper Canada as quickly as possible. He withdrew first from Detroit and Fort Malden. On September 27, with the 6,000 men of Harrison's army, Procter and his soldiers – with Tecumseh and his warriors, along with many refugees, who slowed down their march – began their retreat eastward along the Thames River. About 3,000 Americans took off in pursuit and caught them at Moraviantown on October 5. Harrison then ordered a charge by the Kentucky Mounted Volunteer Regiment commanded by Lieutenant-Colonel Richard Johnson. For the British forces, who were exhausted and unprepared, it was a disaster. The 41st Regiment was cut to pieces and Tecumseh fell, along with 33 of his warriors. No fewer than 634 British officers and soldiers were killed, wounded or taken prisoner. The Americans, with losses of only 12 dead and 17 wounded, also took six cannons. However, Procter was able to escape with 246 officers and men, bearing the colours of the 41st; 12 days later he took

In 1813 the soldiers of the Upper Canada Incorporated Militia and several battalions of the Lower Canada Select Embodied Militia wore green coats because of a shortage of red cloth. Reconstitution by G. A. Embleton.

Canadian Department of National Defence.

up a position further east at Ancaster. In spite of their great numerical superiority, the Americans did not dare attack, and remained in their positions.

Meanwhile, the defeats of 1812 had great repercussions in Washington. General John Armstrong was appointed Secretary of State for War. He was an experienced soldier and diplomat who had spent several years in France, where he had had the opportunity to meet Napoleon and study the

operations of the French army, then at its zenith. Under his supervision, the American army made considerable progress. But Armstrong had to deal with poorly led and inadequately trained troops. With no real staff, he was burdened with administrative details and often had to run campaigns rather than concentrate on strategy proper. Therefore, in 1813 the Americans expended considerable effort in an attempt to conquer Upper Canada, while neglecting the principal objective, Montreal. This scattering of their forces could only work in favour of Canada's defenders.

Since the autumn of 1812, the American navy had been completing considerable work at Sackets Harbor. In the spring of 1813 its squadron, under the command of Commodore Isaac Chauncey, became the most powerful on Lake Ontario. This allowed General Dearborn to order a contingent of 1,700 regular soldiers of the Chauncey fleet to attack York (Toronto). On April 27, although it had defended itself honourably, the small garrison of approximately 200 soldiers, supported by 500 militiamen and 50 Amerindians, had to withdraw. But the victory

Trooper of the Canadian Light Dragoons in 1813. Reconstitution by G. A. Embleton.
Canadian Department of National Defence.

was to cost the Americans dearly. Not long after they had entered the city, a powder magazine exploded accidentally, causing the death of Brigadier Zebulon Montgomery Pike, a promising and highly-rated officer, along with 38 soldiers. The explosion also injured 222 men. The American losses totalled approximately 320 dead and wounded. Dearborn, who initially believed that this amounted to a betrayal by the British, turned a blind eye to the pillaging of the city by the soldiers and sailors. They

did show respect for the women – there were no rapes reported afterward – and pillaged only houses that had been abandoned by their occupants. Before leaving, the Americans burned down Parliament and all public buildings.

One month later, on May 27, Dearborn attacked Fort George, the principal British stronghold on the Niagara Peninsula. Given the numerical superiority of the Americans, the Anglo-Canadian soldiers and militiamen abandoned the fort after defending it vigorously. British General John Vincent then withdrew along with his troops all the way to Burlington Bay, not far from Hamilton. The Americans sent a contingent of approximately 3,500 men after him. Soon afterwards, scouts reported to Vincent that the American camp at Stoney Creek was being guarded by only a few sentinels. On June 6, in the middle of the night, the 49th Regiment and five companies of the 8th charged into the American camp with fixed bayonets! General Winder, the Baltimore lawyer who owed his military rank to his political connections, was captured along with

MILITARY COSTUMES

Royal Staff Corps officer's sabretache, c. 1820; the sabretache was a leather document case worn by the officer on the left, suspended from the sabre belt. Watercolour.
Parks Canada.

Officer's uniform of the Royal Artillery, c. 1833. Watercolour.
Anne S. K. Brown Military Collection, Brown University, Providence.

Officer's uniform of the Light Infantry, c. 1830. Watercolour.
Anne S. K. Brown Military Collection, Brown University, Providence.

Soldier's uniform of the British 9th Regiment, c. 1814.

Musée royal de l'Armée, Brussels.

Officer's uniform of the King's Royal Regiment of New York, between 1780 and 1784.

Canadian War Museum, Ottawa.

Officer's uniform of the York Light Cavalry of Toronto, between 1838 and 1850.

Canadian War Museum, Ottawa.

Soldier's uniform of the 104th British Regiment, 1812.

Cape Ann Historical Society.

Sergeant's uniform of the 6th Battalion of the Canadian Volunteer Militia, 1862-63.

Sheldon Kasman Collection, Toronto.

Officer's uniform of the Commissariat, c. 1830. Watercolour.
Anne S. K. Brown Military Collection, Brown University, Providence.

Officer's uniform of the Royal Engineers, c. 1830. Watercolour.
Anne S. K. Brown Military Collection, Brown University, Providence.

Uniform of the Royal Montreal Cavalry, between 1832 and 1850.
Canadian War Museum, Ottawa.

Infantry uniform of the Canadian Volunteer Militia worn from 1863 to 1870.
Canadian War Museum, Ottawa.

Soldier's uniform of the British 26th Regiment, c. 1814.
Musée royal de l'Armée, Brussels.

British officer's shakos,
c. 1820. Watercolour.
Parks Canada.

Pattern to be used in putting braid
on a rifleman officer's coat, c. 1825.
Drawing.
Parks Canada.

Royal Artillery officer's uniform,
1828. Watercolour.
Anne S. K. Brown Military Collection,
Brown University, Providence.

his artillery, and his soldiers scattered.

Meanwhile, to the east of Lake Ontario, the arrival at Kingston of Sir James Lucas Yeo, accompanied by sailors of the Royal Navy, enabled the British squadron to regain the upper hand. With some control over the lake, Governor Prevost took command of a raid against Sackets Harbor, the main American naval base on the lake. The attack was launched on May 28 by a column of 750 men who disembarked from Commodore Yeo's ships. It was defended by only 400 regular army men and 500 militiamen who had come to their aid, under the command of a young and brilliant general in the New York militia, Jacob Brown. For two days, he spurred on his men and was able to resist two assaults. There were considerable British losses: 47 dead and 1,954 wounded, compared to 41 dead and 85 wounded for the Americans. Brown's conduct earned him a commission as a brigadier in the regular army.

Laura Secord and Beaver Dams

On the Niagara Peninsula, after their defeat at Stoney Creek, the American soldiers regrouped at Forty Mile Creek. But on June 7 Yeo's flotilla shelled their camp, forcing them to retreat precipitately to Fort George, which thus became the final fort in the peninsula to harbour American soldiers. Dearborn nevertheless sent a contingent of 575 men, under the command of Colonel Charles Boerstler, to attack the British outpost at Beaver Dams (Thorold) by surprise. Their effort failed to account for the actions of a genuine Canadian heroine, Laura Secord.

Laura Secord, née Ingersoll, a humble housewife in the village of Queenston, had like so many other women of her time to deal with the horrors of war. In the early summer of 1813 her life was not easy, with her husband James disabled following an injury sustained at Queenston Heights. On June 21 some American officers arrived at their door demanding food. During the meal, the Secords heard them discuss the surprise attack they were preparing. Laura decided to go and warn the British at Beaver Dams. She left the following morning at dawn, making a wide detour to avoid the American patrols. Following a stream through the woods, she kept walking until nightfall, uncertain of the way, until she arrived at an Amerindian camp. By chance, the Amerindians were British army scouts who led her to Lieutenant James FitzGibbon, commander of a small detachment of 50 men from the 49th Regiment at Beaver Dams. FitzGibbon immediately instructed the scouts to cut off the Americans' route.

The following day at dawn the Amerindian scouts commanded by Captain Dominique Ducharme spotted the Americans. At 9 a.m. Ducharme, with some 300 well-hidden Iroquois, opened fire on the rear of the American column. A hundred additional Iroquois, led by Captain William Johnson Kerr, arrived as reinforcements. For three hours they sniped at the Americans, shouting their terrible war cries. Terrorized, Boerstler and his soldiers wanted to surrender, but not to the Amerindians. FitzGibbon arrived with his 49th Detachment, just in time to enable them to do so! No fewer than 462 officers and soldiers of the regular army, along with 30 American militiamen, were taken prisoner. The colours of the 14th Infantry Regiment, along with two

Lower Canada Sedentary militiaman in 1813. Reconstitution by G. A. Embleton.
Parks Canada.

cannon, were taken. FitzGibbon received virtually all the glory from the victory, while the Amerindians and Ducharme and Kerr were forgotten.

It is usually said that the Amerindians did the fighting and that FitzGibbon took all the credit for this feat. As for Laura Secord, without whose efforts it could not have occurred, her story became known only at the end of her life. Her act eventually came to symbolize not only Upper Canada's resistance, but also the patriotism and abnegation suffered by so many Canadian women during these sombre years of repeated invasions.

Objective: Montreal!

In 1813 the Niagara Peninsula remained the theatre for several additional battles and skirmishes that alone could not seal the fate of the country. In the fall, however, the danger worsened when the Americans sent not one but two armies to attack Montreal! The operation was led by General James Wilkinson, a seasoned veteran who replaced Dearborn as commander-in-chief of the American army. He would lead the main army of 8,800 men equipped with 38 field cannons and 20 siege cannons; they advanced on Montreal from the west along the St. Lawrence. The second army, commanded by General Wade Hampton, consisted of 5,500 men and 10 field cannons. This army came up the Châteauguay River to Montreal, where it joined the first. The two armies were primarily regular troops, supported by volunteers.

The menace was a major one: Montreal, the strategic key to Canada, did not have any fortifications. Its old crumbling walls dated from the French regime and had been razed in 1810. In any event, such fortifications would be unable to withstand a large, well-equipped siege artillery. The enemy had to be stopped at the outposts. Approximately 6,000 British and Canadians attempted to do just that to the south of the city from Laprairie to Île-aux-Noix.

When the British commander learned that Hampton's army was preparing to cross the border, some 8,000 men of the Lower Canada Sedentary Militia were mobilized for active duty. These were excellent militiamen, according to William Dunlop, surgeon for the 89th, who encountered several of their regiments along his way one October day in 1813:

"We came up with several regiments of militia on their line of march. They had all a serviceable appearance – all had been pretty well drilled, and their arms being direct from the tower, were in perfectly good order, nor had they the mobbish appearance that such a levy in any other country would have had. Their capots and trousers of home-spun stuff, and their blue tuques [night caps] were all of the same cut and color, which gave them an air of uniformity that added much to their military look.... They

marched merrily along to the music of their voyageur songs, and as they perceived our uniform as we came up, they set up the Indian War-whoop, followed by a shout of *Vive le Roi* along the whole line...."[66]

The Battle of Châteauguay

General Hampton's American soldiers were also on the march. On October 21 they crossed the border and followed the Châteauguay River. The next day General Louis de Watteville, the Swiss officer in the service of the British who was commanding the area southwest of Montreal, was informed of this. He ordered Lieutenant-Colonel de Salaberry to immediately establish an outpost along the river with companies of Canadian Voltigeurs, the light company of the Canadian Fencibles, detachments of the militia and a few Amerindians, representing approximately 1,800 men in all. Salaberry had seven consecutive lines of barricades made out of trees across the narrow road along the west coast of the river close to where Allan's Corners is now. In addition, even

Canadian Voltigeurs on the march in 1813; an Amerindian scout (left) accompanies the soldiers. Reconstitution by G. A. Embleton.
Parks Canada.

though the other shore was completely wooded, he placed two militia companies there.

On the morning of October 26 Hampton's army came into a clearing across from the first barricade defended by about 175 men. General Izard's American infantry brigade placed itself in attack formation. An American officer on horseback approached the barricade and, in French, invited the "Braves Canadiens" to join the soldiers of freedom to shake free of the British yoke. In response, Salaberry stood on a tree trunk, shouldered the musket of one of his Voltigeurs and put an end to his speech! Gunfire then broke out everywhere. While part of the American

army was advancing towards the first line of barricades on the west shore, a column of 1,500 men under the command of Colonel Purdy, which was more or less lost, was slithering through the woods on the eastern shore to get around the Canadian position. These men suddenly came up against the two Canadian militia companies, who immediately fired a salvo at them and charged the American column. Surprised and confused, the Americans hesitated and then began to weaken, with several heading for the riverbank, where they were immediately met by gunfire from the Canadians on the other shore, which forced them to retreat.

Part of the American brigade attempted to go around the first barricade – a movement that appeared to succeed, because the Canadian soldiers began to withdraw. But no sooner had the Americans reached

Soldier of the Light Infantry Company of the 3rd Battalion of Lower Canada Select Embodied Militia, in 1813. Reconstitution by G. A. Embleton.
Parks Canada.

the edge of the woods than the war cries of the Amerindians waiting in ambush were heard, along with their gunfire; at the same time, bugles could be heard everywhere, along with the shouts of hundreds of men hidden beyond in the woods. Salaberry had asked Lieutenant-Colonel George Macdonell, who was commanding the lines of barricades behind, to make as much noise as possible.

That was all it took for the Americans to believe that the woods were full of Amerindians and that the entire British army was on their trail! They beat a retreat. The next day Hampton and his army took the road to the United States. Thus ended the short American offensive against Montreal.

With only one man to every 10 Americans, victory initially appeared improbable to Salaberry and Watteville. For three days they even awaited a further assault. The Canadians – no British corps took part in the action – had only four dead and eight wounded out of the 300 men who took part in the combat. The Americans, who deployed approximately 3,000 men during the confrontation, had at least 50 dead. The battle was to have an enormous impact among the French-Canadian population, who saw in it indisputable evidence of their military prowess.

The Battle of Crysler's Farm

But where was General Wilkinson's army? At the beginning of November, after many delays, it was moving up the St. Lawrence River towards Montreal. Wilkinson still did not know about Hampton's defeat. Part of his army, approximately 3,700 men, disembarked on the Canadian side of the river east of Prescott. An Anglo-Canadian "observation corps" followed them, having been assigned the task of slowing their march. The corps consisted of some 900 officers and soldiers under the command of Lieutenant-Colonel Joseph Wanton Morrison. On the 11th the Americans decided to drive away the troops that were harassing them, and 2,000 American soldiers attacked the Morrison contingent on the farm of one John Crysler, which today is in Morrisburg, Ontario. The American infantry and cavalry attacks were repeatedly beaten back by the British line. The Americans eventually withdrew after having incurred heavy losses: 102 dead, 237 wounded and over 100 taken prisoner. Morrison had only 22 dead and 148 wounded. The next day Wilkinson abandoned the invasion plan and the American troops crossed to the other side of the border.

The British Take Fort Niagara

To protect the naval base at Sackets Harbor, most of the American army stationed on the Niagara Peninsula was transferred there; the troops that had remained in the Niagara area were of inadequate

strength and had to abandon Fort George in December because they could no longer maintain its defence. They did not leave Canada quietly, however, burning Newark (present-day Niagara-on-the-Lake) and much of Queenston, a cruel act that left civilians without shelter as winter approached.

This devastation was not, however, the work of American soldiers alone. Some Canadians played a major role in this affair by wielding the torch with enthusiasm: these were the Canadian Volunteers, commanded by Lieutenant-Colonel Joseph Willcocks. Willcocks, a member of the Assembly of Upper Canada when he joined the Americans in July 1813, had immediately been awarded an officer's commission to recruit a corps of Canadians. The Canadian Volunteers in the regular American army consisted of approximately 100 men who served as scouts in the Niagara Peninsula, as well as informers in the zone occupied by the Americans. This corps of renegades was to continue to function until the end of the war.

The Newark and Queenston burnings infuriated the British, and they responded promptly. Early on the morning of December 16 some 550 men of the 1st, 41st and 100th regiments silently crossed the Niagara River in boats piloted by militiamen and attacked Fort Niagara with fixed bayonets. The Americans lost 67 soldiers, the British only five. The neighbouring village of Lewiston was then burnt to the ground as Newark had been a few days earlier. On December 29 there was a new incursion of 1,500 British at Black Rock and Buffalo on Lake Erie. The Americans were unable to withstand the attack: the villages were torched, as were four small navy gunboats and military supply stores. On January 12, 1814, Governor Prevost asked the Americans to conduct themselves in a more civilized manner, warning that he would not hesitate to take revenge immediately for any further barbarous acts. The belligerents thereafter behaved more moderately.

At the time, Great Britain was unable to send many reinforcements to Canada, for the very good reason that much of its army was busy battling Napoleonic troops in Spain. It did, however, send six infantry regiments and two marine battalions to North America in 1813. An additional regiment of Fencibles was also recruited in New Brunswick. The number of regular officers and soldiers in North America thus increased to about 18,000, 14,000 of whom were deployed in Upper and Lower Canada. In 1813 the American regular army had reached approximately 25,000 men, not to mention several thousand volunteers.

Canadian volunteers or conscripts were also needed to reinforce the regular British army. Lower Canada raised a fifth battalion of Select Embodied militia, which was incorporated in Montreal in September 1812, as well as a sixth battalion in March 1813, to guard Quebec City. There were also three light infantry companies, three light cavalry units, a company of artillery drivers, a half company of artillerymen and 200-300 Amerindian scouts. Finally, there were approximately 400 men who belonged to a corps that was typical of the country, the Canadian Voyageurs. In all, the army of Lower Canada consisted of some 5,500 officers and soldiers.

In many counties of Upper Canada the Flank companies of the militia regiments were mobilized. Several served along with British troops until the end of 1812, when these soldier-citizens were able to return home. A steadier source of troops was nevertheless needed until

the end of the war. In the spring of 1813, therefore, a volunteer militia battalion was incorporated, as well as an artillery company, an artillery driver company, an artificer company, two other light cavalry and a corps of Western Rangers, for a total of approximately 1,000 officers and soldiers, in addition to several hundred Amerindians – it is difficult to know the exact number – mobilized for indeterminate periods of time.

The 1814 Invasion of Canada

In the spring of 1814 President James Madison and the War Hawks received bad news. A succession of major events had upset the whole international scene: Napoleon's great army had foundered in the Russian snows and France was overrun. On March 31, 1814, the allied armies entered Paris, welcomed triumphantly by a people tired of the wars of the Empire. On May 11 Napoleon abdicated and withdrew to the island of Elba. Peace was proclaimed and the Bourbon monarchy was restored. The Americans had thus lost their greatest ally, although there had never been any formal alliance with France, and England could now concentrate all its efforts against the United States.

Soldier of the British 1st Regiment, between 1813 and 1816. Reconstitution by G. A. Embleton. Parks Canada.

The Americans therefore tried to score points as quickly as possible: to invade Canada before large numbers of reinforcements arrived. The invasion plan was heatedly debated in the American Cabinet, though, and did not pass until June 7. The objective was to invade Upper Canada through the Niagara Peninsula.

Before the plan could even be approved, things began to go wrong. At the end of March General Wilkinson, hoping to improve his reputation after the fiasco of the previous autumn, crossed the border into Lower Canada, in command of approximately 2,000 men,

to take a position to the south of Montreal. When he reached Lacolle, Wilkinson met fierce resistance. Faced with such determination, the Americans turned back over the border, with 154 dead, wounded and missing, whereas the British and Canadians suffered only 59 losses.

Not long after the defeat at Lacolle, Wilkinson was relieved of his command. Representing a disappearing species, the old, incompetent American generals who continually argued among themselves, displaying virtually no talent for strategy or tactics but excelling in the back rooms of political power, Wilkinson was beyond a doubt the worst of them all, for it would later be revealed that he was also a traitor.[67] In 1814 the wind shifted, and politicians insisted on young, dynamic generals. They already had William Henry Harrison, who was commanding western Upper Canada, as well as Izard and Macomb at Plattsburgh. In the Niagara Peninsula, Jacob Brown was made commanding general, assisted by Winfield Scott, James Ripley and Peter Porter, all excellent officers.

Even though they had only 3,500 men instead of the 8,000 hoped for to invade Upper Canada, Brown and his generals were confident. For the

first time, the Americans were preparing properly for battle by doing tactical exercises under the watchful eye of Winfield Scott. According to Scott, it was essential that the American soldiers be able to stand up to the British soldiers in European-style battles; otherwise, the whole invasion of Canada would be nothing more than a pious hope. Although he had identified the root of the tactical problem, the fact remained that defeating the redcoats presented a considerable challenge. At Scott's request, the American Army of the Niagara River adopted the French 1791 drill that had proved its worth in Europe.[68] A few weeks of training eventually gave the American soldiers confidence, and all they wanted was an opportunity to take on the British.

Brown, an excellent strategist, avoided attacking Fort Niagara and forced the British to deploy along the border. On July 3 he had his army cross into Canada on both sides of Fort Erie, which, defended as it was by barely two companies of British soldiers, surrendered immediately. When the news reached him, British General Phineas Riall left Fort George with 1,800 men, 1,500 of whom were regular soldiers. They met the Americans on July 5 at Chippewa, with the British attacking General Winfield Scott and his 2,000 men. Riall moved the 1st, 8th and 100th regiments forward towards the enemy lines. But this time the usual rout did not occur. The American line held in perfect order, and its salvos, which were well organized, rapid and murderous, forced the British to retreat. Scott then moved his regiments forward, and the British were defeated, losing more than 500 men, with 148 dead, against only 48 dead and 227 wounded for the Americans.

The defeat worried General Gordon Drummond, in command of the British troops in Upper Canada. Of the three regiments engaged in the battle, two – the 1st, the famous Royal Scots, and the 8th, the King's – were famed for their bravery and excellence. Therefore something had obviously changed on the American side. Drummond immediately requested reinforcements from Lower Canada and had troops brought in from Kingston to Fort George and to York (Toronto).

Officer of the British 100th Infantry Regiment, c. 1812. Charles Buncombe. Silhouette.
Parks Canada.

On July 25 Riall's and Scott's brigades met once again at Lundy's Lane, not far from Niagara Falls, and engaged in the bloodiest battle of the war. Reinforcements reached both camps soon afterwards, along with commanding generals Drummond and Brown. The battle raged fiercely even after sundown. In spite of the smoke, which masked the moonlight, the battalions attacked and counterattacked through the evening, in the glare of musket and cannon fire. Generals Riall, Drummond,

Brown and Scott were all seriously injured. The battle ended after midnight with both armies at the end of their tether. Losses were heavy: 853 Americans and 878 British were missing, but the battle was a draw. As the British continued to receive reinforcements, unlike the Americans, General Ripley ordered a retreat to Fort Erie.

It was not long before the two armies faced one another again, because General Drummond surrounded Fort Erie and began a siege on August 13. After only two days of shelling, the British attempted to take the fort with approximately 1,300 soldiers, but they had not banked on the Americans' determination. They suffered heavy losses when an underground powder magazine exploded, killing hundreds of men. There was no choice but to withdraw. They had lost more than 900 men, killed, wounded or missing, against only 84 on the American side. Drummond nevertheless received reinforcements and continued the siege.

On September 17 a raid by some 1,600 Americans took the British by surprise, with their lines insufficiently protected. The American attack was

Colour-officer and sergeant of the 9th Regiment, in 1814. Charles Hamilton Smith. Engraving.
Anne S. K. Brown Military Collection, Brown University, Providence.

eventually warded off after fierce fighting. The losses were heavier for the British, with 115 dead, than for the Americans, with only 79. The Americans had also succeeded in destroying six of the British heavy cannons.

After the carnage Drummond decided to lift the siege, and his troops withdrew to Chippewa on September 21. On November 5 the Americans blew up Fort Erie after evacuating their troops to Buffalo. Thus ended this third attempt to invade Canada via the Niagara Peninsula.

The Battle for the Northwest

The American 1814 invasion plan called for them to take Fort Mackinac. But the British proved to be more aggressive and they took the small post at Prairie du Chien, Wisconsin, on the Mississippi. The Americans surrendered on July 17 without fighting.

During this time, a corps of approximately 700 American regular soldiers and militiamen, under the command of Lieutenant-Colonel George Croghan, reached the vicinity of Mackinac Island. After razing the small undefended post of Sault Ste. Marie (Ontario), they decided to attack Fort Mackinac. Croghan disembarked his troops, but Lieutenant-Colonel Robert McDouall did not wait for him in the fort itself, and he had hidden his garrison in the woods surrounding a clearing. The Americans entered confidently and McDouall's men opened fire on these easy targets, killing 15 and wounding 51. The Americans re-embarked the next day for Detroit, leaving two gunboats behind, the *Scorpion* and the *Tigress*, to prevent the garrison from receiving supplies. On the return trip the rest of the American flotilla destroyed the only British ship on Lake Huron, the schooner *Nancy*. Its commander, Lieutenant Miller Worsley, nevertheless managed to escape with his sailors and reach Fort Mackinac. In early September, with the help of the latter and the soldiers of the Michigan Fencibles, Worsley captured the *Scorpion* and the *Tigress*, thereby giving the British some naval strength on Lake Huron.

The Race to Build Ships

As the Americans were once again driven back from the West and the Niagara Peninsula, both camps decided, with a view to maintaining naval supremacy on Lake Ontario, to build large warships in record time, each side rivalling the other. Kingston and Sackets Harbor became major shipyards, and the battle for control of Lake Ontario became a race to build large vessels. In May, the HMS *Prince Regent* and the HMS *Princess Charlotte*, with 58 and 40 guns respectively, left Kingston, while the Americans had completed the USS *Superior*, with 62 guns, at Sackets Harbor. The British sent Royal Navy reinforcements to Kingston and spent great amounts of money. In the summer of 1814 an enormous structure took shape in

their shipyard: the HMS *St. Lawrence*, a gigantic ship capable of carrying 110 guns, was launched in September. This sailing ship, the largest ever built in Canada, required a crew of 800 men.

The British, who already had two even larger vessels under construction at the shipyard (with a capacity of 120 guns each), therefore had a clear advantage. The Americans attempted to catch up by building two ships of this capacity at Sackets Harbor. But building large warships has always been an onerous undertaking. With Europe at peace, England could afford to invest immense amounts of money in this operation, employing thousands of men – for this was the way to regain naval superiority on the Great Lakes. In the fall of 1814 work began at the Chippewa shipyard on two gunboats for Lake Erie. Plans were also in the works to build gunboats and a frigate at Penetanguishene on Lake Huron. The British were on the right track to regain control over the Great Lakes and to win the race.

Soldier of the Meuron Regiment, a Swiss corps in the service of the British, between 1813 and 1816. Reconstitution by G. A. Embleton.
Parks Canada.

The British Defeat at Plattsburgh

With peace reigning in Europe once again, it was possible in the summer of 1814 to send a large number of British soldiers to America. In both Upper and Lower Canada, the army increased from approximately 15,000 regular officers and soldiers in May 1814 to some 28,000 by mid-August. During the same period the garrison in the Maritime colonies increased from about 4,300 to 7,500 men. As a consequence, the British adopted a much more bellicose strategy.

Sir George Prevost assembled some 11,000 men in early September to take Plattsburgh and

occupy northeastern New York State. Most of the men belonged to regiments of the British army, but the Canadian Voltigeurs, the Canadian Chasseurs and four Select Embodied Militia battalions incorporated in Lower Canada were also among them. On the American side, General Alexander Macomb had only 3,000 militiamen and soldiers to defend the small town. On September 7 the Anglo-Canadian army arrived within view of Plattsburgh.

But instead of attacking, Prevost decided to wait until the British fleet arrived from Île-aux-Noix to neutralize the American fleet anchored in Plattsburgh Bay. This was a major tactical error, giving the enemy time to dig; an immediate attack would have quickly broken down the town's wooden fortifications, and the fleet would have been forced to evacuate the bay to avoid being taken. Prevost's inaction tied the fate of the land campaign to the outcome of a naval battle.

Captain George Downie's English fleet arrived on September 11 and, on Prevost's orders, attacked the American gunboats of Captain

Thomas Macdonough in Plattsburgh Bay. Downie would have preferred to hold the battle on Lake Champlain, because he was afraid of being blocked in the port, but he had to follow orders. The Americans awaited him resolutely and the battle was a disaster for the British. Downie was killed and his fleet was wiped out. Prevost then recalled the brigade, which was just beginning to attack the town, and returned along the road to Lower Canada that very evening. The Americans were jubilant. A handful of their own had beaten seasoned soldiers who had chased the French out of Spain. This was an extraordinary windfall for their propaganda mill. The evidence was conclusive: despite his political and administrative abilities, Prevost had proved to be a terrible general on the battlefield. The main quality required of a governor of Canada was military ability. Prevost was discredited and recalled to England.

The War at Sea

The War of 1812 took place not only on land and within the Great Lakes, but on the sea as well. Unlike its army, the modest American navy had excellent officers and extremely well trained sailors. At the beginning of the hostilities, the Royal

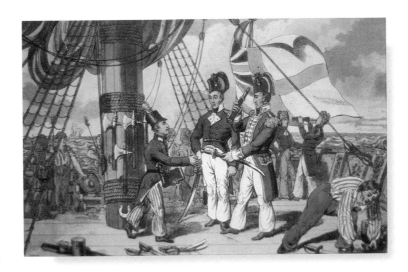

Midshipman and officers of the Royal Navy, c. 1814.

Anne S. K. Brown Military Collection, Brown University, Providence.

Navy was defeated on several occasions in single combat between frigates, to the great surprise of the British. They recovered, however, and on June 1, 1813, the frigate HMS *Shannon* captured the American frigate USS *Chesapeake*. The honour of the Royal Navy had been upheld.

These battles between frigates – which the Americans to this day describe as great naval battles – were nothing more than single engagements with no real effect on the outcome of the war. The security of the Maritime colonies and the Gulf of St. Lawrence was never really compromised, because the Americans did not have vessels that could take on the British fleet in the North Atlantic anchored at Halifax, with secondary bases at St. John's, Newfoundland, and the Bermuda islands.

The British ordered a blockade of the American coasts on November 27, 1812. At the beginning, the measure affected only the coastline between Delaware and Chesapeake bays. But on March 30, 1813, the Royal Navy extended it from Savannah, Georgia, to north of the city of New York, and then all the way to Louisiana. Then, on November 16, the blockade became broader still, from Connecticut to Florida, which was then a Spanish possession. Finally, in May 1814 the ships of the Royal Navy began to patrol offshore from Rhode Island to New Brunswick. From that point on, the entire United States Atlantic coastline from New Brunswick to Mexico was subjected to a blockade that cut off American international trade.

But the British were not content to blockade the coastlines; they also launched increasingly ambitious raids on American coastal towns, including Washington and Baltimore.[69] In August and September 1814 they took Castine (in Maine) and occupied it until the end of hostilities.

Sea warfare inevitably meant privateers as well. Their services were used by both sides. Thus the Americans hurriedly armed more than 500 ships, which took approximately 1,330 British merchant vessels. This was less impressive than it might appear, because the British merchant fleet comprised some 25,000 ships.

As for the British, Royal Navy ships patrolling the American coasts seized hundreds of enemy merchant vessels. And they were not alone in doing so! As soon as war erupted, Nova Scotia shipowners became particularly interested in obtaining "letters of marque," an official commission entitling a privateer ship to pursue enemy ships in wartime. Without such a document, privateers were

considered pirates and outlaws. Once the letters had been obtained, several small, very fast ships hurriedly armed themselves and were remarkably successful. Approximately 50 privateer ships, which had left mainly from Liverpool and Lunenburg, Nova Scotia, captured at least 207 American ships, which compares favourably to the number of privateer ships taken by the Americans. The most redoubtable of the Canadian privateers was the *Liverpool Packet*, which alone took approximately 50 ships – exploits worthy of the best adventure films.

In the United States, however, pressure was mounting to negotiate a peace treaty with the British, particularly in the northeastern states, which were the most hostile to the conflict. Even though the war being fought in America was not its main concern, Great Britain was interested in putting an end to the crisis and renewing its commercial ties with the United States. On December 24, 1814, British and American diplomats negotiated and signed a peace treaty at Ghent, Belgium.[70]

Under the treaty, the two belligerent nations agreed to keep the boundaries in effect prior to 1812 and to defer negotiations on thorny matters to a later date. The Anglo-Canadians were therefore required to evacuate the West and Maine, and to return to the status quo. News of the treaty reached New York on February 8, 1815, and the Senate unanimously endorsed it on the 16th. This information reached Canada in early March and orders were given to disband the corps of volunteers and demobilize the militias.

The Legacy of the War of 1812

Today the War of 1812 has been virtually forgotten. Even in Canada it is barely mentioned in the schools. Yet it was a crucial event in the history of this country. It is in fact what made possible the survival of a separate country to the north of the United States, that powerful nation with grandiose continental ambitions. It was also the first conflict to unite French and English Canadians, in spite of their profound differences, against a common enemy, and it was the last such conflict in which eastern Amerindians had the opportunity to exercise their military might. Another special feature of that war is that it marked the first time Blacks made an appearance in Canadian militia units.

If the Americans had achieved their ends, one thing is certain: the new conquest would have led to the death of Anglophone Loyalist values and very likely undermined the cultural values of Francophones in Canada. Francophones would have been absorbed, either willingly or by force, into the American "melting pot," which would have meant the end of many of their rights. And what would have been the fate of the Blacks who took refuge north of the American border to escape the large-scale slavery of the South, or of the Amerindians in Canada, at the hands of the American soldiers? Would they have been deported like their American brothers who marched along the "trail of tears"?[71] Would they have fallen victim to the interminable wars against them throughout the nineteenth century, when American soldiers told anyone who would listen, "The only good Indian is a dead Indian"?

The Americans sometimes describe the 1812-15 period as the "second war of independence" against Great Britain. What a distortion! For three years running, Canada had to defend itself against many invasion attempts. It would be more accurate to call it the "Canadian war of independence" against the American invader.

Admiral (right) being welcomed by officers and a midshipman, c. 1848. R. Ubsdell. Engraving.

Anne S. K. Brown Military Collection, Brown University, Providence.

THE BRITISH ARMED FORCES

The British armed forces were organized somewhat differently from other major European armies. Because of their island location, the British were not as concerned about land invasions. As long as their navy was able to fend off enemy fleets, they did not really need fortifications or major armies on their own territory. The navy was their principal and preferred line of defence. The Royal Navy was truly the senior service, in terms of both size and prestige.

The Royal Navy

Ultimate authority for major strategic policies concerning the Royal Navy around the world rested with the Admiralty Board. Then came a number of agencies such as the Navy Board, which was responsible for

119

Colours of the British 41st Regiment.
Parks Canada.

financial and technical matters, the Marine infantry, supply, health and hydrography, and finally the Transport Board, which organized convoys.

The hundreds of ships in the Royal Navy were grouped into squadrons. The admiral of a squadron lived on board a large warship flying his pennant, with subordinate admirals or captains, depending on the size of the squadron, under his command. Every ship, large or small, was commanded by an officer. For a large ship, command went to a seasoned captain supported by numerous lieutenants and ensigns; a young ensign could be placed in command of an armed schooner. Under the officers came the midshipmen, or officer cadets, youngsters who experienced the school of hard knocks for several years before obtaining their certificates. Lower down were the non-commissioned officers

specializing in sailing, artillery, etc., who supervised the seamen. Finally, to defend the ship and keep order among the crew, each ship carried a marine detachment.

The Royal Navy had numerous naval bases in Great Britain and around the world. From the Canadian coasts, it controlled the North Atlantic and the North Pacific to provide security not only to the British but to Canadians as well. Thus the Royal Navy played a very important role in Canadian military heritage. It guarded Canadian coasts for a long time, while benefiting from the outstanding geostrategic positioning of the bases – an unparalleled advantage that Canada owed to its links with Great Britain. The ships and seamen posted to Canadian bases were British, but they played a role identical to that of the Canadian navy in the twentieth century.

The British Army

Prior to the mid-nineteenth century, the structure of the British army was relatively archaic. It did of course have a good reputation in Great Britain, but to a lesser degree than its navy did. There was curious overlapping of certain tasks and there were many peculiar practices.

Confusion was already felt at the top of the chain of command, because even in Parliament there was a Secretary for War and a Secretary at War. The latter was a Member of Parliament responsible for

A general accompanied by his staff, Montreal, c. 1865.
F. G. Coleridge. Watercolour.
National Archives of Canada, C102478.

ensuring that the House voted the required budget. The actual Minister was the Secretary for War, who was also, beginning in 1801, responsible for managing the colonies. Army headquarters was in the King's Horse Guards building in London. It was there that the Secretary for War, the Commander-in-Chief, the Adjutant-General and the other staff officers worked. A variety of other organizations governed the army, such as the Board of General Officers, which consisted of half a dozen generals as well as the Adjutant-General. There was also a medical board, a pensions board, a financial audit board and various other organizations.

Immediately under this administrative level came the cavalry and infantry regiments. A cavalry regiment could have

121

from three to five squadrons, with two companies in each squadron. An infantry regiment generally consisted of a single battalion of 10 companies, eight fusiliers and two Flank companies, which were elite companies. The grenadiers took the right flank on the line, the light infantry the left. The number of soldiers varied considerably, depending on the period and the regiment.

Some functions, though, did not fall under the authority of Army Headquarters. Thus the Treasury exercised some financial control over the army through its civil servants in uniform, who belonged to the Commissariat Department. The officers in the Commissariat Department accompanied the army on all its movements, assuming responsibility for rations, transportation and, particularly in Canada, barracks. The Commissariat was not, however, the only organization to procure supplies for the army: the personnel of the Quartermaster General and the Storekeeper General were also authorized to do so.

The Board of Ordnance, a powerful agency whose origins went back to the Middle Ages, was an autonomous ministry with a Secretary in Parliament directed by the Master of Ordnance, invariably an experienced general from the upper echelons of the aristocracy. The position was a very prestigious one, and with good reason: the Board of Ordnance supplied cannons, weapons of all kinds, powder and ammunition to the Royal Navy and the army. It was also responsible for building and maintaining fortifications and all other military construction wherever the British flag flew. It supplied equipment and furniture for forts and barracks, as well as all equipment needed by the army and the navy, and was responsible for maintaining it. All weapons and other items belonging to the Board of Ordnance were identified by a small arrow and the letters "B. O."

The Board of Ordnance had its own small army of artillerymen and engineers. The artillerymen belonged to the Royal Artillery. The engineers belonged to the Corps of Royal Engineers, which since the end of the eighteenth century have had the support of regular companies of artificers, engineers and sappers, consisting of non-commissioned officers and soldiers specialized in this type of work. Lastly, the Board of Ordnance included a number of non-combatant officers who managed the stores and barracks. These people were spread throughout the British Empire. In Canada the Board of Ordnance headquarters was located at Artillery Park in Quebec City.

In principle, all these men were under the command of the Commander-in-Chief in England, or of the commanding generals of the armies in the colonies. In fact, because the expected services were not always provided, a small parallel corps of engineers known as the Royal Staff Corps existed from 1799 to 1838, raised by the Duke of York, who was exasperated by the sluggishness of the Board of Ordnance. The Royal Navy established its own naval artillery corps in 1804.

This archaic organization with its bureaucratic fiefdoms survived until 1854, when the War Department became a separate entity independent of the Colonial Office. The Commissariat and the Board of Ordnance were thus incorporated into the new ministry and weapons and other items were identified from then on by the initials "W. D.," for War Department. Profound changes were introduced the following year. At the top of the chain of command was now a single secretary: the minister. The army itself was reorganized from top to bottom; specialized corps were established for medical care, transportation, logistics and armament, and the composition of the regiments was made more consistent.

British soldier of the 29th Regiment and his wife, in Hamilton, Ontario, in 1868.
D. Blyth Collection, Guelph.

DAILY LIFE OF SOLDIERS AND OFFICERS

SOLDIERS

Until 1871 British soldiers could be seen just about everywhere in Canada. A young boy living in Quebec in the 1860s told how fascinated he was by the infantry sentry who "attracted looks and admiration" because of his scarlet uniform, his shako and his long musket, which gave "an impressive stature to this magnificent soldier when he stood as erect and rigid as a statue."[72] This "magnificent soldier" so admired by the public nevertheless led a life few people would envy.

Recruitment

Soldiers were generally recruited in the British Isles and most recruits were of English, Scottish, Welsh or Irish descent. The number of Irish was increasing, and by the mid-nineteenth century they represented one third of the army, with the English and Welsh accounting for half and the Scots for the rest. Regular British troops were also occasionally recruited in North America. Three line regiments were raised in Canada: the 84th during the American Revolution, the 104th during the War of 1812 and the 100th in 1858. Colonial corps were added to the regular troops in times of war.

The Recruiting Party generally consisted of an officer accompanied by a sergeant, a drummer and two soldiers from the regiment for which the recruiting was being carried out. After announcing in the public square that they were seeking young "heroes" to thrash the enemies of the King and to take booty, they would say, "...if any prentices have severe masters, any children have undutiful parents; if any servants have too little wages, or any husband too much wife; let them repair to the Noble Sergeant..."[73] at the tavern. In wartime, when recruiting could not do the job, the team became a "press gang," which forcibly enlisted "vagabonds" who were not necessarily really vagabonds, thus practising a form of

In the Regiment

legalized abduction. Sometimes prisoners were recruited, their sentences cut short in exchange for the life of a soldier. The recruiters could be helped by "crimps," intermediaries who found recruits (often kidnapped adolescents) and "exchanged" them for a share of the bounty money. In Canada, particularly from 1840 to 1860, some crimps even encouraged British soldiers to desert and join the American army!

A soldier could sign up for a limited period or for life. The latter was more common until the mid-nineteenth century. Beginning in 1847, men were recruited for a period of 12 years, which was shortened to 10 years in 1867.

Once signed up, the recruits were rounded up at the regimental depot and given a medical examination, which they would pass unless they were in a sorry plight indeed, and then assigned a place in the barracks. Clothed and equipped, the new soldier immediately began to learn how to operate and handle his musket. The formal enlistment took place somewhat afterwards before a magistrate, who advised him of his legal obligations in the army. He then received his enlistment bonus, which disappeared immediately because, according to custom, he had to "treat" his new companions. He would learn soon afterwards that he would have to pay for a variety of small items and minor services such as laundry. It also would not take him long to discover that army uniforms came in only two sizes, too large and too small, which meant that he would have to pay the company tailor to make the appropriate alterations.

Infantrymen at drill, c. 1807. J. Atkinson. Engraving.
Anne S. K. Brown Military Collection, Brown University, Providence.

Pay

From 1660 to 1783 an enlisted man's pay was eight pence per day, for an annual amount in British funds of 12 pounds, three shillings and four pence. But after deductions for food, clothing and a host of small expenses he would have only two pounds and eight shillings left at the end of the year, the equivalent of a few pennies a day. The pay was raised to one shilling and one pence per day at the end of the eighteenth century, which meant a yearly total of 18 pounds and five shillings. From 1797 to 1867 it remained the same, one shilling per day, and was increased by twopence in 1867 – prior to deductions, of course – so that soldiers were no richer than they had been a century earlier. The pay for cavalry troopers, artillerymen, veterans, corporals and others was slightly higher. But all in all the income was laughable, and if the soldier had a family to feed it meant abject poverty – for example, a pound of butter at the Laprairie barracks in 1838 cost 10 pence!

The Crossing

Under the garrison rotation system, each regiment usually recruited as many men as possible during its tour in Great Britain or Ireland, and then packed up to head for a port where they would embark for their overseas destination.

Travel in troop transport ships was not exactly comfortable. The soldiers were crammed together under the deck, where they tried to sleep six in a bunk for four. If the ceiling was low it was impossible for them to stand or sit on their bunk. If the

Troops embarking, c. 1820.

Anne S. K. Brown Military Collection, Brown University, Providence.

ceiling was higher hammocks were hung above their heads. Their rations were reduced by a third because they were deemed to be less active, thus requiring less food. Fresh air was scarce, even when the hatches were left open in fine weather. Good weather provided an opportunity to air out the bedding on the deck, where the soldiers also went frequently for exercise. But if the weather turned bad and the ship was pitching, everybody was sent below deck and the hatches were closed. Thus the soldiers existed in airless confinement, crammed together in unsanitary conditions, all the more so because many of them suffered from seasickness. Risk of epidemic was therefore proportionate to the number of days of bad weather.

The officers and their families lived in more spacious conditions than enlisted men, but even they had to share small cabins. In the days of sailing ships the trip to North America took two or three months, longer if the winds were particularly unkind. The use of steamships to transport troops, which began in the 1850s, considerably shortened the journey across the Atlantic, even though it did nothing to improve comfort levels.

Barracks

British soldiers in garrison in Canada mostly lived in barracks. In Quebec City after the Conquest, for example, the Collège des Jésuites was transformed into an infantry barracks, while the Artillery and Engineers set up in the "New Barracks" of the French, which eventually became Artillery Park. The British

authorities feared that the soldiers would be encouraged to desert and that their discipline would flag if they lodged with local civilians, so they avoided this practice as much as possible; it had been much more common under the French regime. Such practice also generally compromised relations with the people, whether French – who would no doubt have given them an icy reception – or English – who were always fiercely opposed to billeting soldiers with civilians. As soon as Canada fell to Great Britain, therefore, Governor Murray stated that barracking was the only way that "discipline and preservation of the troops will be ensured."[74]

The British soldiers in Canada therefore lived in isolation. They had a kind of separate society, because their manner of lodging differed from that of the French in one major respect: the wives and children of the soldiers were allowed to live in the barracks, although in limited numbers.

The soldier's farewell, c. 1810; when the soldiers of a British regiment were posted to another garrison, their women and children were in most cases abandoned without resources.

Anne S. K. Brown Military Collection, Brown University, Providence.

Soldiers' Wives

At the end of the seventeenth century a maximum of three wives per company could accompany soldiers overseas, a figure that was raised to six in the eighteenth century. They travelled at army expense and were entitled to their rations, because they were deemed useful for washing, cooking and sewing. Some learned on their own to be nurses.

Many more women lived in the vicinity of each regiment in garrison in the British Isles, but their status was not secure. Just before the regiments would leave for another country, the soldiers' wives would gather and hold a lottery to see who would go. One ballot for each woman present would be tossed into a hat. Most of the ballots said "not to go," while the prescribed number, three or six per company, depending on the era, said "to go." A woman who drew a "to go" ballot was authorized to embark with her children and accompany her husband to his new post.

The others remained on the dock with their children, with no resources. As it was virtually certain that families separated in this manner would never see each other again, many wives left behind simply awaited the next regiment to find a new husband. But this solution caused sad tales, such as that of one Rachel Heap, who, believing her husband dead, remarried in Halifax in 1802 and gave birth to three children when suddenly her "dead" husband resurfaced. Other women, heartbroken, attempted to return to their families; they were not always welcome, however, often being considered dishonourable for having kept company with soldiers. Some fell into alcoholism and prostitution. There were even cases of suicide, both by the women and by the soldiers who could not live without ever again seeing their loved ones.

Those who were able to follow the soldiers in their travels needed to be strong of character, because they had to work

hard to survive under conditions that can barely be imagined today. Yet many of these women preferred such a life to the even more horrible conditions of the disadvantaged in civilian society. Living with a regiment could be difficult, but there was a certain gaiety and social life, a kind of extended family life that was often warmer than anything they had known before – not to mention love, of course.

The Military Wedding

When a relationship became serious enough, a form of wedding called "leaping over the sword" took place. In this ancient custom, the company would gather around a sword on the floor, in front of which stood the couple, hand-in-hand. A corporal or sergeant acting as the clergyman would order, "Leap, rogue, and jump, whore, and then you are married for evermore."[75] The happy couple would jump over the sword hand-in-hand as the drum beat. From this moment, they were considered man and wife. The event was sometimes followed by a "hoisting," a ceremonial burial of bachelorhood ending in a small parade during which the groom was carried by two of his mates, preceded by a fife and drum playing "The Cuckold's March."[76]

In principle, every soldier had to request official permission to marry. Very few did so, however, because the authorities did not look favourably upon their soldiers marrying. Not until the 1830s did they find a connection between the low desertion rate among married soldiers and the stabilizing influence of their wives. But even in 1863, after the social reforms had been introduced in the mid-nineteenth century, only eight percent of soldiers sent overseas were formally married. Given the many problems involved, it would appear that the vast majority preferred to remain single.

Housing

There was nothing luxurious about British army barracks in Canada. Until the middle of the nineteenth century the practice was to cram as many people as possible into the available space. In 1845, however, minimum space requirements were established for each soldier, although it would take another 15 years before the measure was implemented, because new barracks had to be built.

The inside of a barrack resembled a large dormitory, with whitewashed walls and wooden floors. Each room would generally contain a whole company of soldiers – between 50 and 100 men; the beds were placed to the sides of the room, with the centre occupied by the tables and benches used for meals. Shelves were placed on the walls above the beds to give the soldier a place to put his haversack and headdress. The uniform and harness were suspended on hooks. The musket was usually placed close to the bed, sometimes in a rack. In Quebec and Ontario, the room had a cast-iron wood stove to ward off the rigours of winter; in the Maritime colonies, which were considered more temperate, fireplaces continued to be the main source of heat until the 1840s, at which time wood stoves were also brought into service. The same

Interior of soldiers' barracks at St. Andrews, New Brunswick, c. 1853. J. C. Clarke. Watercolour.
National Archives of Canada, C8404.

bucket was used as a urinal and for washing, which led to many eye infections. In 1840 the authorities began to provide the soldiers with washbasins.

Until 1824, wooden beds were designed for two soldiers. Double bunk beds were also occasionally used. Then the single bed came into use; it was made of iron and could be folded to create more space. However, it took some 30 years for the single bed to be introduced in Canada, because wood was plentiful. Each bed had a straw mattress, a pillow, two sheets, two blankets and a small woven rug, usually green.

The married soldiers' wives and children lived in the barracks, in virtually total promiscuity. The rules granted them no rights, and everyone managed as best they could. Married couples generally occupied the corners of the room and hung a blanket or sheets on a line as a partition to give them some privacy, a privilege that could be withdrawn at any time. Children had to find space for themselves, often taking the bed of a soldier who was on guard duty. This state of affairs continued until 1856, when the army finally agreed to provide beds and bedding for children living in barracks.[77]

Married soldiers often obtained permission to live in town, where, although they could afford nothing more than a hovel, they at least had some privacy. Beginning in 1848, the army allocated a few pence per day for their rent, and also began providing rooms in barracks to accommodate two or three families. In Canada the first barrack allocating one small room per soldier's family was erected in Halifax in 1868; this was the forerunner of the well-known PMQs on our military bases, which were initially called "pavilions" rather than "Private Married Quarters."

Meals

In North America daily rations for the British soldier usually consisted of one pound (489 g) of bread or flour and one pound of beef or a half pound (244 g) of salt pork, with a little butter and cheese. This represents between 2,600 and 3,200 calories, enough food for moderate effort. To vary the menu, soldiers added "groceries" like tea, coffee, sugar and vegetables, at their own expense. In Canada, particularly outside the major cities, some were able to benefit from the rich land and took up gardening or fishing to augment their fare. Each man was also entitled to a beer ration. It is therefore impossible to estimate the nutritive value of the food consumed by British soldiers in Canada, but they generally appear to have been relatively well fed. Women whose marriages were officially recognized, and whose children were under 14 years of age, were entitled to a half ration.

The manner in which the food was prepared was not exactly haute cuisine. Until the 1860s, virtually the only way of cooking was to boil food in large pots in the rooms or in the barrack kitchen. It was therefore a monotonous succession of soups and boiled stews. Tea and coffee were prepared in the same pot. There were only two meals a day, at 7:30 a.m. and at 12:30 p.m.; in principle, then, the barracks residents did not eat for 19 hours straight.

Daily Routine

The soldier's daily timetable is difficult to reconstruct, since information kept on the subject is fragmentary. As a general rule, reveille was sounded at approximately 5 a.m., followed by roll-call some 15 minutes later; then came the men's washing up and the cleaning of the barracks for inspection, held one hour after roll-call. There were then drills, which lasted until the breakfast call was heard at 7:30 a.m. After the first meal, everything was put away for another barracks inspection.

128

Women and children marched with the troops.
T. Rowlandson. Engraving, c. 1811.

Anne S. K. Brown Military Collection, Brown University, Providence.

Each soldier then went to work on his assignments for the day; some relieved sentries; others did maintenance duties; a few groups acted as military police, patrolling areas where soldiers gathered, especially taverns; and others still spent these hours at drill. Towards 12:30 p.m., the dinner call was sounded; after dinner there was another barracks inspection towards 2 p.m., after which, unless they were on duty, the soldiers appear to have been free until the "Tattoo," which sounded at 8 p.m. in winter and 8:30 in summer. The details of the service may have varied considerably, depending on the location and the era, but the British soldier was always watched closely and subjected to iron discipline, possibly more rigorously than his counterpart in any other Western European army.

Drink and Women

The only escape, for many soldiers, from such an implacably regulated and structured life was liquor. Among other spirits, they consumed incredibly large quantities of bad but highly alcoholic rum.[78] The taverns in the towns where the garrisons were located – Quebec City had 500 of them in 1830 – were patronized mainly by soldiers and seamen. In addition, mobile canteens followed the regiments into the field.

From the late eighteenth century on, the army, in an attempt to control the problem of alcoholism, favoured the establishment of "regimental canteens," which were no more than drinking establishments designed to satisfy the unquenchable thirst of soldiers in barracks. In the 1830s regulations became stricter; alcohol could no longer be served between noon and curfew, and never to soldiers who were drunk, nor to women nor children – which says a great deal about practices up to that point. It did not cost much to get drunk: in 1842, at the Laprairie barracks, a glass of beer or a glass of rum cost a cent and a half. To encourage the men to drink beer, which is less intoxicating, an increase in the price of alcohol was ordered. But in 1848, with this measure largely unsuccessful, the selling of liquor was simply banned in the canteens.

The prohibition did not change much, however: alcoholism continued to be a major problem in the army.

Approximately nine out of 10 British soldiers were young bachelors. There is no doubt that many sought the company of women who could give them easy and quick access to their favours with no strings attached. Throughout the British Empire prostitutes therefore haunted the taverns patronized by soldiers and seamen. There were many women in Canada who practised "the world's oldest profession." At the beginning of the nineteenth century it is estimated that there were 500 to 600 prostitutes in Quebec City alone. There were probably even more in Halifax, where there was a large naval base in addition to a major garrison. Venereal disease thus became one of the scourges of the army.

Between 1837 and 1847 more than 25 percent of all soldiers admitted to military hospitals suffered from sexually transmitted diseases. Twelve years later the proportion was 42 percent, a level that could be defined as epidemic. While also having to find a way to deal with the moralistic arguments of the Victorian era, military surgeons combatted these diseases practically: inspecting the prostitutes in the garrison towns and treating preventively. Their efforts yielded solid results, because the rate had declined to 29 percent in 1864 and 20 percent three years later. The army also finally saw that the best way of preventing such epidemics, and of solving other problems as well,

was to make it easier for soldiers to marry by providing them with a proper living environment.

Entertainment

Alcohol and the favours of prostitutes were far from the only forms of garrison recreation. In addition to the card games and dice found in all armies, the British soldiers had their own repertoire of songs, and some even played musical instruments. In the nineteenth century they performed much more than drinking songs, with soldiers taking part in concerts and plays to raise funds for charity. The organizers of these events were primarily officers, but non-commissioned officers and soldiers also participated. An example is the comedy performed in 1835 in Quebec City by the soldiers of the 79th Regiment, which included Scottish dances and bagpipe music; the profits went to the widows and orphans of the regiment.

Beginning in 1840, the military tried to encourage reading by establishing libraries and reading rooms in the barracks, hoping to keep the soldiers out of the taverns. This effort was only moderately successful, however, because 60 percent of the soldiers were illiterate. In 1849 schools were established to teach them to read, but another factor helped develop reading in the army: the religious revival that began to appear in the 1820s, particularly among the lower classes. In some regiments, bible-reading and catechism groups were formed. However, the books and

Soldiers were regular tavern patrons. T. Rowlandson. Engraving, c. 1805.

Anne S. K. Brown Military Collection, Brown University, Providence.

Flogging a soldier with the cat-o'-nine-tails, c. 1820.

Anne S. K. Brown Military Collection, Brown University, Providence.

sermons do not appear to have caught on with the majority of soldiers, who by all accounts preferred to go and have a drink with the boys and meet the girls.

Discipline and Punishment

In the British army, the slightest lapse in conduct was mercilessly punished following the summary judgement of a regimental court-martial, and there was no possibility of an appeal. Even minor offences were punished "cruelly and barbarously," in a manner unequalled in Western Europe: the purpose was to inspire terror by setting an example. "There were few Saturdays," related Philippe Aubert de Gaspé, "on which those who went to the market in Upper Town in Quebec City were not saddened to hear cries of pain emanating from the barracks yard." The soldiers were frequently whipped, and the cat-o'-nine-tails was the instrument of punishment par excellence. Any minor offence could call for this. In 1810-11 at Fort George in Upper Canada sentences of 75 lashings for the loss of a shirt, 100 for the loss of a razor and 295 for having left the barracks without permission were reported. The most common offence was drunkenness, which could merit 100 or 150 lashes.

The sentence was carried out in front of the whole regiment. Stripped to the waist, the soldier was tied up by the wrists. Behind him was a drummer in charge of administering the punishment, with the drum major in turn behind the drummer to strike him with a cane if he failed to whip the prisoner hard enough. After 25 lashes, another drummer took over and so on until the assigned number of lashes had been administered. After the 50th lash the back becomes a horrible mass of bleeding gelatin, and after the 100th blood flows freely. When the soldier lost consciousness he was revived with a bucket of water. The spectacle was so distressing that young soldiers sometimes fainted when they witnessed it for the first time.

According to Aubert de Gaspé, who frequently spoke with officers of the British army on the use of the whip, "they all agreed that 25 to 30 bad apples in each regiment were the only ones to receive this cruel punishment. Most, they said, became insensitive to pain after frequent flagellations. Their skin became so hardened that the cat-o'-nine-tails struck only dry skin resembling parchment stuck onto the bone. They added that the judges at courts-martial avoided to the greatest extent possible inflicting the whip on those who had never had it before, because, after undergoing the experience only once, they became incorrigible."[79] This inhuman punishment, which people wanted abolished as early as the late eighteenth century, continued for much of the following century. The number of

A disabled veteran reduced to begging. Engraving dated 1795.

Anne S. K. Brown Military Collection, Brown University, Providence.

lashes was limited to 1,000 in 1813 and to 200 in 1833; it was restricted to repeat offenders after 1859, after which it was rarely used. However, the whip was not officially abolished until 1881.

The militiamen, volunteers and soldiers of the "provincial" regiments raised in a colony, such as the Royal Canadian Volunteers or the Canadian Voltigeurs, were not subject to this punishment. It was, however, applicable to soldiers in colonial regiments raised by authority of the British Parliament under the rules of the regular army, such as the regiments of Fencibles or the Royal Canadian Rifle Regiment.

Other punishments inflicted on British soldiers and colonial troops were more in keeping with military punishments meted out in other armies of the period: solitary confinement, forced labour, branding, caning and the ultimate penalty, the firing squad.

Mutinies and Desertion

The severity of such treatment might well, one may think, have caused frequent mutinies. The very opposite is true. Uprisings among British troops in Canada appear to have been few, and to have had causes other than the rigours of discipline. They were caused by a few isolated soldiers. For example, a letter dated September 1763 states that there was in Quebec "a mutiny of the Garrison on the Eighteenth instance [September 18], which was entirely amongst the private men,"[80] who were protesting the excessive deductions from their pay. Thirty years later, a mutiny plot was uncovered within the 7th Regiment in garrison at Quebec City. The leader was executed by firing squad and two other soldiers were sentenced to 700 and 400 lashes.

Although mutinies may have been few, the same cannot be said of desertion. Prior to the 1830s, only some five percent of British soldiers deserted the regular army in Canada. In 1830, however, the rate jumped to more than 12 percent and remained high until 1837, when it dropped because of the rebellions. In 1848 it began to rise, reaching 18 percent in 1854 with the new war in the Crimea and peaking at more than 28 percent in 1857 during the revolt in India. The number of deserters then declined but rose again to more than eight percent in 1864 when the Americans offered generous amounts of money to those who enlisted in the Union army.

These figures are directly related to the noteworthy improvements made to the roads and railways linking Lower Canada, Upper Canada and the United States in the middle third of the nineteenth century. In the more isolated Atlantic colonies there

OFFICERS

Origins

It has often been said that in the British army a social chasm separated officers from their men. This is indeed true, but it must not be forgotten that this is true of most armies. Living conditions in the army always reflect conditions in the society which spawned it.

British officers were recruited from the four peoples of the United Kingdom. During the second half of the eighteenth century approximately 40 percent were of English and Welsh descent, 30 percent Irish and 25 percent Scottish. Officers born in the colonies, in particular in North America and the West Indies, and those of foreign descent – i.e., Swiss or German – accounted for only five percent. From the standpoint of social status, only 15 percent came from the aristocracy, but these were the most politically influential; lastly, 15 percent of officers' fathers had been in the military. The majority, some 65 percent, came from families in the minor nobility, the clergy and the relatively well off bourgeoisie for whom a military career was

Officer of the 60th Rifle Regiment, c. 1817.
A. Dickinson. Miniature.
Musée du Québec.

were far fewer desertions. The problem was serious in central Canada and was never really eliminated despite measures taken to guard the borders more carefully. As soon as exciting news arrived, such as the gold rush to California, or when there were fears that the army would be mobilized to fight in the Crimea, or worse still in India, the exodus began. What could the authorities do in 1857, when 955 of the 3,000 soldiers deserted, or in 1864, when 831 of the 9,900 men in garrison took to the fields? Not much, in truth. In London in the 1860s it was thought prudent not to send too many troops to Canada for fear of swelling the ranks of the Americans.

Demobilization and Retirement

Prior to the mid-nineteenth century, most soldiers left the service when their unit was disbanded, usually right after a war. If the demobilized regiment was in Canada the men were generally offered land to encourage them to settle in the colony. Those who wished to were allowed to return to the United Kingdom, it would appear, even though such a right was not granted unconditionally until 1867. Invalid soldiers could claim a small disability pension from the Royal Hospital. It was not unusual, however, to see old blind or amputee soldiers begging in the streets. As for the able-bodied among the demobilized, they could request a pension, which, if granted, was sure to be paltry.

considered very honourable. However, such families usually had neither the birth, the fortune nor the influence needed for rapid promotion, and these officers had to live within their means and accumulate many years of service before being promoted. Finally, some five percent of officers were enlisted men who, with luck and outstanding ability, had obtained a commission.

Promotions and Training

British officers could rise in rank either through seniority or by purchasing rank. In wartime many commissions were issued without the need to buy them, and the high mortality rate among officers led to rapid promotion among the survivors. During long periods of peacetime, on the other hand, there was a return to promotion on the basis of years of service or purchase, for those who could afford it. This method of obtaining rank was severely criticized throughout the nineteenth century before being done away with once and for all in 1871. One celebrated case was that of a poor captain who had 47 years of service and had been in the Battle of Waterloo finding himself under the command of a rich lieutenant-colonel who had been only two years old at the time of the famous battle! Towards

The examination for the post of Acting Major, Montreal, 1866. F. G. Coleridge. Watercolour.
National Archives of Canada, C102547.

1840 a lieutenant-colonel's commission cost approximately £7,000 – a small fortune at the time. Most officers could not pay such an amount; promotion by seniority was their only option.

In the infantry and cavalry in the eighteenth century there was virtually no academic training. The profession was learned in the regiment through contact with experienced officers, a system that generally produced a remarkably competent officer corps.[81] However, the need to establish a military college was becoming increasingly clear during the Napoleonic wars and in 1802 the Royal Military College opened its doors at Great Marlow, moving to Sandhurst 10 years later. Édouard-Alphonse d'Irumberry de Salaberry appears to have been the first Canadian cadet admitted there, in 1807. Officers in the artillery and engineers could not purchase their commissions and had to attend the Woolwich Royal Military Academy, founded in 1741, for in-depth technical and scientific training. Canada had no academy issuing officer's commissions in the regular army between 1760 and 1876.

Because their regiment's stay in Canada was temporary, British officers, like their soldiers, did not form lasting links with the people of the colony. Without exception they lived in barracks built specially for them; their servants, called "batmen," were soldiers, and generally speaking the regiment was their society. It consisted essentially of a group of bachelors, because only a quarter of them got married – nearly always to British women of their class. One of the duties of regimental colonels was in fact to discreetly ensure that young officers did not enter into ill-considered liaisons. Marrying a woman from the colonies was tacitly prohibited. Every officer who did so

was forced to leave the army. They socialized with the families of the colonial elite at balls, the theatre and dinners, but these cordial contacts would remain superficial. In Quebec City between 1760 and 1836 there were only about 30 marriages between officers serving in British line regiments and Canadian women, nearly all of British descent. It is not surprising, then, that many young women of the colonies were deceived by these gallant young men in uniform; such occurrences were even the subject of poetic duels published in the Quebec City press.[82]

The Mess

The social hub for officers was the mess. The word originated from the custom among officers of sharing costs to improve the standard of meals they took together. The practice was known as "messing." It spread, and in the 1760s commanding officers were encouraged to establish officers' messes, not only for the material advantages they brought, but also to develop regimental spirit and for the men to live "together like a family."[83] Little by little, the regimental messes became more sophisticated; first they procured their own dishes and glassware, then silverware, luxurious furniture and their own personnel. The costs were covered by a deduction from each officer's salary, in

Toasting the King at an officers' mess dinner, c. 1797. James Gillray. Engraving.

Anne S. K. Brown Military Collection, Brown University, Providence.

proportion to his rank, in addition to a contribution from the sovereign, beginning in 1818.

In the nineteenth century, the mess became a comfortable place where an officer could find books, newspapers, board games and a fine wine cellar and where he could discuss matters with his colleagues in a warm and pleasant atmosphere. It was the military equivalent of a good private club. In several garrisons the officers' mess was far from inferior to establishments found locally; in fact it was probably superior in terms of refined living and in terms of the intellectual matters discussed. Of course there were obligations, chief among which was that members had to behave like gentlemen. The first regulations appeared at the beginning of the nineteenth century; single members were generally required to dine there three or four times per week, with married members and civilian gentlemen entitled to visit as a guest once a week. An unannounced visit by a woman would cause an absolute scandal. Women were, however, admitted once a month for a gala dinner in their honour. The regimental musicians usually played at the

dinner for guests and at the ladies' dinner, the latter concluding with dancing.

Amusements

British officers were keen on art and literature; some mounted theatre productions and several were good actors, such as one Artillery Lieutenant Marlay, who around 1830 acted "with considerable poise and energy."[84] Some were also musicians. One evening in 1785 there was a small concert at Fort Niagara at which two officers played "charming overtures and symphonies"[85] on the violin, accompanied by the horns, bassoons, oboes and clarinets of the band of the 29th Regiment.

If one is to believe the travel diaries they kept, officers had a veritable passion for fishing and hunting. It may be surprising to find that they had enough leisure time to engage in these sports, but it was an excellent way to keep in shape, practise shooting, and familiarize themselves with

Breakfast at the officers' mess, c. 1840.
Anne S. K. Brown Military Collection, Brown University, Providence.

the surrounding fields and woods where they would perhaps one day have to deploy their troops. Some painted watercolours of the landscapes and towns, which was very useful from the strategic standpoint because it gave the officers the opportunity to familiarize themselves with the local topography.

Of the many games of chance, horse racing was the most popular. Races were organized by officers with the assistance of local gentlemen, in accordance with the prevailing English Jockey Club rules and ceremonies.

Duties and Honours

Like their French predecessors, British officers supervised the military activities of their men, taking part in exercises, guard duty, parades and various other duties. The pride they took in their soldiers and their regiment encouraged emulation and esprit de corps. The end result was usually well-disciplined troops who were fearless fighters because of their determination and bravery.

Unlike the French, British officers were not at first awarded medals such as the Croix de Saint-Louis. Towards the end of the eighteenth century, though, their victories were beginning to be recognized. Sometimes the legislatures or a number of associations also awarded ceremonial weapons to commanding officers. In Canada the first medals, which were for officers only, appeared for the battles of the War of 1812. The rank and file became eligible for good conduct medals in 1830, but for campaign medals only in 1847. The practice of awarding military medals and decorations, which was a source of great pride, then became more widespread.

Chapter 5

DEMOBILIZATION

In 1815 a world tired of more than 20 years of conflict welcomed the end of the Napoleonic wars. Throughout the long period of peace that followed, all the countries involved in these confrontations were relieved to be able to make huge cuts in their military spending, which was swallowing up most of their budgets. In Great Britain the Royal Navy was reduced from 140,000 to 17,000 men. Army personnel were cut to 110,000, the minimum required to maintain British garrisons in Great Britain and the colonies. With the exception of those in India, regular colonial troops were disbanded.

Some believed, rightly, that the people of British North America would lose interest in defence matters unless one or more Canadian regiments were kept active. But Great Britain retained its strict cost-saving measures and applied them rigorously. All the Fencibles regiments, including the 104th, which had been raised in New Brunswick, were disbanded in 1816-17. Henceforth all defence would be the responsibility of the home British army sent to the colony.

The American Threat

The American army was reduced to 10,000 men and reformed from top to bottom to become a truly professional force. There remained many sources of animosity between the United States and Great Britain, and a new war was still possible. In London, after the signing of the peace treaty, the staff considered the problem of how to defend British North America.

The War of 1812 had unfolded to a great extent in accordance with the rules of European war. At the beginning the armies were still covering long distances by travelling along rivers and lakes, but as time went by overland troop movements had become possible in some areas. The armies also no longer consisted solely of infantrymen, but also artillery, cavalry, a train and baggage. This meant that future battles would likely occur increasingly on open land as in Europe, rather than in the woods where the Canadians excelled.

It so happened that European-style war gave the Americans an advantage. In fact, they would likely be the first to favour an invasion of British North America to satisfy their ambitions of hegemony, because neither the Canadians nor the British had anything to gain from attacking them. The regular American army, although modest, did have an enormous number of volunteers and militiamen they could call on, all of whom would be more at ease in a conventional campaign. The British garrison, supported by Canadian militiamen, could hold out for a while but would probably eventually collapse simply because of the difference in numbers.

With such prospects, the staff saw only one way to safeguard British North America: to build impressive fortifications.

The Great Fortifications

Defending a strip of land from the Atlantic to the west of the Great Lakes involved difficult choices. What areas should be given defence priority? Where should the great forts be located? From the very first, Quebec City, Kingston and Montreal were identified as strategic points for safeguarding the country, and it was imperative that these cities be made virtually impregnable. Citadels were therefore built in Quebec City and Kingston. Montreal was to be defended by forts to the south and an army in the field. Communications could be improved by digging various canals along the Richelieu River and around Montreal Island, and particularly by building locks on the Ottawa River and canals along the Rideau River. A second navigable channel between Montreal and Kingston was considered desirable in the event that the Americans took control of the St. Lawrence River between these two cities. Secondary works, consisting of strengthening almost every existing fort and erecting a citadel in the Niagara Peninsula, were also planned, to ensure that "the inhabitants would not think that we had abandoned them."[86]

The estimated cost of this ambitious programme caused the authorities to scale it down to the essentials. At the insistence of the Duke of Wellington, funds were immediately made available to the army and in 1819 several works were begun: construction of Fort Lennox on Île-aux-Noix and another fort on

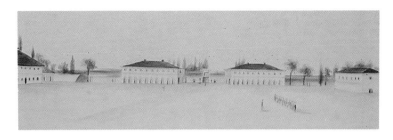

Interior of Fort Lennox. J. D. MacDiarmid. Watercolour, c. 1838.
Royal Ontario Museum, Toronto.

Île Sainte-Hélène, facing the port of Montreal, which would house the "military stores and buildings"[87] of the city. In 1820 work was begun on the Quebec Citadel.

The years went by, and in April 1825 the Duke of Wellington became impatient and sent a military commission to Canada under the command of Colonel James Carmichael-Smyth to identify the reasons for the delay and to recommend solutions. After carrying out inspections during the summer and fall, the commissioners returned to England and submitted their report. Fort Lennox and the fort on Île Sainte-Hélène were virtually complete, but the Quebec Citadel was only one third built. And nothing had been done along the Rideau River nor at Kingston. Not only had the 1819 plan not been completed, according to the commission, but a citadel remained to be built at Halifax. They found it unacceptable that this city, the home port of the Royal Navy in the North Atlantic, should be so poorly fortified. On the basis of the report, the Duke of Wellington approached the government once again,

maintaining that not two but three large citadels were required, in Halifax, Quebec City and Kingston; he also felt that the Rideau Canal should be built, whatever the cost. Although apprehensive, with good reason, about the exorbitant costs of such works, the government approved the plan in 1826.

Huge Expenses!

Construction of the Quebec Citadel continued apace but it would take several years before it was completed, in 1831, after which there were still many additional expenses. Instead of the projected £70,000, it cost £236,000. Work on the Halifax Citadel, which began in 1828, was to total £116,000 and to be completed in 1834; instead it took 28 years to build and cost £242,000. Work on the Kingston Citadel, called Fort Henry, began in 1832. It took the form of an enormous redoubt, and the

plan called for five similar redoubts around the city. Work went smoothly, and it was almost complete in 1837 at a cost of £73,000. However, the final touches were not completed until 1848, raising the total to £88,000. The British government then deemed that it had spent enough and the other redoubts were never built.

At Quebec, and particularly at Halifax, the building of the citadels raised unexpected problems requiring considerable changes from the initial plans and many costly delays. However, it was probably the Rideau Canal that caused the most problems for the officers and men of the engineers. Work began with the building of locks at Carillon on the Ottawa River before construction of the canal proper began in 1827, not far from the current location of the federal Parliament in Ottawa. The undertaking proved to be exceedingly arduous, and hundreds of workers died, primarily from malaria transmitted by the mosquitoes in the swamps. Problems of all kinds plagued Lieutenant-

139

Colonel John By of the Corps of Royal Engineers, who was in charge of the work. But he persevered, and the Rideau Canal, with its 47 masonry locks and 52 dams, was finally ready in 1832. The matter of the costs raised a political storm in the British Parliament, however, particularly since England was in a serious economic crisis. The initial £169,000 had already been increased to £474,000. By the time it was completed, the Rideau Canal cost more than a million pounds sterling, a phenomenal amount for the time. For comparison, the total budget of the Royal Navy for 1832 was five million. When called to England to explain, By successfully defended himself against the accusations against him: the Duke of Wellington had ordered him to go ahead with the work without waiting for the vote from Parliament. By was nevertheless a victim of political quarrels and his reputation was never restored to its former lustre.[88]

The fact remains that Great Britain provided Canada with a formidable chain of fortifications, which undoubtedly had the desired effect on the Americans. To take these fortresses would have required resources that their army simply did not have. An officer from the United States visiting Quebec City was very much impressed with its citadel; he said that the only way to take it would be to have the troops brought in by hot-air balloon![89]

The Great Lakes –
Neutral Territory

These fortifications were now the first line of defence for the country's interior, a role previously played by fleets of warships on the Great Lakes. Both Great Britain and the United States were keen to avoid a repetition of the 1814 costly race to build ships. In 1817 American Secretary of State Richard Rush and British ambassador to Washington Charles Bagot signed an agreement to this end. Under the Rush-Bagot agreement, each country would henceforth maintain only a small ship with a single 18-pound cannon on Lake Champlain and Lake Ontario, and two such ships on lakes Erie, Huron and Superior. The existing ships would be disarmed and no more would be built.

It was also understood that the Royal Navy would maintain small naval bases at Île-aux-Noix, Kingston and Penetanguishene until the mid-1830s. If a dispute were to arise, the British Admiralty would send small ships from the North Atlantic Squadron to the Great Lakes through the new canals. The agreement in fact proclaimed military neutrality on the Great Lakes, which suited both countries perfectly.

Although there were a few snags during certain tense periods, the spirit of the Rush-Bagot agreement was respected, and it contributed greatly to the harmony that exists to this day between Canada and the United States.

Nevertheless, the existence of impressive fortifications, and the fact that the Great Lakes were recognized as neutral

adequate to face the regular American army would, however, not be equal to the task of dealing

Officers of the Royal Engineers Corps, in 1846. H. Martens. Engraving.
Anne S. K. Brown Military Collection, Brown University, Providence.

territory, required many men to defend British North America. Great Britain kept a contingent of 3,000 to 3,500 soldiers in Upper and Lower Canada and 2,000 to 2,500 in the Maritime colonies. What may have been

with the hordes of militiamen who would undoubtedly attack the country in the event of a new conflict. There was no doubt that the invaders would be better prepared than they had been in 1812.

Volunteers of the Montreal Rifle Corps wore the uniform of the 60th Rifle Regiment from 1820 to 1830. Reconstitution by P. W. Reynolds.
Canadian Department of National Defence Library.

Military theorists all reached the same conclusion: it was essential to have a large number of willing and properly trained militiamen. It so happens that at the time many of the men who were eligible for the militia in British North America were of French descent, and most of them lived in Lower Canada. At the beginning of the 1820s the colony had approximately 80,000 men capable of bearing arms, whereas there were only 17,000 in Upper Canada and 30,000 in the Maritime colonies. It was felt that one quarter of the militiamen could be armed.

In 1820, when Lord Dalhousie arrived in Quebec as governor-in-chief, the training of the militia was one of his priorities. Although he was a talented administrator in the autocratic style, he did not have the patience to recognize the political factions. He supported the oligarchies of the upper bourgeoisie, whether the Family Compact in Upper Canada or the Clique du Château in Lower Canada, and opposed progressive politicians like Louis-Joseph Papineau and William Lyon Mackenzie, who were demanding reforms, including the abolition of privileges.

Dalhousie believed that to be effective the Upper and Lower Canada militia should correspond in every respect with his idyllic vision of the volunteer militia in England: brave yeomen – i.e., prosperous farmers – led by their squires, beneficent noblemen, both wearing bright uniforms and going off to war as if they were going on a hunting expedition!

Because of its familiarity with English institutions, Upper Canada adapted better to the programme than did Lower Canada. In the 1820s several companies of volunteers were established in various parts of the province and in May 1829 each regiment was even ordered to have two companies of volunteer riflemen. The first task of all of these men was to obtain uniforms at their own expense in order to receive weapons from the government. No uniform, no weapon. That was the rule.

At first sight, these active volunteers appeared to strengthen the militia, but this was merely an illusion. Because they were generally from the well-to-do classes, they represented only a small proportion of men able to bear arms. The mass of militiamen was completely neglected except for the annual review.

Annual Review of the Upper Canada Militia

For each volunteer, in uniform and armed, who enlisted, there were 10 others who were forsaking a militia that was becoming a social club for the right-thinking people in their county. Most were content to show up for the annual review of the garrison militia, an event that had been relatively

serious in the past but which in the new line of thinking had become a kind of country picnic, if not a veritable circus.

Every June 4 the militia regiment assembled in a field. But it really was more of a disparate band of men wearing all manner of clothing and armed with pitchforks, sticks, umbrellas... and even some old guns. The officers did their best to look like officers, attempting not to trip over their scabbards! After separating the men into groups – those armed with umbrellas would constitute one group, those with old hunting muskets another – attempts were made to have them do drill. The usual result was a kind of chaotic square dance with people coming and going in all directions, to the great dismay of the officers, who went hoarse shouting orders that no one was listening to, or at least hearing. In the ranks it was all jokes and laughter. The men then quenched their thirst, ending each day more or less pickled and deeply convinced that every Canadian was worth 10 Yankees! Sometimes, thanks to the alcohol, fights would break out and the entire assembly would turn into a free-for-all.

Officers of the Royal Artillery in 1828; the volunteer artillerymen adopted the uniform of the regular artillery. E. Hull. Engraving.
Anne S. K. Brown Military Collection, Brown University, Providence.

The Militia of Lower Canada

In Lower Canada, the Francophone population appeared to have a more respectful and pragmatic view of the militia, because it still played an important social role. It was mandatory to be part of the militia, but being an officer or a non-commissioned officer was always considered an honour. Moreover, many of the French-Canadian elite had an officer's commission.

Of course during the 1820s militia exercises and tasks could be no more than tedious duties like those performed in the other colonies. But the militia gatherings still resembled shooting competitions and were generally held on May 1, as they had been under the French regime. The gatherings ended with a proper party given by the captain (see *Canadian Military Heritage*, Volume 1). On St. Peter's Day, the militiamen assembled after Mass at the doors of the church. The captain then had them shout, "Vive le roi!" and "Le pays était sauf, la paix assurée."[90]

Many French-Canadian militiamen thus continued to practise their shooting and relations with officers were cordial. The organization was relatively egalitarian and did not really have volunteers in the British or American sense of the word; being a part of the militia was considered a community duty. Except in some staffs and a few city companies, French-Canadian militiamen, officers and soldiers were all considered equal and did not see the need to wear the uniform.

When he came up against this peculiar institution, Lord Dalhousie thought it "in truth, more

143

of a police force similar to the Gendarmerie in France than a Militia of British formation."[91] This perception stemmed from the fact that the duties of the militia in Lower Canada included civil duties such as escorting prisoners and criminals. He was very disappointed to see so little of what "is found in almost every other part of the British Empire."[92] Lord Dalhousie was clearly thinking of the uniformed volunteers of the English Yeomanry. He therefore encouraged the training of volunteer militia companies in Quebec City and Montreal.

However, he committed one major error at the ouset – admitting only young people from the Anglophone bourgeoisie. Thus the Royal Montreal Cavalry was to be a military version of the Montreal Hunt Club – a club for riding to the hounds. While the Gregorys and the Molsons were asked to form their companies, His Excellency found it preferable "for several [unspecified] reasons not to accept"[93] the offers of the French-Canadian bourgeois to form companies of volunteer riflemen and artillerymen. How would these bourgeois distinguish themselves in the new militia when they were not even authorized to establish their own companies of volunteers? The experience was

mortifying for those among them interested in military matters.

But that was only the beginning. It was then decided to replace French county names with English ones; for example, the Terrebonne Militia became the Effingham Militia. In addition, in 1828 Dalhousie ordered that the city militias be divided by district, which in many instances meant that officer positions would go to English Canadians while most of the militiamen were French Canadian. This decision once again raised the sensitive issue of French as a language of command. Worst of all, the governor-in-chief, in a fit of anger against the Legislative Assembly, eliminated militia officer commissions for many of the members of the Opposition. Perhaps he was hoping to discredit them in the eyes of the voters, but it was the militia itself that would suffer. The result was deep discontent, confirmed in a special investigative committee in a report dated 1829.

Demobilization of the French-Canadian Militia

But the Francophone militia in Lower Canada still existed on paper and continued to meet. In 1828, at the request of the governor-in-chief, some

men were even able to obtain uniforms. Even more striking, in Dorchester County, Beauce, a Francophone horse company dressed in grey with black collar and cuffs, armed by the government, pursued deserters as a police force would. But none of this activity could hide a deep malaise.[94]

In reality, the French Canadians were seriously questioning the values of the militia. Control over this institution, which in the past had been so central to its interests and so dear to its heart, was being lost. In the end, French Canadians turned away from an organization that no longer represented them. Because they were being assimilated and humiliated, they would isolate themselves socially in order to keep their identity and to truly belong only to the institutions they could control: their Church and their political parties. The militia, and more generally the very idea of military service, became a matter "for others" from then on, their only concern being to defend their immediate territory. In 1830, the French-Canadian militia organization, although it continued to subsist, was virtually wiped out. This situation, aggravated by a political landscape resembling a minefield, encouraged the rebellions of 1837 and 1838.

Political Confrontation and Secret Societies

During the 1820s and 1830s the political situation in Upper and Lower Canada deteriorated. In each colony, groups of reformers began to stridently demand powers for the Legislative Assemblies. But although they formed the Parliamentary majority all their bills were rejected by the Legislative Councils, which were controlled by the existing cliques.

The British garrison was tied to this explosive political situation in spite of itself, because it was responsible for maintaining the public order. When a serious incident occurred in 1832 in Montreal during elections, a detachment of the 15th Regiment called to the aid of the civil power opened fire on a mob that had refused to disperse, killing three Francophones, including the editor of an opposition newspaper. This discredited the army in the eyes of many French Canadians.

The situation worsened as the reform partisans, led by Louis-Joseph Papineau, began demanding political autonomy ever more stridently. They assumed the name Patriotes. Most were of French descent, but among them could also be found Irish nationalists and a few Americans. Most Canadians of English

Officer of the Queen's Light Dragoon, a corps raised in Montreal in December 1837.

Anne S. K. Brown Military Collection, Brown University, Providence.

origin identified with the conservative elements in place, even though some of them also favoured reforms. In 1834-35 a number of political clubs were created with a view to taking up arms. At the end of 1835 the British Party, taking an openly paramilitary stance, established the 393-member British Rifle Corps and demanded that the government provide them with weapons.[95] The new governor-in-chief, Lord Gosford, was aware of the danger this represented and ordered the corps disbanded on January 15, 1836.

Opposing factions responded by founding

semi-secret societies. The conservatives founded the Doric Club and the Patriotes created their own paramilitary association called Les Fils de la Liberté. Officially, the latter claimed to be a civilian political association, but in reality its whole structure was military. Its sections were organized into companies and battalions, and the heads of each level had a rank. Brawls became ever more frequent. In the summer of 1837 many

An old Patriote of 1837.
Reconstitution by Henri Julien.
National Archives of Canada, C17937.

large political meetings were organized by Patriote politicians. The Church encouraged people to be calm, condemning any idea of rebellion against the legitimate authority and the law. But passions had been inflamed.

In view of this agitation and the ever more persistent rumours of an armed uprising, General John Colborne, commander of the British forces in Canada, discreetly took action to place the troops in a state of readiness in the Montreal area. He also requested the establishment of a police force consisting of constables in Montreal and Quebec City, for in the fall of 1837 only the British troops were capable of keeping order. Upper Canada, striving to accede to greater autonomy, was also experiencing political tensions. This did not prevent Lieutenant-Governor Sir Francis Bond Head, in 1837, from believing that any danger had passed and sending the Toronto garrison to lend a hand to Colborne's troops in Montreal.

The 1837 Lower Canada Rebellion

On November 6, 1837, in Montreal, members of the Doric Club attacked the Fils de la Liberté, and the confrontation spread. After being called in to quell the riot, Lieutenant-Colonel George Augustus Wetherall's troops were able to disperse the crowd. The response from the Fils de la Liberté was quick: squads of armed Patriotes sprang up from everywhere to guard the house of their leader, Papineau, and in the neighbouring counties hundreds of others mobilized, disarming government supporters, intimidating magistrates and demanding neutrality from militia officers. The situation got out of control.

The governor-in-chief called for reinforcements, and on November 16 he issued warrants for the arrest of 36 Patriote leaders. Companies of volunteer militiamen were mobilized to bring them in. Papineau and Edmund Bailey O'Callaghan, who had been warned in time, were able to flee, but the president of the Fils de la Liberté, André Ouimet, was arrested and imprisoned. That very day a detachment of the Royal Montreal Cavalry, which was bringing to Montreal Patriotes arrested in Saint-Jean, was attacked and forced to release its prisoners. It had become clear to the Patriotes that the armed forces were giving full support to the oligarchy in power. To Sir John Colborne the essential thing was to restore order. But to do so he could not depend on the militia, which had been discredited and had fallen apart.

The population of Montreal was approximately half Francophone and half Anglophone. Peter McGill, founder of the university bearing his name, president of the Bank of Montreal and president of the country's first railway, suggested to Lord Gosford that companies of volunteers be formed in various districts of the city. Such a step would release the army to go and restore order in the countryside. Lord Gosford agreed and in

The Patriotes capture a piece of British artillery during the Battle of Saint-Denis, November 22, 1837. Reconstitution by Henri Julien.
National Archives of Canada, C18294.

The Horrors of War

People sometimes think that war in the time of our ancestors was a more noble undertaking than it is today. The following lines, written in the days of the colourful uniforms, serve to question any such notions.

The scene is Saint-Charles on Sunday November 26, 1837, the day after the battle between the Patriotes and the British troops. At the scene is Captain George Bell of the 1st British Regiment, who sadly sees parents and friends coming to look for the bodies of their loved ones. Two distinguished-looking girls approach Bell and ask if he can help them find their father, which he agrees to do:

"I went along with them, and, alas! he was indeed found with his head shattered to pieces, and a most dreadful corpse, frozen like a log, with his limbs extended in the manner in which he fell, and the blood and brain congealed and forming a part of the horrid mass. These poor girls, with some assistance, had him placed upon a sleigh, and covered up. One of them never shed a tear, the other was in agony. I could fancy their inward feelings, and I pitied them from my heart, poor souls! It is such scenes as these that make war so awful."

---

record time units of volunteers were raised. All the "loyal subjects" who had been waiting for this moment were able to take up arms and do away with their Patriote opponents who had been accused of treason! Most of these volunteers were English Canadians, of course, but a few Canadians of French descent were among them.

Saint-Denis and Saint-Charles

The first task was to subdue the Patriote counties around Montreal. A column of 300 British soldiers, consisting of detachments from the 24th, 32nd and 66th regiments, artillerymen with a 12-pound howitzer and members of the Royal Montreal Cavalry, left Sorel under the command of Lieutenant-Colonel Charles Stephen Gore. It was to join up at Saint-Charles with another column from Chambly, under the command of Lieutenant-Colonel Wetherall in the heart of Patriote country. But when they reached Saint-Denis on November 23, Gore

found himself facing approximately 800 barricaded Patriotes under the command of Dr. Wolfred Nelson. Although only 200 of them had muskets, their accurate fire soon forced the British scouts to turn tail. Gore then decided to shell the village, but even at a distance of 320 metres four artillerymen were shot before the howitzer could fire a single shell. The British nevertheless succeeded in taking a few houses. In the end, after six hours of combat, Gore was forced to order a retreat, abandoning the howitzer to the Patriotes. The losses were not heavy: six dead, 10 wounded and six missing among the British; 12 dead and seven wounded among the Patriotes. Nelson's men were jubilant; the farmers armed with pitchforks and old muskets, some of which dated back to the French regime, had beaten the well-trained and properly armed British soldiers.

But the triumph of the Patriotes was to be short-lived. On November 25 Lieutenant-Colonel Wetherall's column of 420 soldiers from the 1st and 66th regiments, with two field artillery pieces, along with a detachment from the Royal Montreal Cavalry, reached Saint-Charles. Approximately 200 to 250 Patriotes, led by Thomas Storrow Brown, were in position. Although

warned of Gore's defeat, Wetherall decided to attack immediately, surprising the Patriotes with his boldness. After two hours of firing, Wetherall ordered the three companies of the 1st Regiment to charge with fixed bayonets. The Patriotes, who did not have bayonets on their guns, were soon at a disadvantage. That is when an incident of disastrous consequences occurred: 50 of them, pretending to surrender in order to get a better shot at the soldiers, killed a sergeant and wounded several men. This treacherous gesture enraged their adversaries, who bayoneted large numbers of Patriotes and then sacked and burned the village. At the Battle of Saint-Charles the English had only three dead and 18 wounded, whereas the Patriotes had about 150 dead.

This victory returned the initiative to the British troops, and two days later Wetherall's column scattered a corps of approximately 300 Patriotes with only a few shots. On December 2 a new column commanded by Gore, consisting of detachments from the 24th, 32nd, 66th and 83rd regiments, with three cannon, had no difficulty entering Saint-Denis and burning part of the village. To the southeast of Montreal the rebellion had been truly quelled.

Saint-Eustache

But the Patriotes to the north of the city still held out. The arrival in Montreal of the 83rd Regiment gave Colborne the men and the resources he needed to march on Saint-Eustache, their headquarters. Colborne thus had the combined forces of the 1st, 32nd and 83rd regiments, 79 artillerymen with five artillery pieces and Congreve rockets, the Royal Montreal Cavalry, a company of the Montreal Rifles and a company of Saint-Eustache loyal volunteers; in all, there were some 1,280 British soldiers and approximately 220 volunteers. The Patriote organization was primitive and many members did not even have firearms. They thought they could get 800 combatants but eventually only 200 men, led by Dr. Jean-Olivier Chénier, lay barricaded in the convent, the church, the rectory and the manor in the centre of the village. To those who requested weapons, Chénier replied, "Relax, some will be killed and you will take their muskets."[96]

Colborne placed his troops around the village and had his soldiers advance systematically to tighten the vise on the defenders. Towards noon he ordered the artillery to open fire on the centre of the village and then to

148

The Battle of Saint-Eustache, December 14, 1837. Lord Charles Beauclerk. Engraving.
National Archives of Canada, C396.

advance up the main street and break down the doors of the church where many Patriotes had taken refuge. Two companies of the 1st Regiment were able to take the rectory nearby, and they set it on fire so that the smoke would make it difficult for those defending the church to see. The grenadiers of the 1st Regiment then took the manor and set it on fire as well, and then were able to enter the church through the vestry, which they also torched prior to withdrawing under the fire of the Patriotes in the balcony. Caught in the burning church, the Patriotes tried to get out by jumping from the windows, at which point the British troops made a final assault in a merciless struggle. This disastrous battle for the Patriotes lasted at least four hours; 70, including Chénier, were killed, against only three British soldiers.

The regular troops and volunteers then burned down the houses that had sheltered the Patriotes. After nightfall, they gave vent to terrible sacking and pillaging. The sacking of Saint-Eustache was so violent that Captain Swinburne of the 83rd Regiment would recount that it "equalled if not surpassed...what he had witnessed at the sack of Badajos."[97] The following day Colborne and his troops invaded the neighbouring village of Saint-Benoît. The Patriotes surrendered without resistance, but this did not prevent Colborne from burning down the village as well as the village of Saint-Hermas (today Mirabel).

In the days that followed, other corps of volunteers who had arrived on the scene after the Battle of Saint-Eustache pillaged the neighbouring farms. The usual practice after taking everything they could carry was to "make the men, women

149

and children undress, leaving them virtually naked at the doors of their burning houses."[98] One company of loyal volunteers, which had come to the area on foot, left on "French" horses, which were called "the Papineau horses."[99] Generally speaking, discipline among the volunteers left a great deal to be desired. According to one Patriote who had been taken prisoner, they "were fanatical partisans or ignorant and uncouth immigrants who believed they would be currying favour from those in authority by showing themselves to be pitiless. The regular British soldiers, on the other hand, were disciplined and showed compassion on occasion. To the greatest extent possible, they alleviated the suffering of those in their care."[100]

The Upper Canada Rebellion

When they learned the news of the Lower Canada Rebellion in Upper Canada, the radical reform followers of William Lyon Mackenzie, also called Patriots, decided to overthrow the government and declare a republic. The timing was particularly good, because there were no regular troops in the capital, Toronto (which in 1834 had dropped the name of York to take an

Amerindian name). On December 5 Mackenzie marched into Toronto and down Yonge Street, with some 800 poorly equipped and undisciplined supporters, when a skirmish with a few Loyalists broke out, leaving two people dead. The incident led to the general mobilization of the city

Volunteers of the Quebec Light Infantry, c. 1837-38.
National Archives of Canada, C40757.

militia and volunteers, because most citizens did not want revolution.

Two days later some 900 Toronto militiamen equipped with two cannon attacked the 500 or so rebels – hundreds of others had already deserted Mackenzie's camp, for he was a superb speaker but a deplorable soldier – at their gathering point on Yonge Street, the Montgomery Tavern. The battle was brief and it ended with most of the rough-and-ready revolutionaries bolting at

the first cannon shots. Only two rebels were killed. Mackenzie managed to escape to the United States but several of his lieutenants were captured.

These events turned the province upside down, because rumours of attacks by rebels were rife. Groups of Patriots met in the London area, but dispersed without fighting at the approach of a column of loyal volunteers commanded by Colonel Allan Napier MacNab.

The militias of the Niagara Peninsula also mobilized, for Mackenzie and his supporters, with the assistance of American sympathizers, set up the provisional government of the Republic of Upper Canada on the small Navy Island on the Canadian side of the Niagara River approximately four kilometres upstream from the famous falls. The *Caroline*, a small American steamboat acquired by the Patriots, served as their supply vessel. On the evening of December 29 some 50 Canadian volunteers led by Captain Andrew Drew of the Royal Navy boarded the ship and took it in a few minutes on the American side of the border. Only one American supporter of Mackenzie was killed. The ship was torched and set adrift. The *Caroline* in flames as it approached the great falls

150

WEAPONS

Naval pistol, early nineteenth century.
Parks Canada.

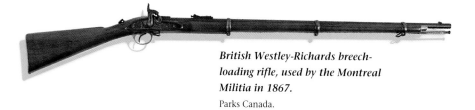

British Westley-Richards breech-loading rifle, used by the Montreal Militia in 1867.
Parks Canada.

British "Short Land Pattern" musket, last third of eighteenth century.
Parks Canada.

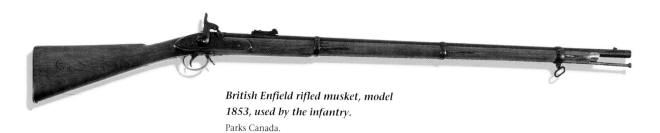

British Enfield rifled musket, model 1853, used by the infantry.
Parks Canada.

British "Long Land Pattern" musket, mid-eighteenth century.
Parks Canada.

British percussion musket, between 1840 and 1850.
Parks Canada.

British "India Pattern" musket, first third of nineteenth century.
Parks Canada.

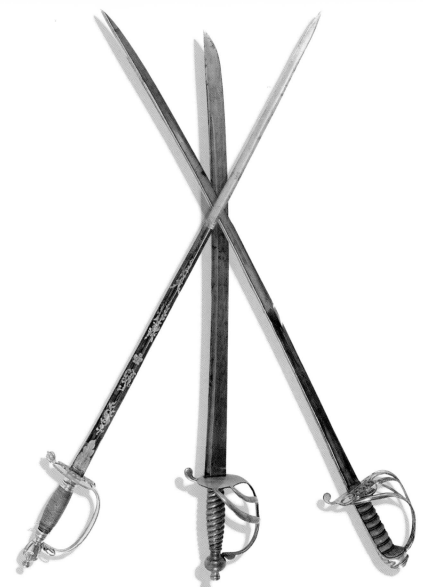

British infantry officer sword, model 1796.
Parks Canada.

British infantryman short sabre, mid-eighteenth century.
Parks Canada.

British infantry officer sword, model 1822.
Parks Canada.

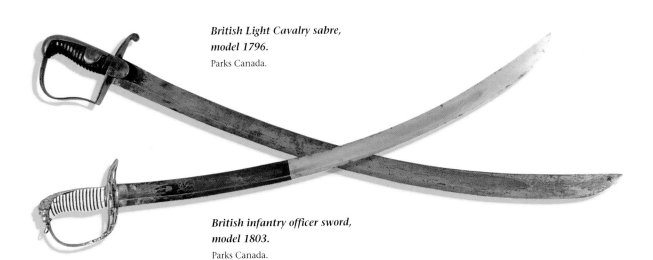

British Light Cavalry sabre, model 1796.
Parks Canada.

British infantry officer sword, model 1803.
Parks Canada.

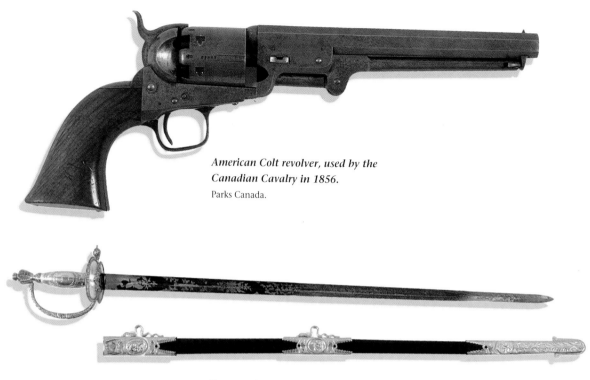

American Colt revolver, used by the Canadian Cavalry in 1856.
Parks Canada.

Presentation sword, in silver, given to General Sir Gordon Drummond by the Legislative Council of Upper Canada in 1814.
Parks Canada.

British Brunswick percussion rifle, with sword-type bayonet, between 1840 and 1850.
Parks Canada.

American Spencer breech-loading rifle, used by the Volunteer Militia in Ontario in 1866-67.
Parks Canada.

must have been an unforgettable sight for inhabitants on both sides that evening. However, it did not plunge into the abyss, as several newspapers would claim, but crashed into a small island at the top of the falls and disintegrated.

Following this manifest violation of United States territory, the American diplomatic response was equally spectacular, and the ambassadors in Washington and London exchanged a few acerbic missives. The Americans, however, did have to admit that a number of their citizens had fomented the invasion of Upper Canada. President Martin Van Buren condemned their actions and ordered the regular troops of General Winfield Scott to patrol the American side of the border along the Niagara

River. On January 13, 1838, realizing that they would be unable to invade Upper Canada, Mackenzie's men evacuated Navy Island. On January 9, to the west of the colony other Patriots who had left from Detroit shelled Amherstburg, but their ship drifted away before being boarded by Canadian militiamen. Thus ended the 1837 Upper Canada Rebellion, a spirited but much less bloody rebellion than the one in Lower Canada.

New Preparations

In Canada, as in London, the authorities were shaken by these two insurrections. With navigation on the St. Lawrence blocked by ice when they broke out, the 34th, 43rd and 85th regiments stationed in New Brunswick were sent to Quebec City through the woods in the middle of winter. But as soon as navigation became possible again, ships full of British soldiers arrived at Quebec. In mid-1838 there were more than 10,000 British soldiers in garrison in the two colonies, four times the number the previous year. But the increase was more spectacular still in the corps of volunteers created and raised in Canada itself. Approximately 6,200 volunteers, on foot and mounted, were mobilized for six months of service in Lower Canada, and some 3,500 volunteers throughout Upper Canada had been equipped with weapons.

The insurgents who had taken refuge in the United States, the supporters of both Papineau and Mackenzie, had considerable support from the Americans. They founded a secret society, the Hunters' Lodges, whose purpose was to organize contingents to invade from the United States and to establish secret groups in Canada who would rise up against the British when the time for the invasion came. The Patriot Hunters took an oath, used secret signs to identify one another, as well as passwords, and had a rather quaint chain of command. A grand eagle designated a general commanding a whole region, an eagle the colonel of a regiment of 500 men, a beaver the captain of a company that had six rackets, each racket commanding nine hunters. Many Americans joined this secret society whose aim was to liberate Canada. But in Canada itself some were doubtful about their altruism, and this did not help the Canadian Patriot cause.

The Start of the 1838 Rebellions

Throughout 1838 the insurgents kept both provinces on the alert. On February 28 some 250 armed men led by Dr. Wolfred Nelson crossed the border at Week's House

and proclaimed the independence of Lower Canada. They then immediately returned to Vermont when the British troops and volunteers approached! Back in the United States, they were disarmed by the American army. At the beginning of March in Upper Canada the Patriots occupied Pelee Island near Windsor. On March 3 a detachment of the 32nd and 83rd regiments, supported by loyal volunteers, attacked and scattered them after a brief and heated battle. Eight Patriots were killed and the British lost six soldiers and a volunteer. In May a small Canadian ship, the *Sir Robert Peel*, was taken and burned in the Thousand Islands. In June between 40 and 70 Patriots, hidden in the Short Hills of the Niagara Peninsula, captured a detachment of a dozen Queen's Lancers. But the alarm was sounded and a search by hundreds of militiamen sent them running.

In Lower Canada, with the situation having calmed somewhat, Sir John Colborne demobilized many of the loyal volunteers in the early summer but kept open the option to recall them in the event of an emergency. He could also count on reinforcements of regular troops from Great Britain and Gibraltar.

But the calm was nothing more than an illusion. Many rumours made the rounds about the secret Patriot societies, and the new governor-in-chief himself, Lord Durham, believed there could be as many as 3,000 partisans in Montreal alone. Pierre-Édouard Leclère, superintendent of the newly created Montreal police force, received scraps of information every day to the effect that a great and terrible revolt was in the offing.

These fears were not without foundation. The strategy of the Hunters' Lodges, which was formulated by their leader Robert Nelson, was to have some of their members take Sorel and then join up with a Patriot army from the United States to take Fort Chambly and Fort Saint-Jean. At the same time in Montreal, other Patriot Hunters would disarm the troops during religious services on Sunday, when the soldiers were armed only with bayonets.101 Uprisings were then to break out simultaneously at several points. But on November 2 the plot was revealed and British troops were placed on alert. The following day a large contingent of regular troops moved towards the American border. At the same time,

156

however, loyal citizens were arriving at Fort Lennox to take refuge: the Patriotes had crossed the border and taken Napierville!

As it happens, Nelson, who had been proclaimed President of the Republic of Lower Canada, had set up his headquarters in this small town. When joined by the republican forces of Dr. Cyrille Côté, he prepared to advance on Montreal. The Hunter Patriots then came out from the shadows and began to gather in several areas to the south of Montreal. But in spite of the plans concocted in Vermont the organization was far from tight. It "consisted simply," reported one Hunter, "in the promise by a number of men to respond, bearing arms, to the call of the chiefs who had just been designated. As for our weaponry...our partisans [at Saint-Timothée] could amount to approximately 100 hunting muskets, most of which dated back to the French regime; others were armed with pitchforks used as spears and 'scythe blades' turned into sabres."[102]

On Sunday morning, November 4, approximately 600 Patriotes, half of whom were armed with muskets, took control of the small town of Beauharnois southwest of Montreal. There, Colborne ordered the militia of the counties of Glengarry and Stormont in eastern Upper Canada to join him, placed the garrison on a war footing and issued an order to mobilize the volunteers. In

157

Napierville

Following Colborne's plan, the British forces approached the rebels from three directions. From the west, the 7th Hussars, the Grenadiers Guards, the 71st Regiment and the militiamen of Glengarry County followed the St. Lawrence River and attacked Saint-Timothée and Beauharnois in succession, finally joining up with the Stormont militiamen and the Huntingdon volunteers who were coming up the Châteauguay River. At Baker's farm on November 9 they quickly routed the Patriotes, and then moved onwards towards Napierville to the east to the sound of bagpipes under the command of General James Macdonell.

To the south near the American border, the loyal volunteers of the neighbouring villages routed the Patriotes at Lacolle on November 7, and then at Odelltown on the 9th. They were joined by the King's Dragoon Guards and the 73rd Regiment. Under the command of Colonel George Cathcart, the British volunteers, infantrymen and troopers headed north for Napierville.

To the northeast, Colborne himself went to Saint-Jean and marched on Napierville leading the 15th and 24th regiments. In all,

Patriotes at Beauharnois in November 1838. Katherine Jane Ellice, who was their prisoner, painted this watercolour.
National Archives of Canada, C13392.

less than a few hours 2,000 volunteers were guarding the entrances to the town and patrolling the streets. Any action by the Hunter Patriots against the garrison was neutralized. In addition, several suspects were taken in by the police and the volunteers, for martial law had taken effect. Colborne, a cautious soldier, waited for reinforcements because it had been estimated that

there were approximately 5,000 Patriotes to the south of Montreal. The actual number was more like 2,500 or 3,000 and they were already riddled with internal conflict and treachery.

approximately 3,300 British soldiers and loyal volunteers converged on the small town. The Patriote army vanished helter-skelter, afraid of being surrounded and massacred by the British troops. The 1838 invasion and insurrection in Lower Canada was over.

The Invasion of Upper Canada

In Upper Canada, meanwhile, the invasion attempt was going forward more resolutely than ever. To the east of Upper Canada on November 11 a powerful contingent of some 400 American Patriots and volunteers swept into an area near Prescott. They were relatively well armed and under the command of a Finnish adventurer who claimed to be Polish, Nils von Schoultz. About 140 volunteers and militiamen from the area were then at Fort Wellington at Prescott. The general alarm was sounded as soon as the Patriots entered Canada. Realizing that he would be unable to take Fort Wellington, where they were resolutely waiting for him, von Schoultz withdrew with his men to a large stone windmill near the St. Lawrence one kilometre to the east of the fort. On November 13 it was surrounded by some 500 soldiers and militiamen who attacked

by land while two steamboats, the *Queen Victoria* and the *Coburg*, shelled it. Many Patriots and American volunteers were able to escape and return to the United States, but 131 were taken prisoner the evening of the 16th. Some 20 British and

A British sentry guards Patriot prisoners in 1838.

Anne S. K. Brown Military Collection, Brown University, Providence.

loyal volunteers were killed in this engagement, against about 30 rebels.

On December 4 some 250 Patriots and American volunteers left from Detroit and took the city of Windsor. Their victory was short-lived, however, because a contingent of approximately 130 Essex County militiamen attacked them and drove

them back almost immediately. Four militiamen were killed and the Patriots lost approximately 27. Infuriated by the insurgents' raids and shaken by the death of his friend, Dr. John James Hume, Colonel John Prince, who commanded the militiamen, had five prisoners executed on the spot, an act that caused a scandal.[103] When the British troops and Amerindians sent from Fort Malden arrived, the rout of the rebels was complete.

The Legacy of the Rebellions

This second rebellion plunged Upper Canada into an unprecedented general mobilization. On November 30 there were 19,318 active volunteers throughout the colony, not including the 2,800 men in the four battalions and one cavalry company of the Embodied Militia. Fear had overtaken much of the population. Independently of political convictions, the general perception of events wavered in the fear that there would be an influx of adventurers of all kinds. Thirteen Patriots and American sympathizers, including von Schoultz, were executed, and 86 others were deported to Australia.

159

Sergeant and officer of the 85ᵗʰ Regiment in 1839. Reconstitution by P. W. Reynolds.

Canadian Department of National Defence Library.

In retrospect, we can see that Ontario's collective memory came to consider this rallying to the cause as a sign of patriotism. This interpretation is all the more credible given that, unlike what took place during the War of 1812, there were very few people killed and there was very little damage done in Upper Canada during the rebellions, probably because the people did not want the changes that revolution and invasion would have brought.

In Lower Canada the situation was different. The 1837 insurrection had been bloody, resulting in the death of almost 300 Patriotes and 10 volunteers, 10 times more casualties than the number of Voltigeurs and militiamen from Lower Canada killed in the War of 1812. In addition, the widespread burning of villages and farms, which plunged families into poverty, traumatized the French-Canadian population.

The repression continued, moreover, in areas that favoured the Patriote movement. At the end of 1838 a corps of Rural Police was raised; it was a kind of paramilitary force, partly mounted and armed with sticks, rifles, pistols and sabres. In addition to seeking out common criminals, this police force intended to "...supply the government with intelligence in those localities where discontent and disaffection appeared to have taken deepest root."[104] Many stations, each with a deputy chief and a few constables, were established in localities around Montreal, all the way to Hull to the northwest, Nicolet to the northeast and Saint-Jean to the south. Police corps with similar objectives had already been set up in Montreal and Quebec City in the summer of 1838.

On another front, there were many trials everywhere: 12 Patriotes were hanged and 58 were deported to Australia. Unlike those convicted in Upper Canada, those found guilty here were nearly all of French descent, and their convictions were felt with pain and consternation by French Canadians, the vast majority of whom had not answered the call to arms. Those convicted, who had stood up to defend their rights, were not considered by the people to be traitors.

From a military standpoint, the professionalism of the British troops, and the action that they took, was never in doubt, all the more so since it was they who did the most fighting. The volunteers, although they were not always models of discipline and moderation, repeatedly showed bravery and fearlessness. They did of course have the advantage of being well armed.

Such was not the case for their compatriots, who raised the flag of revolt. The politicians who encouraged their fellow citizens to armed insurrection totally failed in their responsibilities when the battles began, having no more pressing matters to attend to than to take refuge in the United States. Left to their own devices, without weapons, without a

strategy and without tactics, and placed under the command of untrained leaders, thousands of people had no choice but to barricade themselves against the approaching troops. Many of these civilians behaved as honourably as the best soldiers. In combat, it is only valour that really counts, and from this

period weakened. Most of the loyal volunteers were in Upper Canada; in Lower Canada, any thought of mobilizing the population was now eliminated, even though it included half the potential able-bodied men in British North America. And it was precisely in this colony that a new American threat arose.

militiamen. No longer able to depend on the Lower Canada militia, four companies of the 11th Regiment were sent from Quebec to Lake Témiscouata to defend the road used in the winter by soldiers moving back and forth between Quebec and New Brunswick.

Self-portrait of Charles Traveller, a soldier of the 70th Regiment, accompanied by his dog, in Laprairie in 1841. At the rear, from left to right: the soldiers' barracks (resembling a barn), the officers' barracks (resembling a villa), the elite soldiers of the 70th in ranks, the guardhouse and the regimental band. This illustration is one of the few paintings by a soldier of the era. Parks Canada.

standpoint they showed exemplary bravery under desperate circumstances.

The Aroostook War

All of this fighting, however, undermined the defence of British North America against the United States. On the surface, the country was more powerful than ever militarily. On January 1, 1839, there were 31,848 armed men in Upper and Lower Canada, excluding the Maritime colonies, 10,686 of whom were British soldiers. But in reality the two Canadas came out of this difficult

The border between the American state of Maine and the colonies of Lower Canada and New Brunswick had always been imprecise. In February 1839 the Governor of Maine heatedly claimed the Aroostook area, which was rich in timber resources, and mobilized 8,000 militiamen to occupy the area in question. It was virtually a declaration of war, and the incident is indeed called the Aroostook War. The American claims came up against resistance in New Brunswick, which itself mobilized 1,200

Fortunately, no one really wanted a war, and in March a diplomatic truce provided for the withdrawal of troops while awaiting a negotiated solution. But other American incursions came in the summer and fall, and in November 1839 two companies of the 11th were sent once again to Lake Témiscouata. This time the British soldiers built a small wooden fort, called Fort Ingall (at Cabano, Quebec). The controversy was finally settled in August 1842 with the signing of a British-American treaty defining

commander-in-chief in British North America, Sir Richard Downes Jackson, considered that the new fortifications built by the Americans near the border the border between Maine and British North America. The Americans were granted part of the disputed area but the military road remained part of the British colonies.

In Quebec there were no illusions about the peaceful intentions of the Americans. In November 1840 Colborne's replacement as were "evidently calculated to form a basis of offensive operations"[105] against Canada.

Canadian Politics and British Withdrawal

During 1840 and 1841 the separate colonies of Upper and Lower Canada were eliminated and the Province of Canada was established. It nevertheless remained divided into Canada East and Canada West, corresponding to the present provinces of Quebec and Ontario.

Nevertheless, the political situation in British North America remained tense and confused. In London, serious questions were being asked about whether the Province of Canada was defensible without the support of a significant proportion of its inhabitants. The Duke of Wellington realized that it was impossible for Great Britain to effectively defend the people under his control. His view was that if the North American colonies could not vigorously defend themselves in the event of an attack it would be wiser, more beneficial and fairer[106] to evacuate the British garrison and to let them negotiate their own arrangements with the Americans!

Although it would have been unthinkable only a few years earlier, the idea of leaving Canada, which was put forward by the commander-in-chief of the army, was attractive to many Britons. Canada was no longer a strategic location and it cost at least twice at much as it raised in taxes. Great Britain changed its policy accordingly and began to disentangle itself from the defence of the Province of Canada.

In Canada, as the threat of a new rebellion faded volunteers were demobilized. Whereas in 1839 the estimates were 21,000 volunteers, there were no more than 4,879 the following year, and 2,766 in 1841-42. By 1843 all provincial troops had been disbanded with the exception of three cavalry companies in Canada East and one infantry company in Canada West, which were kept for another seven years.

In Canada East the Rural Police and the police corps in Montreal and Quebec City gradually became not a paramilitary political police force but a civilian one. But the costs of maintaining these companies, and in particular their repressive origins, were reason enough to suppress them. In December 1842 the Legislative Assembly ordered the dissolution of all police corps raised during the rebellion.[107] This decision did, however, leave a gap for crime-fighting, and circumstances made it necessary to establish other police forces.

In 1842 and 1843 the regiments that had been brought in to deal with the 1838 emergency withdrew. In 1844, however, the regular British garrison in the Province of Canada, with its 7,700 soldiers, was still three times larger than it had been in 1837. But each year there were a few hundred fewer soldiers. Some did not wait for their regiment to return to England before they left Canada, preferring to go to the United States! The Royal Canadian Rifle Regiment was formed in 1840-41 precisely to put a stop to the exodus. It was not a Canadian regiment, as its name would suggest, but rather a unit of veterans from line regiments, and it was part of the regular army. But its soldiers were not rotated: it was a Sedentary regiment whose companies were placed along the border to watch the United States, of course, but even more so to prevent deserters from going there.

Reorganization of the Militia

The whole issue of the Canadian militia remained confused during these years. It was almost impossible to raise the subject in Parliament because the arguments became so heated. Things remained this way until 1845, when a major crisis with the United States occured, over Oregon. Elected to the rallying cry of "Fifty-four Forty or Fight," President James Knox Polk encouraged Americans to fight if Great Britain refused to cede the territory west of the Rockies up to the 54°40′ line. The fever pitch of American Manifest Destiny, with Texas annexed and war declared against Mexico, led Canadian legislators in the end to vote in June 1846 for a new Militia Act. The Act's intent was to harmonize and extend most of the provisions of earlier statutes. Henceforth, all men aged 18 to 60 would be required to serve in Sedentary Militia regiments, but they would be divided into two classes, the first consisting of men under 40 years of age. In the event of an emergency, up to 30,000 militiamen could be called to serve in active militia battalions.

The Act was innovative insofar as it officially recognized the existence of the volunteer corps. It thus legalized a de facto situation and enshrined the principle of voluntarism for the universal requirement to bear arms. It is in effect a reasonably sound principle to count on men who wish to serve their community to be citizen soldiers. But the Canadian government gave them virtually no assistance. They had to train and procure uniforms and horses at their own expense before receiving weapons from the government. These conditions limited the number of potential candidates to a minority with the time and money needed to be volunteers.

163

Nevertheless, a noteworthy effort was made to revive the militia, particularly in Canada East, which had not organized a review since 1837. French asserted itself as an official language on a par with English in the Legislative Assembly, and the Deputy Adjutant-General of the militia for Canada East was henceforth to have two clerks "sufficiently familiar in the knowledge of French"[108] to be able to correspond in French with the battalion officers. In September 1846 the militia staff began to allocate the approximately 246,000 militiamen to 57 regiments with 334 battalions, and to appoint senior officers who would in turn recommend officers for their battalions.

To render French Canadians in the cities less hostile to the militia, the measures introduced by Lord Dalhousie were dispensed with. Once again, the battalions could reflect each language group and the number of officers was to be equitable within joint regiments, as the staff of the 4th militia battalion of Carleton County in Bytown (Ottawa) were to learn to their cost. When the governor-in-chief discovered that all the officers in this regiment were English Canadians and that half the militiamen were of French descent, he simply revoked all the officers' commissions! The 1846

statute thus represented the beginning of reconciliation. It was, however, given a rather cool reception in French Canada, which ought not to have been surprising. French Canadians, who had been excluded for a quarter century, remained distrustful.

In the field itself, the question may be asked whether the militia's wartime effectiveness was truly improved by these measures. Poet Louis Fréchette reported on a review of militiamen in Lévis after Mass when he was a child. First there was roll-call and then: "...after that came drill – Oh! drill reduced to its simplest expression: – Face right!... Face left!... Three steps forward!... Three steps back!... To which all the kids added: 'If you're not happy, go say your prayers!'... They liked rhyme, the kids of my day. I can still hear them stamping their feet in time, crying out to the militiamen: 'Face! face! face!...to the shop of Gnace!'..." The "shop of Gnace" was the blacksmith's, a man named Ignace Samson, across from the church on the public square. After a few minutes of parade and drill the militiamen broke ranks, lit their pipes and dispersed, while one child, more brazen than the others, and in spite of people's attempts to hush him up,

ran away shouting, "Hooray for Papineau!"[109]

The state of the Sedentary Militia in Canada West was no brighter. Waterloo County, for example, also had its practical jokers. One parade day, during roll-call a militiaman threw a football onto the ground. Within a few minutes the review had turned into a giant football game! On another occasion, a regimental officer, a farmer by profession, was calling out orders to the battalion as it marched along. He could not remember the command "Halt" so he shouted, "Whoa! Whoa!"[110] as if calling to his horses. The line of militiamen collapsed in laughter and the review was cancelled. Obviously much effort was still required to deal with the American threat.

Fortunately, though, tensions between Great Britain and the United States faded as the years went by. The Oregon Crisis was settled by an agreement that extended the border along the 49th parallel all the way to the Pacific. In 1846 the American troops deployed along the Canadian border were nearly all sent to fight the Mexicans.

Great Britain continued to reduce the size of its regular garrison in North America, particularly since in Europe the situation was seriously worsening for the

164

first time since 1815. In 1854 the Crimean War showed the English that their army, although brave and disciplined, was in a pitiful state and urgently needed modernizing.

All of these events had an impact on the Province of Canada. The British garrison deployed in North America declined from more than 6,000 men in 1853 to fewer than 3,300 two years later. On the other hand, the Sedentary Militia was growing. Throughout the 1840s the arrival in the Province of Canada of hundreds of thousands of immigrants, mainly from Ireland and Scotland, considerably increased the population of Canada West. In 1851 the

Officer of the British 4th Light Dragoon Regiment in 1856; the first and second companies of the Montreal Volunteer Cavalry and the Port Hope Cavalry adopted this uniform. H. Martens. Engraving. Anne S. K. Brown Military Collection, Brown University, Providence.

Province of Canada had 534,000 men aged 18 to 60 years, 317,000 of them in Canada West. French Canadians were no longer the majority.

Paradoxically, this demographic shift encouraged the establishment of responsible government in 1849, the enshrining principle of the supremacy of the Legislative Assembly. Henceforth the Governor

General of Canada would "reign," but the House would govern politically. For national defence, though, Canadian parliamentarians proved to be exceptionally cautious, leaving responsibility and expenses for defence to Great Britain.

In November 1854 the Canadian government nonetheless appointed a commission to investigate ways of improving the militia. In French Canada some even favoured the establishment of a permanent Canadian corps "to replace the regular troops that the English government had to bring home," according to Montreal's *La Patrie*. The editor added that "it would

open a new career to Canadian youth. We are sure that many of our young compatriots would prefer a captain's epaulettes, even with all the dangers involved, to the gown [of a lawyer] or the cassock [of a notary] that are so highly prized these days."[111] Resurfacing here was no less than the old dream of a French-Canadian regiment, which had been proposed as early as 1763 to replace the Compagnies franches de la Marine.

The 1855 Volunteers

The commission's conclusions, which were put into effect in a Militia Act passed in 1855, were not at all along these lines, opposing the idea of the Province of Canada maintaining regular troops. However, the legislators in the end agreed to free up some money to help the volunteers, called the Active Militia. Henceforth, the government would be responsible for supplying weapons and ammunition, for paying for the days set aside for drill, and for allocating compensation to cover the costs of the uniforms for the 5,000 volunteers spread among a number of companies of riflemen, cavalry and artillery.

Volunteer rifleman of the Halifax Rifles, in 1859. Reconstitution by Ron Volstad.
Canadian Department of National Defence.

These measures were welcomed enthusiastically. All the planned companies were recruited quickly, while hundreds of other volunteers demanded from the government the right to establish supplementary companies, which they were granted in 1856. Designated class B companies, they were supplied with weapons and were paid for the uniform. As an economy measure, however, they were not paid for drill days.

Nevertheless, in 1857, an unprecedented number of volunteers – 5,300 – enlisted, and were armed, clothed and trained. The new system required that all these companies be registered with the Office of the Militia Adjutant-General if they were to benefit from the provisions of the 1855 and 1856 statutes. This requirement led to "unjust" situations in terms of precedents and seniority. For example, a company of riflemen established in 1854 in Montreal was registered first and thereby became the volunteer militia company with the most seniority, whereas in the same city there had been a volunteer cavalry company since 1812! To this very day the unexpected repercussions of this act sometimes cause public servants working for the Department of National Defence and the unit commanders some grief.

Independently of their seniority, all the companies were suitably armed. The riflemen were given the model 1853 Enfield with a rifled barrel, which had recently been adopted by the regular army. Along with their sabres, the troopers were given the new Colt six-shot revolver. The artillery pieces were also the latest models being used in the regular army.

In the Maritimes

Because the Maritimes were distinct colonies during this period, the militia for each was governed by its own laws and regulations. But these laws were generally similar. They required men between the ages of 18 to 60 to enlist in the militia regiment of their county and to take part in the reviews. They also enabled the existing authorities to mobilize the men for active duty and interested citizens to establish uniformed volunteer companies.

In the first half of the nineteenth century the development of militias in the Maritime colonies generally followed the pattern seen in central Canada. However, the Sedentary Militia regimental reviews appear to have been performed more seriously than in central Canada, and onlookers were generally full of praise for the efforts of these militiamen. County militia regiments, particularly in the cities, usually had one or more elite companies who supplied uniforms at their own expense. As in central Canada, the volunteers became more important in the 1840s and 1850s. The Volunteer Movement,[112] which was growing in Great Britain in 1858, had a marked impact in the Maritimes, where the people were very much

Anglophiles, so much so that by the following year laws were passed to encourage the establishment of volunteer corps. These measures were very successful and in the early 1860s some 4,000 to 5,000 well-armed volunteers wearing a wide variety of uniforms were given military training in this region.

Nova Scotia was the most populous of the Maritime colonies, with approximately 14,000 militiamen in 1821, 26,000 in 1830, 41,000 in 1845 and 44,000 around 1860. Apart from the regiments of the Sedentary Militia organized throughout the colony, there was a Nova Scotia Volunteer Artillery corps at Halifax to assist the regular artillerymen of the Royal Artillery who operated the cannon at the many forts defending the port. Around 1840, the elite companies of this prosperous city's regiments were probably the best trained and equipped in the colony. The 1859 statute on the volunteer companies led to the creation of many such companies throughout the colony. So enthusiastic was their reception that the number of volunteers had to be restricted to 2,000, although the number was increased to 2,600 in 1862. The colony's government supplied modern weapons

and ammunition and paid the instructors as well as part of the costs of the uniforms.

New Brunswick had approximately 14,000 Sedentary militiamen in 1825 and 27,000 in 1844. The 1837-38 rebellions, the Aroostook War and the Oregon Crisis spurred on the militia, who beginning in this period supported the training of volunteer corps in the southern part of the colony by issuing weapons and uniforms for a lump sum. There was then a period when things were allowed to drift, until 1859, when measures were taken similar to those adopted in Nova Scotia to encourage the training of volunteer companies. These were an immediate success and in the middle of the following year 1,237 volunteers, divided into 23 companies, two cavalry and seven artillery, began holding practices and drill twice a week.

The Prince Edward Island Sedentary Militia included all men from the age of 16 to 60 living in the three counties of the small colony. This militia consisted primarily of infantry companies, but there were also a few artillery and cavalry companies in Charlottetown. In 1829 the militia totalled 5,400. Most were unarmed, a situation that would change little in the 30 years to follow. In 1859 the creation of

Volunteers and militiamen of Prince Edward Island, between 1859 and 1863. On the left, a soldier and officer of the Irish Rifles; in the centre, an officer of the Royalty Rifles; on the right, an officer of the Queen's County 1st Regiment. Reconstitution by David Webber.
Canadian War Museum, Ottawa.

volunteer companies was given a considerable boost when 1,000 Enfield rifled guns were sent to the colony. The following year there were 800 well-armed volunteers wearing a great variety of uniforms.

In Newfoundland, the Maritime colony par excellence, the population was so sparse and so busy with the business of offshore fishing that there would never to be an organized Sedentary Militia. Corps of volunteers were raised from time to time, such as the St. John's Volunteer Rangers from 1805 to 1814. Beginning in 1824, even the regular troops had only veterans in the three Royal Newfoundland companies to perform garrison duties. The Volunteer Movement of Great Britain led to the establishment, in 1860, of four companies of volunteers in St. John's, who wore red uniforms, and a company of riflemen at Harbour Grace, who wore blue uniforms. But these units were very short-lived because protecting Newfoundland was not really a land matter but a sea one, thanks to the warships of the Royal Navy, which kept surveillance over the island and its fisheries. Indeed the Royal Navy defended not only Newfoundland but all the coasts of British North America on three oceans.

Chapter 6

THE ROYAL NAVY: RULER OF THE SEAS

British North America was defended not only by soldiers guarding forts. Alone, they would not have been able to fend off American ambitions, which were contained in large measure because of the superiority of the Royal Navy. In fact the seamen and ships of the British navy played a defensive role of the first magnitude throughout the first half of the nineteenth century, even though most Canadians rarely or never saw them anywhere but at the main ports. At most, fishermen and other people living along the coasts would occasionally see frigates cruising offshore and sometimes be treated to the impressive spectacle of a large ship of the line majestically hovering on the horizon. This discretion no doubt explains why the role of seamen is sometimes neglected in Canada's military heritage.

As long as the Royal Navy ruled the seas, a major naval attack against any part of the British North American colonies was unlikely. Any adversary would indeed be subject to naval raids by the British! In North America the only serious potential enemy was the United States, and the War of 1812 had shown the extent to which the Royal Navy could, through its deadly incursions and its coastal blockade, upset the commercial and military life of that country. In peacetime the British Admiralty always kept in reserve some plan of retaliation against a major city such as Boston in the event of any attempted invasion of one of its colonies by the United States. During periods of tension between the American republic and Great Britain, such prospects were always on the minds of American diplomats, and no doubt encouraged them always to find solutions.

Until the end of the Napoleonic wars, the Royal Navy had many squadrons around the world, including several in America. In Newfoundland there was a small squadron of a few frigates and corvettes based in St. John's, called the Newfoundland Squadron, responsible for protecting the fisheries. Other, more powerful, squadrons had at least one ship of the line, supported by large numbers of frigates, corvettes and other small

gunboats. These included the North American Squadron, which patrolled the American coastline from its main base in Halifax all the way to a secondary base in Bermuda. Immediately after the wars against France and the United States, all squadrons in America were incorporated into one. Halifax thus became the headquarters and the most important base for the Royal Navy in America. There were secondary bases in Bermuda and the West Indies.[113]

From Sail to Steam

At the dawn of the nineteenth century, naval technology had not undergone a major transformation for 200 years. Then in 1807 the *Clermont*, a small steamship invented by the American Robert Fulton, went up the Hudson River from New York to Albany in 32 hours. This was an incredible speed record, and it marked the beginning of a naval revolution. For the first time since the beginning of navigation, man was now able to free himself from the winds. A few visionary traders, including the Canadian brewer John

Molson, immediately saw the usefulness of the invention. In 1809, in Montreal, Molson launched the second steamship in the world; it was called the *Accommodation* and it made its maiden round-trip voyage between Montreal and Quebec City in 33 hours. Other steamships were brought into service in the following years. In Quebec City the British staff saw how useful these ships could be for the rapid transportation of troops. During the War of 1812 the *Swiftsure*, also built by Molson, often transported soldiers between Quebec City and Montreal, a practice that continued in peacetime on the *Lady Sherbrooke*, among other ships.

In military circles there was initial scepticism that these small steamships could constitute a serious threat. The admirals of the Royal Navy were particularly doubtful about the innovation, but in 1822 they were convinced by the arguments of the famous inventor Marc Isambard Brunel and ordered construction of the first Royal Navy steamship, the HMS *Comet*. Like all boats of its type, it was a small sailing ship, in the centre of which was an engine and a tall chimney stack, and it was propelled by paddle wheels on either side of the ship.

The first armoured battleship of the Royal Navy, the HMS Warrior, *in 1861. Reconstitution by N. L. Wilkinson.*
Canadian Department of National Defence Library.

But the Royal Navy delayed the adoption of steam for its large warships until the end of the 1840s. The reluctance of the military navies was justified. First, paddle wheels were very vulnerable to enemy fire and took up space where the cannon ought to be mounted. Not least, the presence on board a warship of the fire required to run a steam engine together with explosive black powder was reason enough for anyone to fear the worst. The introduction of screw propulsion and the taking on board of mechanical engineering specialists gradually eliminated any such reservations. By the end of the 1840s the Royal Navy was beginning to install screw propulsion engines on several old line vessels. In 1849 the 80-cannon *Agamemnon* became the first warship specifically built with a screw propeller. It was incorrectly believed that iron hulls would be more difficult to maintain than wooden hulls; during the 1850s wooden hulls were therefore retained, as well as sails, even though engines had been installed and the most vulnerable parts of the ship were protected by iron plates.

The first armour-plated ship in the world appeared in 1859; it was the French warship *La Gloire*, a 5,600-ton colossus packed with cannon, its wooden hull completely covered in 10- to 12-centimetre-thick iron plate. The Royal Navy was thus instantly outmoded, which caused keen reaction in England and in Canada and contributed powerfully to the Volunteer Movement. The Admiralty responded immediately by ordering armour-plated vessels from the shipyards, and in 1860 the HMS *Warrior* was launched. This British ship, which drew 9,000 tons, had a hull made completely of iron and armour covered more than half its surface.

Master gunner of the Royal Navy in 1829. E. Hull. Engraving.
Anne S. K. Brown Military Collection, Brown University, Providence.

A Revolution in Artillery

While advances were being made in naval technology, there was remarkable progress in artillery as well, both on land and on the sea. There had been no fundamental

A naval artilleryman with an Armstrong gun, in the second half of the nineteenth century.
W. Christian Symons. Engraving.
Canadian Department of National Defence Library.

changes since the sixteenth century. At the end of the 1850s cannons were still simple muzzle-loaded cast-iron tubes that fired cannonballs. Variations, such as howitzers and carronades, appeared, and even rifling was attempted in the muzzle-loaders. But these innovations did not lead to any dramatic changes. Then in 1858-59 a British artillery committee studied a revolutionary gun design by a British civil engineer, William G. Armstrong. Instead of being cast, the gun was made of steel plates welded around a rifled iron tube; it was breech-loaded and fired a conically shaped shell a distance of some two kilometres with extraordinary accuracy. The shell even had the capacity to pierce a dozen centimetres of armour before exploding. The Armstrong gun was immediately adopted by the British navy and army.[114]

The appearance of such a powerful weapon significantly influenced the design of warships and fortifications; ship armour and casemates for forts had to be much more elaborate. The last great forts built by the British south of Quebec City between 1865 and 1870 reflected the influence of these new types of guns, because the Americans Thomas Rodman and Robert Parrott had invented similar guns for their army as early as 1861. The new forts were clearly designed to fend off a land attack, because on the sea the Royal Navy remained invincible, having rapidly equipped itself with an impressive fleet of steam-propelled armoured ships against which no country had a chance.

Arctic Exploration

Another facet of Royal Navy activities during the long period of peace in the first half of the nineteenth century took place in the Arctic, with a renewed interest in discovering a Northwest Passage and in making reliable maps.

In 1818 an initial expedition, led by Captain John Ross, explored the coast of Baffin Island. The following year Lieutenant William Edward Parry, commanding the HMS *Hecla* and the HMS *Griper*, sailed westward into the Arctic Ocean with two objectives in mind: to go as far west as possible beyond Lancaster Sound and to spend the winter in the Arctic. The latter objective was unprecedented. Parry's expedition had gone some 1,300 kilometres into the Sound and lay between Banks Island and Melville Island when the two ships were locked into the ice in October 1819. Temporary roofs were built on the bridges, and the interiors of the ships were heated by a kind of central heating system, the pipes generating heat from the kitchen ovens. Ten months later they were able to free themselves, and the members of the expedition were given a triumphant welcome when they returned to England; they were even awarded £5,000 for having reached 110° longitude west. Parry had failed by only a small

margin. The Beaufort Sea and the Pacific Ocean lay west of Melville Island, but no one knew it yet.

The next quarter century witnessed many expeditions led by officers of the Royal Navy. Whalers, now that new whaling grounds were opened to them to hunt the great cetaceans, quickly followed their lead. In 1829 Captain John Ross embarked on a search for the Northwest Passage, but the ice in the Gulf of Boothia firmly imprisoned his steamship, which had to be abandoned in May 1832. The crew survived by living like the Inuit, with whom they had become friends, and they were rescued by whalers the following year. During the voyage, Ross noted that at 72° North his compass read 90° North, and he thereby discovered the magnetic North Pole! The research passionately interested Sir James Beaufort, chief hydrographer of the Royal Navy, who did everything he could to encourage Arctic exploration. There were other reconnaissance trips, and then in 1845 a large-scale expedition was formed to settle, once and for all, the mystery of the Northwest Passage.

Franklin's Tragic Expedition

The new expedition, led by Sir John Franklin, an experienced 58-year-old captain, was prepared meticulously: provisions for three years, clothes specially designed for winter, ships equipped with auxiliary steam engines and bows covered in iron plate to break the ice. In short, every foreseeable factor was taken into account. In May 1845 the HMS *Erebus*[115] and the HMS *Terror* sailed, the 134 men on board convinced they would find

the famous passage. Whalers saw them for the last time at Baffin Bay on July 26.

In 1847 British opinion began to show concern. The following year, the last for which Franklin had provisions, two expeditions went searching for him, one from the Bering Strait, the other from the Atlantic, both unsuccessfully. Other attempts followed. In 1850 some debris and three graves were found on Beechey Island, where Franklin had wintered in 1845. But where were the ships and their crews? The whole world was caught up in the mystery. For the next four years no fewer than 38 expeditions left by land and by sea to search for them before any sign was found. Some Inuit reported to Dr. John Rae of the Hudson's Bay Company that in 1848 they had seen to the west some 40 white men pulling provisions and a row-boat over the ice. Their bodies were finally found on the Adelaide Peninsula of King William Island. Another expedition, sponsored by Lady Franklin, who still hoped to find her husband alive, discovered a message dated April 25, 1848, reporting Franklin's death on June 11, 1847, and the abandonment of the two ships caught in the ice. All members of the expedition had perished, then, martyrs of Canadian Arctic exploration.

Discovery of a Northwest Passage

The tragic fate of Franklin and his men had not been in vain. In 1852 one of the many expeditions that had gone searching for them, that of Commodore Robert McClure on the HMS *Investigator*, reached Banks Island through the Bering Strait. McClure abandoned his ship there and went eastward on foot all the way to Melville Island, where he met another search ship that had arrived via the Atlantic. He returned to England on board the latter. A Northwest Passage had finally been found! But the "passage" was not navigable and from a strategic naval and military standpoint had no value.[116] But the Arctic Ocean played a significant role in defending the Canadian Prairies.

In fact, part of the fur trade was conducted through the Arctic Ocean. From the end of the eighteenth century onward, the rivalling North West Company and Hudson's Bay Company controlled this trade. Beginning in 1816, people were upset by a number of bloody incidents, including the terrible massacre by the men of the North West Company of a group of Scottish colonists established by Lord Thomas Selkirk at Seven

Oaks, today the city of Winnipeg. Lord Selkirk recruited some 80 demobilized Swiss soldiers from the Meuron and Watteville regiments, took Fort William, and re-established his colony on the banks of the Red River. In the end, in 1821 the Hudson's Bay Company took over its rival and found itself operating an immense network of trading posts from the Great Lakes to the Pacific Ocean. Most furs and goods for trading from this point on came through Hudson Bay, and hence via the Arctic Ocean, on both the outbound and the return journey to England.

Lord Selkirk's colony along the Red River eventually grew, although the presence of colonists was more or less incompatible with the Company's activities. During the 1820s and 1830s the Company erected Lower Fort Garry (at Selkirk, Manitoba) and Fort Garry (in Winnipeg).[117] These two trading posts differed from the others in that they were designed as large-scale forts and were built of stone rather than wood. They were the company's administrative centre for Rupert's Land, an immense territory stretching from Labrador to the Rockies, and also served as the residence of its governor.

The North West and Hudson's Bay companies did not maintain troops. At the very most, some posts kept a few Amerindian guards, called the Home Guards, who were armed well enough to maintain a basic level of order adequate for the forts used for trading. After withdrawal of the small detachments of French colonial troops in the mid-eighteenth century, there was therefore no permanent military presence in the Prairies until the mid-nineteenth century.

The Red River Volunteers

However, the region to the south of Lake Winnipeg grew steadily in population, and on February 12, 1835, the Governor of the Hudson's Bay Company, Sir George Simpson, ordered the raising of a corps of 60 men, called the Red River Volunteers, to defend and police the colony. Each member agreed to "well and truly serve the same double office of Private in the Volunteer Corps and Peace Officer."[118] They were to be ready to serve at all times, in exchange for which they were paid a

Soldier of the Royal Canadian Rifle Regiment, between 1857 and 1862. Reconstitution by Derek FitzJames.
Anne S. K. Brown Military Collection, Brown University, Providence.

modest annual sum. The commander of the unit, Alexander Ross, was also sheriff of the district.

Based on their names, approximately one third of these Red River Volunteers were of French descent, with most of British descent and a few, such as Gaspard Bruce and John Baptiste Wilke, of both. It is virtually certain that several of them also had Amerindian roots.

The Red River Volunteers probably did not wear a uniform, and they used hunting weapons, but they nevertheless represented the first militia corps recruited in the Prairies. But a militia formation like this one, however useful it may have been, could not replace regular troops in the event of major problems.

Thus in 1845, when the Oregon Crisis arose, the presence of American troops was signalled at Pembina along the disputed border with the United States only 100 kilometres to the south of Fort Garry. The Hudson's Bay Company was forced to ask London for regular troops, and these were indeed sent. In the summer of 1846 a portion of the 6th Regiment, along with artillery and engineering detachments consisting of 17 officers and 364 non-commissioned officers and men accompanied by 17 women and 19 children, left Ireland for Fort Garry via Hudson Bay. They remained in garrison until 1848 and then returned to Great Britain. Given that the crisis had been dealt with in the meantime, the British government did not replace the 6th Regiment, but instead sent Enrolled Pensioners – retired soldiers – to keep watch in the two forts in Rupert's Land.

Great Snake, Chief of the Blackfoot, recounting his exploits to five subordinate chiefs, between 1851 and 1856. Paul Kane. Oil.

National Gallery of Canada, Ottawa.

The integrity of the land north of the 49th parallel remained precarious. In 1856 a detachment of American cavalry visiting Pembina revived the old fears of an invasion, and the following year 120 officers and soldiers of the Royal Canadian Rifle Regiment were sent to the Red River. Consideration was even given to adding a company of Amerindians and Métis, but the idea was abandoned. Once there, however, the commander of the troops deemed the "threat" to be exaggerated because the closest American military post, Fort Riley, was nearly 700 kilometres away. The Royal Canadian Rifles detachment was nevertheless maintained in garrison for four years at Red River.

The presence of regular troops in garrison in the Canadian West in the first half of the nineteenth century was limited to these exceptions. In reality, the 49th parallel as a border between Canada and the United States all the way to the Rocky Mountains, beginning in 1818, crossed vast expanses, the true masters of which were neither British nor American, but Plains Amerindians. The proud nomadic nations, whose warriors were fierce fighters and outstanding riders, were confronted first with the inexorable advance of the American soldiers and colonists, whom they opposed. But they do not appear to have been threatened by the white men who occupied the Hudson's Bay Company post further to the north, because these white men apparently sought only to trade with them, and not to colonize the land. Relations were generally smooth and there was no need for troops. And since the Royal Navy protected access to Rupert's Land by sea, the security of this vast area was assured.

The Pacific Coast

Circumstances were different on the Pacific coast, which the Hudson's Bay Company's network of posts extended to as well, because the British were not the only white men there. Even before the Spanish had withdrawn from Nootka, an American navigator had discovered the Columbia River, in 1792, and the American army officers Lewis and Clark had reached the Pacific through Oregon in 1805. In 1811 American fur traders built Fort Astoria at the mouth of the Columbia River, which the British took during the War of 1812 and renamed Fort George.

The British considered that the entire Pacific coast from California to Alaska belonged to them, but the Americans felt it was theirs. Believing firmly in its right to do so, the Hudson's Bay Company established a relatively large number of posts in northern California, and in 1845 the dispute degenerated into the Oregon Crisis, which was finally settled by extending the border along the 49th parallel to the Pacific, with the exception of Vancouver Island, which remained British territory.

It was then up to Royal Navy warships to defend the interests of England on the Pacific coast, because the army had no military garrison there. Thanks to an agreement with Chile, the British navy had a base at Valparaiso as of 1837, and from there the HMS *Pandora* left for Vancouver Island in 1846. Two years later the HMS *Constance* used the excellent Esquimalt Harbour as a temporary base. Immediately following the Oregon Crisis, however, it became important for the British to have a real colony on the west coast to counter any American or Russian claims. In 1849 Vancouver Island was turned over to the Hudson's Bay Company in return for a commitment to settle it. The capital became Victoria, a trading post erected by the company in 1843, and the government appointed a royal governor who was independent of the company. At this point the British navy began its frequent patrols along the west coast.

The Victoria Voltigeurs

The royal governor did not, however, have any troops to enforce regulations or to perform guard duty when needed. And in fact there were justifiable fears about the west coast Amerindians. In mid-1851 the Victoria Voltigeurs were thus formed. This was a small corps of volunteers, the first in British Columbia, intended to lend an occasional hand in enforcing justice. The Voltigeurs were mostly French-Canadian voyageurs or "half-breeds" – Métis of French-Canadian and Iroquois descent – who were mobilized as circumstances required. Their numbers could vary considerably from a half dozen to 30 or so; they were paid and fed for their periods of service and were given trade guns and a company "uniform." This was not, however, a European-style military uniform, but a sky-blue Canadian capote with a red woollen sash.

Around the 1850s, detachments of Victoria Voltigeurs frequently accompanied Royal Navy expeditions to intimidate the Amerindians. These volunteers were well disciplined and reliable. In 1853 Governor James Douglas praised them highly, reporting that they "imitated their noble example,"[119] speaking of the seamen and marines of the HMS *Beaver* on a punitive expedition to the mouth of the Cowichan River. This first military unit and police force in British Columbia existed until March 1858.

The Purported Russian Threat

In the first half of the nineteenth century the Russians were busy consolidating their settlements in Alaska, making Sitka an administrative centre and regularly patrolling the coast with frigates from the Imperial Russian Navy. A few Russian officers had completed some remarkable explorations, among them naval Lieutenant Lukin who in 1832-33 had reached as far as the site of what is today Dawson by going down the Yukon River.

The war against Russia, which was declared in 1854, thus fed the worst fears of the colonists on Vancouver Island. Governor Douglas urgently called for troops, cannons, rifles, ammunition and provisions to battle his Russian neighbours to the north. His requests were given the cold shoulder in London. According to the staff, England had "no such interest in the maintenance and support of this outlying settlement," which was costing it a great deal. As for "taking possession of the Russian settlements," it was not clear to them "whether it would be worth our having." Douglas was thus advised in August that "H. M. Govt. deems it to be at once both unnecessary and unadvisable"[120] but that the warships would continue do patrol the coast.

Douglas was nevertheless convinced that his fears were well founded. The Russians had, as it happens, sent a Siberian infantry battalion to Sitka, but – and Douglas could not have known this – for the sole purpose of protecting their colony, and not to attack their British neighbours. In fact neither the British nor the Russians wished to do battle on the northwest coast. The two countries thus agreed not to fight in this part of the globe during the war, which ended in 1856. Eleven years later the Russians sold Alaska to the United States, making it Canada's only immediate neighbour.

The Gold Rush and the Royal Engineers

At the end of 1857 the discovery of gold in the Fraser River Valley led to a gold rush that shook up the peaceful young colony. Thousands of adventurers, primarily American, flowed in, and tensions over the exact location of the

*Construction of the Cariboo Road
by the Royal Engineers in 1862.
Reconstitution by Rex Woods.*
Confederation Life Collection, Toronto.

*Construction of the Cariboo Road
by the Royal Engineers in 1862.
Reconstitution by Rex Woods.*
Confederation Life Collection, Toronto.

border with the United States resurfaced. The situation led the British government to take direct control of the territories, which had until then been administered by the Hudson's Bay Company – which meant not only Vancouver Island, but also the coastline and the interior, creating the colony of British Columbia on November 19, 1858.

British and American commissions were appointed to settle the problem of the land border. In July 1858, 60 officers and soldiers of the Royal Engineers arrived. Over the next four years they systematically surveyed southern British Columbia in great detail. This was the first detachment of regular troops to be posted to the

west coast since the departure of the Spanish soldiers in 1795.

A second detachment of Royal Engineers was later dispatched to build the colony's infrastructures. These consisted of 165 officers and soldiers, accompanied by 37 women and 38 children, who arrived in British Columbia between October 1858 and June 1859. They founded

the town of New Westminster, built schools, churches, the first theatre, a library, and roads and bridges, drew maps of the region, designed the coat of arms and the first postage stamp of the colony, published an official gazette, and even printed a newspaper. Finally, in 1862-63 they supervised the building of the famous Cariboo Road, some 700 kilometres long, which opened the interior to colonization. After completing all this work, the detachment was disbanded in November 1863 and the vast majority of its members took up the offer to settle in British Columbia.[121]

"The Pig War"

In 1859 a harmless incident almost caused a new war between the United States and Great Britain. San Juan Island was part of the territory disputed in determining the border. On June 15, 1859, an American farmer shot and killed a pig that had come to feed on his field of potatoes on the island. But the pig was British, and it belonged to the Hudson's Bay Company; this led to an incredible series of false rumours and unfounded accusations that inflamed American opinion.

On July 18 American General W. S. Harney, giving credence to the

Seaman of the Royal Navy raising signal flags during the second half of the nineteenth century.
W. Christian Symons. Engraving.
Canadian Department of National Defence Library.

rumours that British seamen had mistreated American citizens, and believing that San Juan Island was an important strategic point, sent a regular infantry detachment. When he heard the news, Governor Douglas called for assistance from the Royal Navy, and at the end of July the American soldiers stationed on the island saw the frigate HMS *Tribune* and its 31 cannon appear,

followed soon afterwards by the corvette HMS *Satellite* with 21 cannon. "The Pig War" was about to be declared! The arrival of an American ship with reinforcements led to a confrontation that was defused only with the providential arrival of instructions from Governor Douglas allowing the Royal Navy to let the American troops disembark. Captain Geoffrey Hornby of the HMS *Tribune* did what he could to calm Governor Douglas and Captain George Pickett,[122] commander of the American troops, and to keep the incident from degenerating into a war. He had the full approval of his superior, Rear-Admiral Robert Lambert Baynes, who arrived in Victoria on August 5 from Valparaiso on board the HMS *Ganges*, an 84-cannon vessel.

Baynes opposed the military views of Governor Douglas, who was in all probability not fully aware of the implications of an armed intervention. The rear-admiral preferred to let the American troops occupy the island. He already had five warships, and two others, the HMS *Topaze* with 51 cannon and the HMS *Clio* with 22, were to join them imminently. If war were to break out, the British, with their naval superiority in the Pacific, would be able to hem the American soldiers in on the island

and bombard cities in Oregon and California. London wanted to avoid war, however, and the Prime Minister made this absolutely clear to Governor Douglas, which did something to cool his ardour. The government in Washington was also not keen to get involved in the matter, and the hot-tempered General Harney was replaced by General Winfield Scott, who had been instructed to negotiate a joint occupation of the island until the two governments could reach agreement, which is precisely what happened in the end. In March 1860 a British marine detachment took up a position in the northern part of the island. The dispute continued for years, and it was only in November 1872, after the signing of the Treaty of Washington, that the British soldiers withdrew once and for all.[123] Fortunately for everyone, only the pig was killed throughout this whole "war."

The Royal Navy Patrols the West Coast

The 1858 gold rush and the Pig War the following year hastened the search for a lasting solution to the problem of defending the new colony. Instead of building fortifications defended by troops, which was a costly undertaking,

the British government opted to establish a naval base at Esquimalt. The permanent presence of warships would, it was felt, suffice to secure the west coast.

The Royal Navy had regularly used Esquimalt Harbour since 1848, and had over the years

Ships of the Royal Navy, between 1850 and 1860. Reconstitution by N. L. Wilkinson.
Canadian Department of National Defence Library.

developed more or less temporary facilities such as foundries, carpentry

workshops, a coal depot and a small hospital. As in all ports, a village had grown nearby, with its taverns and its brothels. Beginning in 1858, there was considerable new construction, including barracks, and in 1860 a lighthouse was built on Fisgard Island at the

entrance to the port, as well as a major depot that could hold some 1,400 tons of coal. This coal, which was essential in those years for steam-powered warships, came from the Nanaimo mines located only 130 kilometres to the north.

Construction of a powder magazine was completed in 1862, the very year in which the British Admiralty moved its headquarters for the Pacific Squadron from Valparaiso to Esquimalt. The North Pacific was growing in importance as trade with the United States, Japan and China increased. The Esquimalt base was ideally located to protect these maritime routes, whereas Valparaiso in Chile and Callao in Peru were used as secondary bases for the South Pacific.

The Royal Navy also played a policing role along the coast of British Columbia. The proud Amerindians of the west coast, those "Vikings of the North Pacific," were not always keen to see Europeans arrive, especially since more and more of them were building small settlements here and there. There were sometimes deadly incidents on both sides. From the Royal Navy's standpoint, such domestic wars, murders, piracy and slavery among the Natives had to end, and they would have to submit, willingly or not, to British law and order. It would appear to have generally been effected willingly, for the elimination of intertribal conflicts and slavery was probably well received by these people. On the other hand, the piracy and murder continued, and a

few merchant ships met a tragic end. In such cases, the Royal Navy used force as a means of intimidation. Misdeeds invariably brought a warship to the area where they had been committed, to track down those responsible. The detroits and bays along the coast, many of which were inaccessible to sailing ships, sometimes made the chase difficult, but this situation changed with the introduction of steamships.

In 1850, following the murder of three seamen who had deserted, the gunboat HMS *Daphne* arrived at the northern end of Vancouver Island searching for the guilty parties. They were Newittys, and they were awaiting the British on Normand Island and opened fire on them. The British in turn shelled the area and landed to destroy the Newittys' dwellings and canoes. This was enough for the Newittys to turn over the mutilated corpses of the three seamen. Further north, the Haida in the Queen Charlotte Islands were busy in 1851, not for the first time, pillaging and torching an American merchant ship, the *Susan Sturgis*. Fortunately, the crew, who had been taken and placed in slavery, were rescued when the Hudson's Bay Company paid their ransom. The British, fearing a diplomatic incident with the

Americans, sent the frigate HMS *Thetis* to patrol the islands, along with a paddle-wheel steamboat, the HMS *Virago*, commanded by Captain James Charles Prevost, to conduct an investigation. It was met by armed Haida, who were expecting an attack. The atmosphere relaxed somewhat when they understood that the British wanted to punish those who had committed the crime and not to make war on their nation. Their chief, Eda'nsa, impressed the British officers with his quick mind. He understood immediately that it would be impossible to resist their warships and that there were benefits to be gained from ongoing cooperation with the powerful English. The guilty were identified. Because no murders had been committed, Prevost opted for moderation, demanding restitution of the stolen goods and their word that the crimes would not be repeated, assuring everyone that they would become loyal subjects of "King George."

The killing of a Scottish shepherd near Victoria by a few Cowichans and Nanaimos in November 1852 led Governor Douglas to organize an expedition to capture the killers. In January 1853, 110 seamen, 20 naval infantry soldiers and 20 Victoria Voltigeurs arrived at the Cowichan settlement and took the guilty men, immediately

*A West Coast warrior wearing
armour made of rope.*
National Archives of Canada, C16779.

trying and hanging them. This same forceful response was used three years later when a colonist was killed by a chief. To counter any resistance by the approximately 1,400 Amerindian warriors, 437 officers, seamen and naval infantry soldiers, as well as 18 Voltigeurs, appeared in the Cowichan Valley. With this show of strength, the Amerindians turned over the troublemakers, who were once again tried and hanged on the spot.

Various similar incidents occurred over the following years. In 1863, for example, a ship's boy was killed on board the HMS *Forward* during an exchange of gunfire. But there was a major incident in August 1864, when Amerindian pirates boarded a small merchant vessel, the *Kingfisher*, killing its crew and then pillaging and setting fire to

the ship. In view of the seriousness of what they had done, the governor asked the Royal Navy to intervene. But when the HMS *Devastation*, a small six-cannon steamship, arrived in the vicinity, it found hundreds of armed Natives and decided to wait for reinforcements in Clayoquot Sound, approximately 50 kilometres south of Nootka. On the evening of October 2 the screw frigate HMS *Sutlej* arrived, captained by Admiral Joseph Denman, commander of the Pacific Squadron and a veteran hunter of slave boats and pirates off the African coasts. The next day the

two warships arrived at the village of Marktosis looking for Chapchah, the purported leader of the pirates. But the area had been abandoned and the pirates had taken refuge nearby.

The HMS *Devastation* then went to the village of Moyat, where the Amerindians immediately opened fire, forcing the ship to move out of range. The HMS *Sutlej* arrived in support, and Denman informed the opponents that he would not shell them if the guilty parties were turned over to him. They cavalierly refused, adding that if Moyat was burned not a single seaman who dared to set foot on land would be spared. The *Sutlej* opened fire in response, and row-boats that kept well away from the ship launched incendiary rockets while others bearing armed

184

The Volunteer Corps

seamen approached the shore. They were welcomed by Amerindian fire, but this was rendered powerless by a few well-aimed British salvos. The seamen disembarked, with fixed bayonets, and found the lifeboats of the unfortunate *Kingfisher*. They burned the place down. In the days that followed, eight other villages were destroyed, with the Amerindians offering only token resistance. Although he was unable to capture Chapchah, Admiral Denman considered the operation a complete success. Not a single British seaman had been killed or injured, whereas the Natives had lost approximately 15 men and had been given a severe warning.

Other incidents would occur, but this swift justice at the muzzle of a cannon discouraged the Amerindians from continuing with their piracy and slavery and they abandoned these practices once and for all in the 1880s.[124]

Although the Royal Navy was able to patrol the coasts, and although the engineers were systematically surveying the southern part of the colony, the new towns had no form of defence. The statutes of Great Britain were well and truly in force in British Columbia,[125] but because the colony had not passed any specific laws concerning the militia and volunteers there was no Sedentary Militia as there was in the eastern part of Canada. However, corps of volunteers were eventually established.

In 1859, at the time of the Pig War, 67 men suggested that a company be formed in Victoria. Governor Douglas refused because he had no weapons to give them, so they formed a company of volunteer firemen. The next year 45 Black Americans who had taken refuge in Victoria created the Victoria Pioneer Rifle Corps, which existed until 1866. In July 1861 the Vancouver Island Volunteer Rifle Corps, with two companies, one of which was an artillery company, was raised from the white population of Victoria, but it was disbanded a year later because of disagreements between the companies. In May 1864 the Victoria Volunteer Rifle Corps came into existence; it was, however, to have a longer life.[126]

In New Westminster, which was founded in 1859, the need for a volunteer corps was felt only after the disbanding of the detachment of Royal Engineers in 1863. In January of the following year the New Westminster Volunteer Rifles were raised. In June 1866 a corps of approximately 60 men, called the Home Guards, as well as the Seymour Artillery Company, named in honour of the colony's governor, were founded. The latter received its first two field guns the following year. Most of these volunteer artillerymen were former Royal Engineers who had settled in New Westminster.[127]

Thus in the mid-nineteenth century, thanks to the Royal Navy, the Hudson's Bay Company, a few British military detachments, and units of Canadian volunteers, British North America, which was destined to become Canada, was able to extend and maintain its sovereignty over an immense expanse of land, both to the north and to the west of the Great Lakes. However, the most worrisome threats during what was perhaps the most turbulent decade in the history of North America would rise in the east.

185

Chapter 7

A DECADE OF TURBULENCE

Until the mid-nineteenth century, there was peace among the great nations of Europe. However, the Crimean War, in 1854-55, was a harbinger of confrontations to come. It would be followed in 1859 by a brief conflict between France and Piedmont and the Austrian Empire, which the French-Piedmontese won. The Italian peninsula, which was divided into several kingdoms surrounding the Papal territories, was the subject of a powerful unification movement led by Giuseppe Garibaldi and Camillo Benso Cavour, the first Prime Minister of Piedmont. Then in 1861 the Kingdom of Italy was proclaimed, but the Pope opposed the creation of this new state, leading to a crisis that would last almost 10 years.

In North America, while Mexico was torn by a civil war followed by a French invasion, tensions worsened in the United States between the northern states, which were becoming increasingly industrialized, and the southern states, which were intensively developing the cotton industry, based to a great extent on the use of Black slaves. The election of abolitionist Abraham Lincoln to the presidency led the southern states to withdraw from the Union in 1861 to establish the Confederate States of America, or the Confederacy. At that point civil war became inevitable. It began with the shelling of Fort Sumter in the port of Charleston, South Carolina, and spread like wildfire. Battles on a scale unheard of in America involved hundreds of thousands of men and caused enormous losses: more than 24,000 killed and wounded at Shiloh and 38,000 at Antietam in 1862, and almost 55,000 at Gettysburg the following year.

A Weapons Revolution

The American Civil War, which could be called the first "modern" war, served as a laboratory for an impressive number of deadly new weapons such as the repeating rifle, the first torpedoes, heavy artillery on railways, and turret-mounted guns on battleships. For the first time, trains were used to transport large numbers of troops. Military communications by telegraph also appeared. The rank and file of both

armies were virtually all relatively untrained volunteers, but they were armed with guns of unprecedented accuracy.

Small arms had not advanced appreciably between the end of the seventeenth century and the 1830s and 1840s, when the percussion mechanism for firing was introduced. This system, which was more reliable than the gun flint, appeared in the British army in 1836 with the adoption of the Brunswick rifle for rifle corps. In 1838 the Guards infantry battalions sent to Canada were equipped with percussion muskets. Because there was unanimity regarding the reliability of the weapon, its use was extended to all of the infantry within a few years. But even though the percussion musket fired reliably, its range remained the same as that of the weapons it replaced.

It was then discovered that a conically shaped bullet fired from a rifled barrel could go much further – with greater accuracy – and this discovery revolutionized weaponry. In 1851 part of the British army adopted the Minié rifled musket; then in 1853 the whole army chose the rifled-barrelled Enfield. The Enfield could shoot a bullet onto a 0.9-metre target at a distance of 825 metres, and onto a 0.6-metre target from approximately 400 metres! The Canadian volunteers were supplied with the Enfield rifled musket from 1856 onward.

However, the rifled gun was still muzzle-loaded, which meant that it could be fired only about three times per minute. The solution for speeding up fire was simple: breech-loading, if possible, with a repeating mechanism. Many inventions designed to do just that were tested during the American Civil War. But repeating cavalry rifles were still too inaccurate for the infantry, which preferred a one-shot breech-loading weapon that fired accurately, approximately six shots per minute. The Prussian army already had such a weapon; the French and American armies would have theirs in 1866. The British army chose the breech-loading system invented by the American Jacob Snider, which could be adapted to the existing Enfield rifled muskets. In 1867-68 some 350,000 guns of this type were modified accordingly, to become the Snider-Enfield rifle.

Officer, sergeant and soldier of a British infantry regiment; this uniform was worn from 1858 to 1868. H. Martens. Watercolour.

Anne S. K. Brown Military Collection, Brown University, Providence.

All these innovations transformed infantry tactics, and more particularly the movements of armies on the field of battle, since during the same period siege and field artillery was also making remarkable progress. Armies still advanced in formation, but they had a longer shooting range. From that point on, cavalries ceased their great charges against infantrymen, but remained ready to exploit any disarray. Soldiers armed with modern weapons and properly sheltered in trenches proved to be highly effective against attackers, as demonstrated in the siege of Vicksburg, in 1863, where the South had 31,000 men killed and wounded, compared to only 4,500 for the North. With the horrifying Civil War in the United States and the terrible Mexican invasion, the whole of North America was being brought to fire and sword. Only Canada remained a peaceful haven. But could it last?

The Trent Affair

Great Britain and Canada both wanted to stay out of the American Civil War. But on November 8, 1861, an incident led people to expect the worst: seamen on the American warship USS *San Jacinto* intercepted at sea and boarded the British ship *Trent* and forcibly took two Confederate commissioners who were travelling on that vessel. The freedom of the seas and maritime neutrality were called into question, and England was indignant. As soon as the news reached Quebec, Governor General Charles Stanley Monck ordered that the troops in garrison in the Province of Canada be placed on alert. Great Britain sent

reinforcements, and in 1862 the garrison was increased from 5,500 officers and soldiers to more than 18,000, a number not seen since the 1812 attempted invasion.

The prospect of a war with the United States was extremely worrisome to the Canadian public; the number of volunteers jumped to more than 13,000 in May 1862 and to some 25,000 by the end of the year. This amounted to one man for every 100 inhabitants of all ages and both sexes, with three times as many volunteers coming from the cities as from the countryside. In addition to the many rifle, cavalry and artillery companies, there were now the engineers and the sailors, the latter supplying the crews for small gunboats – which were

often no more than armed yachts – assigned to Lake Ontario and Lake Erie.

In the end, there was a diplomatic solution to the Trent affair, because the United States could not afford to fight on two fronts, especially given that it was already at the mercy of the Royal Navy. In Halifax, Admiral Alexander Milne planned to break the blockade of the southern states by the North, to introduce his own blockade of the northern states and to help the Confederate army in Virginia. And his squadron was powerful enough to rout the American navy.

Volunteer militiaman, probably a member of the Cobourg Cavalry, the only corps to wear the red dragoon uniform with the metal helmet. Colour photograph c. 1858.
D. Blyth Collection, Guelph.

Vulnerability of the Province of Canada

Having got over the shock of the crisis, the authorities had to quickly think of ways in which to repulse any American land invasion of Canada. In February 1862 Lord Monck appointed a commission of inquiry to study the Province of Canada's system of fortifications and defence, to be chaired by Colonel John William Gordon of the Engineers. Their report was submitted on September 2. The commissioners expected that the Americans would attack Collingwood, Windsor, the Niagara Peninsula, Prescott and Montreal initially, followed by Kingston and Quebec City. They therefore recommended the building of fortifications in 16 locations, at a cost of approximately £1.6 million ($8.5 million), and to keep 65,000 soldiers and volunteers on a war footing. They also felt it eminently desirable to build a railway between Halifax and Montreal, which would complete to the east the network that already reached as far as Windsor to the west. Railways were being built everywhere around the world and military staffs recognized their importance for the rapid transport and deployment of troops, just as they were aware of the need for telegraph lines, which usually ran along the train tracks.

While the commission was completing its work, a bill to considerably expand the volunteer militia at a cost of $500,000 caused a public outcry and plunged Canada into a political crisis. The bill, sponsored by John Alexander Macdonald and Georges-Étienne Cartier, was defeated in Parliament, which caused the fall of the Conservative government. But the defeat of the bill shocked the British, who had promptly sent troops and modern weapons and had seen their expenses for the North American garrison increase in a single year from £300,000 ($1.5 million) to approximately £1 million ($5 million), only to be refused assistance from those they had come to defend! Stormy debates followed in Parliament in London and the British press flew into a rage. The new Liberal government of John Sandfield Macdonald and Louis-Victor Sicotte attempted to calm British opinion by increasing the militia budget to $250,000, but the British were not taken in. That was only enough to mobilize 25,000 volunteers in an emergency; the Canadian government was thus not recruiting any permanent corps to support the British soldiers. In England, *The*

Spectator summed up the reaction, which was that the British should not have to "defend men who will not defend themselves."[128]

The British were thus in no mood to adopt the commission's costly recommendations of 1862. Yet in Canada the situation generally remained calm in 1863-64, although a Militia Act passed in 1863 provided for a total of 35,000 volunteers as well as for something new: the government of the Province of Canada would now be supplying uniforms as well as weapons. The riflemen's uniform was dark green with scarlet facings, the infantrymen's scarlet with blue facings, white lace and piping – relatively similar to the uniforms worn by British troops. The volunteer artillerymen would also wear a uniform similar to that of the British artillery, and the naval companies' uniforms resembled those of the Royal Navy. The idea was to lead the enemy to think from a distance that the volunteers were redoubtable soldiers of the British army. The cavalry continued to wear different uniforms until 1866, at which time it was supplied with a uniform similar to that of the 13th Hussars Regiment, no doubt in anticipation of its forthcoming arrival in Canada.

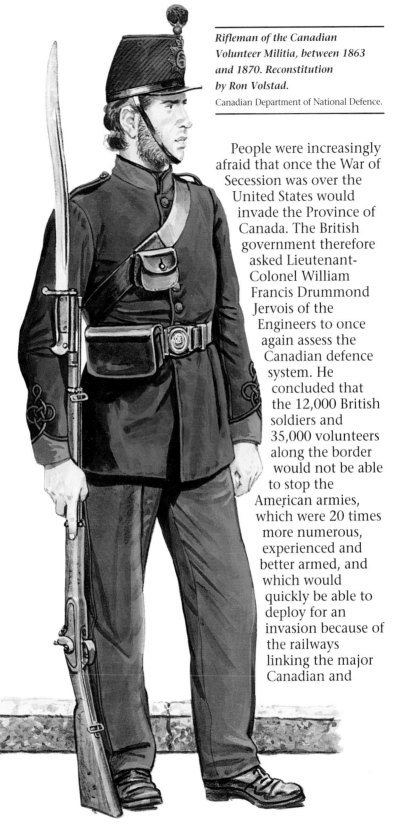

People were increasingly afraid that once the War of Secession was over the United States would invade the Province of Canada. The British government therefore asked Lieutenant-Colonel William Francis Drummond Jervois of the Engineers to once again assess the Canadian defence system. He concluded that the 12,000 British soldiers and 35,000 volunteers along the border would not be able to stop the American armies, which were 20 times more numerous, experienced and better armed, and which would quickly be able to deploy for an invasion because of the railways linking the major Canadian and

American cities. Most of the fortification plans proposed in 1862 were now obsolete; the American armies were so numerous that some could lay siege to cities while others crossed the country. To resist such a force effectively it was necessary to consolidate the available forces in a few virtually impregnable fortresses. Jervois considered Canada West virtually indefensible. In one of his scenarios, Kingston, Montreal and Quebec City could be made impregnable, but at an impossible political cost of some £1.7 million ($8.75 million)! A less expensive plan would require that at least Quebec City be defended, which would require defending the south shore with large modern forts to prevent the Americans from setting up batteries there and shelling the Citadel and the city at point-blank range.

The other stronghold that obviously needed defending was Halifax, whose fortifications also had to be renovated. Lastly, as the British government had already advocated, it was necessary to harmonize the defence of the various colonies in North America. Jervois explained to the Fathers of Confederation, who met in Quebec City in November 1864, that it was of the utmost importance to have a single national administration for the defence of British North America. To the benefits of political union would thus be added the advantages of military union, for the British would not remain in Canada indefinitely.

Gunner of the Canadian Volunteer Artillery, between 1863 and 1870. Reconstitution by Barry Rich.
Parks Canada.

The St. Albans Raid

The defence of the Province of Canada resurfaced as an issue in the fall of 1864. In September a group of Confederates based in the Province of Canada captured two American merchant ships on Lake Erie. A more serious incident occurred in October when some 20 Southerners left Montreal and took the small border town of St. Albans, Vermont, killing a civilian, robbing banks and attempting to burn down the town before taking refuge in the Province of Canada. Indignant that a neighbouring country should be used as a base for Confederate raids, the United States government threatened to take action. The border states were particularly outraged at Canada's tolerance, which they perceived as a betrayal. In Vermont 2,200 volunteers were mobilized, and a regular cavalry regiment was posted to Burlington and St. Albans. The state of New York sent 13 regiments on active duty to its border with Canada and Michigan mobilized a few companies.

This time the Canadian government was truly worried. On December 19 it mobilized 30 companies of volunteers into three "administrative battalions," with headquarters in Windsor, Niagara and Laprairie, to stave off any further raids along the border. This was the first time since the 1837-38 rebellions that the volunteers were called up for active duty. The companies in these battalions came from a

variety of regions. For example, three of the 10 companies stationed at Windsor were from Montreal. The three battalions spent a quiet winter and were disbanded on March 28, 1865.

On April 9, 1865, General Robert E. Lee's Confederate Army surrendered at the Appomattox Court House, putting an end to the American Civil War. Now fears of an invasion of Canada reached a fever pitch. Work on the three large forts recommended for Pointe de Lévy (Lauzon) began that very month, after heated debate in the House of Commons and the House of Lords in London. The British Opposition believed Canada to be indefensible. It contended that maintaining a garrison provoked the Americans to inflict a military defeat on Great Britain and that building forts amounted to waste, pure and simple.

Fortunately, though, the Americans were exhausted by their terrible Civil War, with its million and a half dead, 700,000 of them killed on the battlefield, and more than 500,000 wounded, out of a population of five and a half million men between the ages of 18 and 45. The Union Army, which stood at a million men in April, was reduced to 350,000 by August. Two years later there were 57,000, with

only 1,300 stationed along the Canadian border. General Sir John Michel, commander of the British army in North America, concluded that the era of military confrontation with the United States had come to an end.

The Fenians

Few Canadians today have heard of the Fenians. Yet they struck fear into the hearts of our ancestors of the 1860s and often made the front pages of Canadian newspapers. They were a more or less secret society of Irish patriots who had emigrated to the United States and whose mission was to secure, by force, Irish independence from Britain. By the end of 1865 some 10,000 Civil War veterans of Irish descent belonged to the Fenians. There were two factions, one in favour of an uprising in Ireland and another intent on taking Canada so that it could be exchanged for Irish independence! They were taken very seriously by the Canadian and British authorities, who planted spies in their midst. Their discoveries were not reassuring: the Fenians were mostly experienced officers and soldiers; they appeared to be well organized, they had money, and not only did they possess rifled guns, but Spencer seven-shot

breech-loading rifles, no less – effective weapons of which there were none in Canada. When it learned of this, the Canadian government immediately ordered 300 such rifles.

It was not long before the intelligence service reported the possibility of an attack on St. Patrick's Day, and in March 1866 the Canadian government called up 14,000 volunteers for active duty. Nothing happened, and the Canadian volunteers were demobilized at the end of the month. In April, however, a failed raid by the Fenians against Campobello Island in New Brunswick caused public alarm and won the people of that colony over to the proposed unification of the various British North American colonies into a single country.

The Invasion of 1866

At the end of May new intelligence reports expected attacks on Canada at the beginning of June. The Canadian government promptly mobilized 20,000 volunteers from May 31 to June 2. Thirteen small steamboats, transformed into gunboats and operated by crews of volunteers under the supervision of the Royal Navy, patrolled the Great Lakes and the St. Lawrence River.

193

The Montreal Volunteer Cavalry in winter dress, 1866. F. G. Coleridge. Watercolour.
National Archives of Canada, C102551.

This time there was an invasion. Approximately 850 Fenians led by General John O'Neill crossed the Niagara River and approached Port Colborne. The 2nd and 13th battalions of Canadian volunteers, along with the York and Caledonia rifle companies, totalling some 900 men, under the command of Lieutenant-Colonel Alfred Booker, intercepted the small Fenian army at Ridgeway on June 2. The battle went well for the Canadian volunteers, who, in spite of their inexperience, had been advancing and firing in sequence – until they were ordered to prepare to receive a cavalry charge! The order caused alarm in the ranks and confusion soon spread; the volunteers became frightened and fled. Nine Canadians were killed and 32 were wounded, with 10 Fenians killed and a few wounded.

There was a second battle the same day at Fort Erie, where the steamship *W. T. Robb*, crewed by the Dunnville naval brigade, landed the Welland Canal Volunteer Artillery Company. Soon afterwards, O'Neill's victorious army arrived and there was a heated exchange of gunfire. Some of the volunteers were able to re-embark before withdrawing. Six Canadians were injured and 36 were taken prisoner, but there were nine Fenians killed and 14 wounded. These Fenian victories did not, however, lead to anything more, because other Canadian troops and part of the 16th and 47th British regiments arrived. O'Neill and his men returned to the United States and were

disarmed by detachments of the American army.

A few days later, on June 8, a second small army of Fenians crossed the border near Huntingdon, south of Montreal. Several corps of volunteers had already been posted nearby but excitement had reached a peak in the Montreal newspapers. *The Gazette* even reported that the number of invaders was around 5,000, when in reality there were only 1,000, and they advanced only a few kilometres into Canadian territory – when they saw that there were several thousand British soldiers and Canadian volunteers converging on them from all sides they beat a hasty retreat. But the British and Canadian troops caught up with approximately 200 Fenians as they were leaving Pidgeon Hill. The Royal Guides, a Montreal volunteer cavalry company, charged them with swords drawn and captured 16. After this episode, the Fenians suspended their attacks for a few years.

An Improved Volunteer Militia

The Canadians gained military knowledge from the Fenian raids. They learned, for example, that the manner in which rural volunteers were organized, into hundreds of independent companies,

Volunteer cavalryman of the Montreal Royal Guides, c. 1866.
Canadian Department of National Defence Library.

made their deployment complicated. Adjutant-General Patrick MacDougall ordered that henceforth they be grouped into battalions, the practice followed by urban companies since 1859. It was also noted that corps of volunteers placed in brigades with regular British troops were clearly superior, because they served side-by-side with professional soldiers and learned a great deal about military cunning. Eight-day training camps were therefore held in the summer, with the help of the British regiments, to teach these battalions the essentials of the art of war. This led to the formation of seven brigades, each consisting of three battalions of volunteers and one British battalion. The Canadians welcomed this innovation because

"they knew that they would be properly led, that they were under the command of professional soldiers, and would have the advice and assistance of men whose trade was war."[129]

It was noted that the weapon used by the Canadian volunteers, the rifled-barrelled, muzzled-loading Enfield, was out of date and needed to be replaced by a breech-loading weapon like that used by many Fenians. In 1866 only a few regiments in the regular army had begun to receive weapons with the Snider-Enfield system. In the second half of the year the government purchased approximately

195

6,000 breech-loading rifles. Then in September it ordered the manufacture of 3,000 Peabody rifles; however, because of troops used the Spencer cavalry carbines until 1872. The Canadian volunteer militia was thus very well armed, equipped and trained for its time.[130] Maritime provinces, Quebec and Ontario. Henceforth all decisions concerning defence, including militia matters, would be the responsibility

The British 13th Hussars Regiment served in Canada from 1867 to 1869; the Canadian Volunteer Cavalry adopted this uniform during this period.

Anne S. K. Brown Military Collection, Brown University, Providence.

production delays these were not delivered until the spring of 1867. Some 30,000 Snider-Enfield rifled weapons were sent free of charge from England that summer, and these were also issued to the infantrymen and artillerymen. Mounted

Confederation

On July 1, 1867, Canada East and Canada West became the provinces of Quebec and Ontario. United with New Brunswick and Nova Scotia, they officially became a new country, Canada, the first autonomous state in the British Empire, maintaining a significant political link with Great Britain. The Militia Act, which was passed in 1868, ratified the unification of the militias of the two

of the federal government. Headquarters was located in Ottawa and military districts were created in the provinces. Districts 1 to 4 covered Ontario, 5 to 7 Quebec, 8 New Brunswick and 9 Nova Scotia.[131] These changes did not alter much for the Ontario and Quebec militiamen, because they were subject to the same regulations and kept their uniforms and their battalions retained their designations. But for the 2,717 volunteers of New Brunswick and Nova Scotia

196

the changes were considerable. Their laws and regulations were replaced by the statutes and regulations of Canada, which in general they welcomed because the new provisions were more favourable to them than the old ones. The only problem was battalion numbering. Some Maritime battalions had to take numbers secondary to those of Ontario and Quebec even though they were the older units.[132]

The Canadian Volunteer Militia officially had 37,170 men, 21,816 in Ontario and 12,637 in Quebec, and cost the Treasury $1 million a year. It consisted largely of infantry, rifle, cavalry and artillery units, in addition to naval units. There were a few in Ontario from 1862 to 1870 and there was one corps of the Sea Fencibles of Saint John, New Brunswick, from 1833 to 1867. But the most important unit of its type was without a doubt the Nova Scotia Naval Brigade. Established in April 1866, with some 550 men, it consisted of several companies of volunteer seamen in the main ports of the province. These companies were disbanded, however, towards the end of 1868 with the exception of one in Halifax, and this 122-man naval brigade was eventually incorporated into the garrison artillery of the city in 1871. All

these troops wore the navy uniform. Finally, from 1869 to 1874 there were two volunteer marine companies wearing the scarlet uniform on the Gaspé Peninsula of Quebec, one at Bonaventure and the other at New Carlisle. This was the first and only time that Canada had marines.

Despite unification and strengthening of the military establishment, there was no doubt in the minds of Canadian politicians that Great Britain would continue to provide the basic defence of the country. Even though Great Britian would eventually be able to reduce the size of its garrison, people believed it would keep a few regiments in Quebec City, Montreal, Kingston and London. London, located between Windsor and the Niagara Peninsula, had since the 1840s been the main British base in western Ontario, its central location making possible the deployment of troops to the east and to the west. The system of a regular British garrison of modest size supported by a volunteer Canadian militia was considered virtually immutable. As it happens, there were several differences of opinion between the British and Canadian governments with respect to the costs involved: the Canadians expected the British to pay

for all the costs of maintaining the regular fortifications and garrisons, whereas the British asked the Canadians – without success – to ease their financial burden.

Canadians Forced to Defend Canada

In the fall of 1868 Georges-Étienne Cartier and William MacDougall were delegated to London to negotiate defence matters. They had many requests with a view to improving the status of the military in Canada, at England's expense. But in Great Britain the new Liberal government of William Gladstone had other priorities, and it announced that within two years British troops would be withdrawn from Canada, Australia and New Zealand. Only the major naval bases would maintain a garrison, which meant that all troops except those stationed at Halifax would be evacuated from Canada.

Caught by surprise, the Canadian delegates did not believe the decision, thinking it a political manoeuvre. Negotiations degenerated to the point where Canada even refused to pay an invoice of $4,000 for the repair of weapons damaged by Canadian volunteers – weapons that had come from British army stores. British taxpayers, over a period of

Canadian volunteer wearing the infantry frock adopted by a few units beginning in 1866. Reconstitution by Ron Volstad.
Canadian Department of National Defence.

Royal Navy continued with the naval defence of overseas British territories, but public opinion demanded that the army be repatriated to Great Britain. Faced with the France of Napoleon III and Germany's increasing power, its anxiety continued to grow.

Canadians Abroad

The people of Canada supported a wide range of political leanings and sympathies. Although the Fenian movement was clearly unsuccessful in attracting nationals of Irish descent, from the 1850s on there were some ethnic tensions between Irish and British volunteer militia companies. In 1856 the Governor General made it clear that he would not permit any intrigue and that he expected complete harmony within the ranks of the volunteer companies. The following year the Adjutant-General confirmed that the Irish company in Kingston would be entitled to celebrate St. Patrick's Day in uniform, just as a Scottish company "or any other company has to observe the festival of their patron saint," adding that "intolerant feeling"[133] among the Kingston volunteers would have to end. Tensions continued,

not only between the Irish and the British, but also among Scottish, English and French Canadians. But the firm position of the authorities concerning ethnic or racial outbursts prevented any serious incident from occurring within the Canadian volunteer forces.

The emotional attachment to the mother country was still strong among many English Canadians, for whom Great Britain and Canada were two parts of the same nation. In 1858, when the decision was taken to recruit a new British line infantry regiment in Canada, the 100th Prince of Wales Royal Canadian Regiment, more than 1,500 men enlisted. The recruits were assembled in Quebec City, and old uniforms, some dating from the War of 1812, were distributed before they left for England.[134] After they were trained, equipped and armed at Shorncliffe and Aldershot, they were sent to Gibraltar and Malta for seven years before returning to Canada in 1866. They were then posted to Montreal and Ottawa. But these Canadians belonged to an imperial line regiment and two years later they left for Scotland. Other English Canadians occasionally enlisted in the Royal Navy. Driven by a desire for adventure and attracted to military life, these

six years, had armed the Canadian volunteers with 40,000 rifled Enfields and 30,000 Snider-Enfields, so it is understandable that such a response should outrage the British ministers, who were more determined than ever to withdraw their garrisons; in 1869-70 the Canadian garrison thus declined from 16,000 to 6,000 soldiers, which brought savings of approximately $10 million (£2 million) to the Royal Treasury. The

Canadians saw the British armed forces as not foreign but rather "family" and themselves as colonial sons serving their mother country.

The patriotism of French Canadians was very different. They saw Canada as their only true native land and as altogether distinct from Great Britain; like their descendants today, they considered France their mother country. They were also familiar with the northeastern United States, tens of thousands of them having gone to work in New England. When the American Civil War broke out thousands of French Canadians volunteered to fight for the Union Army.[135] One of them, who signed on as a musician in the 4th Rhode Island Regiment and was injured in the Battle of Antietam in 1862, is known to all Canadians: Calixa Lavallée, who would later compose the music for the national anthem, "O Canada."

Other French Canadians, though far less numerous, joined the Confederate Army, particularly in Louisiana. A few even sought adventure further south, as far afield as Mexico. France had invaded Mexico – which Napoleon III had called a "generous intervention" – to establish a vassal empire in America.[136] Two French Canadians who were to

make their mark in the world of literature took part in the war. Narcisse-Henri-Édouard Faucher de Saint-Maurice, an unconditional Francophile, campaigned with the French army as a sub-

Calixa Lavallée in the musician's uniform of the 4th Rhode Island Regiment, c. 1862.
Société historique de Montréal.

lieutenant in 1864-65. He was injured and received the Mexican Medal and the Cross of the Military Order of Guadeloupe. He later wrote a great deal about his campaigns. During the same period, Honoré

Beaugrand, future mayor of Montreal and author of the celebrated legend "La Chasse-galerie," was a young sergeant of the redoubtable Corps de Contre-guérillas of the French army. Faucher de Saint-Maurice and Beaugrand were not the only Canadian military men in Mexico; a staff officer in the Mexican republican army reported that other, less famous, Canadians had also served with the republicans.

The Pontifical Zouaves

In 1860 the French-Canadian writer Arthur Buies volunteered to serve in Garibaldi's army. This was an extraordinary act, since many of Buies's compatriots enlisted in the opposing camp. In the early 1860s some devout Catholic French Canadians went to Italy to enlist in the pontifical army. The Pontifical States, with Rome as their capital, held the centre of the country and fought against the unification of Italy by the supporters of Piedmont and Garibaldi. The most fervent Catholics – the ultramontane – considered that the loss of Pope Pius IX's temporal power over his states would constitute a sacrilege. The pontifical army included a corps specially formed in 1860 for volunteers from various Catholic countries, particularly France and

Belgium: the Pontifical Zouave Regiment. In November 1867 the Bishop of Montreal, Monseigneur Ignace Bourget, launched an appeal for volunteers to go and defend the Pope. The idea was taken up by other prelates and was received enthusiastically across Quebec.

In only a few weeks [135] recruits were selected from among 429 volunteers. These men left Montreal on February 19, 1868, to the cheers of some 20,000 people, a fifth of the city's total and a third of its French-speaking population. Other

Canadian Zouave of the Pontifical Army in Italy, between 1868 and 1870. Reconstitution by Ron Volstad.
Canadian Department of National Defence.

contingents followed, and of the 500 men selected 388 were to serve in the Pontifical Zouave Regiment. But for the strict eligibility criteria and the costs involved – it was necessary, by means of gifts and collections, to cover the cost of transportation of these Zouaves and their pay while in Rome – thousands of French Canadians would no doubt have been recruited. As it was, the operation cost at least $112,000, a considerable amount for the period. The Canadians in Rome had a peaceful time of it, their war efforts limited to chasing after guerillas in the surrounding hills. Only eight of them died, most owing to illness. In the spring of 1870 most of the Zouaves in the first contingent returned to Montreal, where they were welcomed by almost 12,000 people. After symbolic resistance, Rome surrendered on September 20, 1870, and the other Canadian Zouaves were repatriated. When they

arrived in Montreal a crowd of approximately 50,000 was there to receive them.

An Anglophile Militia

While people were rushing to cheer the Zouaves, there were only 7,000 volunteer militiamen of French descent out of 12,600 volunteers in Quebec – from a population of 1.3 million, 80 percent of which was French Canadian. How can this disproportion be explained?

Many French Canadians were uncomfortable with the volunteer militia. They felt excluded from an institution that had been designed and managed by and for "the English" and for those among them who wished to get involved in "a sort of playing at soldiers"[137] of the British Empire. The language of the high command was English, although there were some efforts to use French – for example, the drill manual was translated. With the exception of Quebec City, all the officer training schools established in 1864 were run in English. During the Fenian invasion the commanding general of the British Forces in North America, Sir John Michel, ordered the Francophone units in the joint brigade to use only English in order to achieve uniformity in the language

of command.[138] In general, however, the units that were completely French Canadian did use French, not only out of pride but also because their members did not understand English at all or not well enough. The fact remains that many French Canadians were offended to see their mother tongue barely tolerated and they turned their backs on the Canadian militia, which appeared to them an instrument of assimilation.

However, many French Canadians showed a

Officers of the Royal Engineers between 1860 and 1870. O. Norrie. Watercolour.
Anne S. K. Brown Military Collection, Brown University, Providence.

genuine interest in the military; of course they asked to be assigned to units that functioned in French and they demanded a "national uniform." In 1862 a grey uniform of "homespun cloth with red cuffs"[139] was suggested, but to no avail. That same year the 4th Battalion attempted to give its dark-green made-in-England uniform the look of "Chasseurs français."[140] Between 1860 and 1870 citizen committees proposed raising French-Canadian battalions wearing the Zouave uniform, a military style that originated in the French army and was spreading to many armies around the world, but the higher authorities always refused such requests.[141]

British officer in winter, c. 1870. Seccombe. Drawing.
Private collection.

Such inflexibility is inexplicable considering that Scottish Canadians were permitted to wear tartan kilts and trousers. Even the Americans had a number of Zouave regiments, one in Plattsburgh, New York. Yet there was no lack of good will on the part of French Canadians. For example, even though they generally avoided wearing the red uniform, the 17th Battalion and several other French-

Canadian battalions did wear it. Even Monseigneur Bourget's paramilitary guard, which was identified with the nationalist ultramontanes, became the corps of volunteers that formed the 65th Battalion in 1868-69, a Francophone unit that nevertheless had to wait until 1904 to have its name gallicized.[142]

The stubborn desire of the authorities to give a thoroughly British character to the Canadian militia finally prevailed; they created an armed force that was closely linked to British military traditions. Their faithfulness to the original model was such that it was sometimes impossible to tell a British soldier from a Canadian one.[143] The fact remains that the British model was an excellent one, and its adoption contributed considerably to the high standard of the many Canadian units that adopted the military traditions of England in a spirit of loyalty to the motherland. The policy, which was in keeping with the patriotic feelings of many Canadians in the Anglophone provinces, thus greatly enriched Canada's military heritage.

But the total imposition of the British model on all Canadians was a mistake. Any truly national army must show respect for the heritage of its people; otherwise it will be perceived negatively by that part of the population that cannot find a place for itself and its traditions. This, unfortunately, is what happened in Canada. Not only were non-British military traditions rejected out of hand, but, even more pernicious, statistics show that the system either kept servicemen who were not English Canadians out of the high command or totally assimilated the few Francophones who reached those heights. The Anglophile senior officers were afraid that a two-headed army would be created. Their decisions excluded from the militia approximately a third of the able-bodied population, which amounted to an incredible waste of Canadian military potential. It was as if the German Swiss cantons had decided to do without the military support of the Francophone cantons – which would have spelled disaster for their national defence.

Canada paid the political and military price for having excluded a significant portion of its population from an institution as fundamental as the national army. The corollary of such a policy was clearly a lack of national cohesiveness and considerable wrangling over the objectives of the armed forces, each group immediately accusing the other whenever problems arose. And that is precisely what happened only three years after Confederation.

The Northwest Expedition

In 1869 the government of Canada recovered vast lands from the Hudson's Bay Company in the West. The following year it created the province of Manitoba, the most populous region of which was the Red River area. No one seems to have worried about the fate of its 10,000 inhabitants, most of whom were French Canadians who had to varying degrees intermarried with Amerindians, until they sent their new lieutenant-governor back to Ottawa and proclaimed a provisional government led by their chief, Louis Riel. English Canadians in Manitoba tried twice to overthrow the Métis, who unfortunately executed one of them, Thomas Scott. When it learned the news, a furious Ontario demanded a punitive expedition to avenge Scott's death and the opening up of Manitoba to colonization and "civilization."

To restore order, the Canadian government arranged for Colonel Garnet Joseph Wolseley of the British army to take command of a military expedition to the Red River. It consisted of a

battalion of the 60th British Rifle Regiment and two battalions of volunteer riflemen, the first recruited in Ontario, the second in Quebec. But the French Canadians found that the Métis were being treated in a very offhand manner and that the operation was sullied by an unacceptable level of racism. They had the impression that by recruiting a battalion from among their ranks the English Canadians, who controlled the volunteer militia, sought moral approval to do what seemed right to them in the name of a purported "national" will. In addition, only a third of the officers' commissions in the Quebec battalion were to go to French Canadians. Cohesiveness was missing, as were the Francophone recruits of the "2nd Battalion, Quebec Rifles." Only 77 French Canadians enlisted out of a total of 362 non-commissioned officers and men. Recruiting for the "Quebec" battalion had to be completed in Ontario. The Ontario battalion obviously had no such recruiting problems.

At the beginning of June 1870 Wolseley assembled his three battalions, as well as some artillery and engineer detachments, for a total of 87 officers, 1,048 soldiers, 256 voyageurs and 15 guides, and headed to the western end of Lake Superior. On August 24, after an exceedingly difficult voyage punctuated by many portages in which the hardiness of the voyageurs greatly impressed Wolseley, the expedition reached Fort Garry only to find that Riel and his supporters had vanished and that everything was quite peaceful. Wolseley and his British soldiers immediately returned eastward without any fighting, leaving the two Canadian battalions in

garrison in Manitoba. With volunteers from the two battalions, a mounted police company was also formed. It wore a dark-blue uniform with brass buttons instead of the dark green of the riflemen. In April and May 1871 the troops were demobilized except for two infantry companies that formed a small "temporary" battalion in Manitoba; it guarded Fort Garry until it was disbanded six years later.

A Final Attempt by the Fenians

In spite of repeated defeats, the Fenians had not been discouraged, and in 1870 they made a new attempt at invading Canada. Spies had reported the possibility of an attack in May. The Canadian government thus mobilized 13,000 volunteers, equally divided between Quebec and Ontario.

On May 25 approximately 600 Fenians,[144] under the command of General John O'Neill, left Franklin, Vermont, and reached Eccles Hill, Quebec, just north of the Canadian border. The 60th Canadian Battalion and approximately 75 farmers in the area, under the command of Lieutenant-Colonel Brown Chamberlin, were waiting for them and were soon joined by some 400 volunteer militiamen

under the command of Lieutenant-Colonel William Osborne Smith. The Fenians had a cannon, but when the Canadian volunteers charged them they took flight and left it in the field along with other equipment. No Canadians were hurt, whereas there were five Fenians killed and 18 wounded.

Two days later the invaders came again, this time crossing the border at Trout River, Quebec, some 15 kilometres west of Eccles Hill. The 50th Canadian Battalion, along with a company of the 69th British Regiment and the Montreal Volunteer Artillery, were already there. The accurate fire of the artillery drove the Fenians from their cover in the woods, while the Anglo-Canadian infantry advanced on them with fixed bayonets. They fled after firing three salvos too high to cause any damage. The Canadians and British suffered losses, but the Fenians had three more dead.

On October 5, 1871, the Fenians made a final attempt. This time O'Neill and 40 men crossed the Manitoba border at Emerson north of Pembina and took the Canadian customs office. The next day Canadian soldiers and volunteers from Winnipeg and Saint-Boniface[145] learned, on their way to battle, that the American

army had arrested O'Neill and his men.

It did not take long for everyone in Canada to realize that the era of the Fenian "invasions" was well and truly over. The movement lost much of its popularity and political weight in the United States, no doubt because of its repeated military defeats. Also, the American government, which was keen to maintain good relations with Canada and Great Britain, appeared to be ready to take more forcible action to disarm such organizations on its territory.

Withdrawal of British Troops from Canada

There was nothing more to prevent the total withdrawal of regular British troops from Canada, as the government in London so ardently wished. In spite of Canadian protests, British diplomats were already negotiating with the Americans to settle all their differences, and they reached a general agreement: the Treaty of Washington was signed on May 8, 1871.

The British garrison had already been withdrawn from Ontario, New Brunswick and Newfoundland the previous year. Several high-ranking British officers encouraged the Canadian government to raise a

small regular army to replace the troops that had left or were about to depart, but without success. Until the spring of 1871 the government did not believe the British garrison would completely withdraw, and it continued to hope that at least one battalion would be left in Quebec, the Gibraltar of North America and a symbol of British power. London had nevertheless very clearly stated that only its naval bases in Halifax and Esquimalt would be kept for the Royal Navy and that only one garrison would be maintained at Halifax.

As the troops were repatriated, the British government turned over to the Canadian government all its property and all its regular army stores of military supplies, weapons and artillery. In the fall of 1871 it was preparing to do the same in Quebec. The Canadian authorities finally resigned themselves to the situation, and on October 20 issued an order to raise two regular units of Canadian artillery to occupy Fort Henry in Kingston and the Quebec Citadel, and to place detachments in the fort at Pointe de Lévy and the fort on Île Sainte-Hélène in Montreal. These troops

would henceforth train and instruct the volunteer artillery corps. There was nothing planned for the infantry or the cavalry.

On the afternoon of November 11, 1871, the officers and soldiers of the 60th Regiment, the Royal Artillery and the Royal Engineers came out of the Quebec Citadel and Artillery Park in full dress and paraded for the last time through the streets, marching from Upper Town to Lower Town singing "Auld Lang Syne" and "Good-bye, Sweetheart, Good-bye." On the dock, with a huge crowd cheering and wishing them "bon voyage," they boarded the troop transport ship *Orontes*, which glided slowly down the St. Lawrence as dusk fell. A major page in Canada's military history had been turned.

The End of an Era

Thus ended what could be called the era of invasion. From 1755 to 1871 the country, governed in turn by the French, the British and the Canadians, was under almost constant threat of real or apprehended invasion. But when all the battles, troop deployments

and ship movements, and all the construction and military exploration, were over, Canada was considerably larger, stretching from the Atlantic to the Pacific. Indeed British Columbia had become a Canadian province on July 20, 1871, which marked a Canadian version of Manifest Destiny. It may have been less turbulent than the Manifest Destiny of its neighbours to the south, but it was not necessarily any less successful.

Fenian infantryman, 1870.
Reconstitution by Ron Volstad.
Canadian Department of National Defence.

The troop transport vessel Orentes
leaving Quebec on November 11, 1871.
National Archives of Canada, C56624.

After all these wars and fears of invasion, all Canadians, no matter where their ancestors may have come from, were tired of armed conflict. Since it had become clear that there would be no war with the United States, the Canadian government no longer showed an interest in military problems. It slashed the army's budget and left its management to a few Anglophile officers.

In any event, the new regular Canadian army consisted of a small battalion in Manitoba and two artillery units posted to Kingston and Quebec City. There were many volunteer militias, but well below the national potential and thus they cost much less than they could have. This situation was undeniably pleasing to the government, which was already attempting to raise the funds needed to complete the railway link to the Maritime provinces and to achieve its great dream of extending the railway all the way to the Pacific, thus opening the West to colonization. All Canadians, whether of old stock or immigrants just off the boat, were clearly more concerned with building an immense country and carving out a better life for themselves in a nation that appeared to be sheltered, in future, from the horrors of war.

NOTES

AC — Archives nationales, Colonies (Paris)
AG — Archives de la Guerre (Service historique de l'armée de terre, Vincennes)
AN — Archives nationales de France (Paris)
ANQQ — Archives nationales du Québec, Quebec City
ANQM — Archives nationales du Québec, Montreal
BL — British Library (London)
NAC — National Archives of Canada (Ottawa)
PRO — Public Records Office (Kew, England)
SRO — Scottish Records Office (Edinburgh, Scotland)

1 There was one company of cannoniers-bombardiers in Canada and one at Île Royale. There were no artillery companies in Louisiana prior to 1759, but until that time some infantrymen were given artillery training at the Mobile school for cannoniers.

2 The Louisiana Garrison consisted of 150 Swiss soldiers from the 4th Company of the Halwyll Swiss Regiment (called the Karrer prior to 1752), half of which was stationed at New Orleans, half at Mobile.

3 Quoted in Frégault, Guy, *La guerre de la Conquête, 1754-1760* (Montreal: Fides, 1975), p. 131.

4 The expression "Régiment de la Marine," used by several French officers in Canada to designate this battalion, often caused confusion among historians of the past century, who believed that it was the regiment in the French army bearing the same name. However, this temporary battalion had absolutely nothing to do with the regiments of "La Marine" or "Royal-Marine" of the French armed forces then serving in Europe.

5 The two de Berry battalions, which were originally supposed to go to India, had only nine companies each, instead of 13. In all, 1,118 men embarked at Brest, of whom 59 were officers and 26 were servants. But disease broke out during the crossing, killing 141 men; when they arrived in Quebec at the end of July, there were still eight officers and 200 men sick in the two battalions (AG, A1, Vol. 3459, No. 49, 100 bis). Moreover, beginning in 1756, many soldiers of Irish extraction had deserted the British army to join the French forces. A small corps of such soldiers accompanied Montcalm's army on the siege of Oswego. Like the Irish regiments serving France, this troop wore a red uniform with distinctive green trim. In June 1757, because of the possible fate of these men if they were captured in Canada by the British, they were reorganized into a company that was stationed in Quebec until it embarked for France on September 16. The nominal roll of these soldiers is reproduced in Roy, Pierre-Georges, *La ville de Québec sous le Régime français* (Quebec City: 1930), Vol. 2, pp. 287-288.

6 General Amherst sent his compliments to Mrs. Drucour with a gift of pineapples from the West Indies, a rare delicacy at the time. Mrs. Drucour thanked him and sent him in return a basket of bottles of good wine.

7 The 11 colours of the other corps were turned over to General Amherst, who immediately sent them to the King. They were placed in St. Paul's Cathedral in London on September 6, 1758. The ceremony was reported in several English and American newspapers, as well as in the Annual Register for 1758, p. 108. They rotted over time because of the moisture, and 70 years later all that remained were a few shreds. Also, fearing that Louisbourg would be turned over to France once again at the end of the war, as it was in 1748, the British raised a special corps of sappers, who blew up all the fortifications in the summer of 1760.

8 Vaudreuil to the Minister of the Navy, Montreal, August 4, 1758, AC, C11A, Vol. 103, fol. 144.

9 Vaudreuil to Minister of the Navy, Montreal, November 1, 1758, NAC series K, Monuments historiques, box 1232, No. 51. Captain Aubry belonged to the Louisiana troops. He had arrived at Fort Duquesne in July with 240 reinforcements from Illinois.

10 Bougainville, Louis-Antoine de, *Écrits sur le Canada: Mémoires - Journal - Lettres*, ed. Roland Lamontagne (Sillery: Pélican, 1993), p. 379.

11 Robert Napier to William Fauquier, London, November 6, 1758, PRO, War Office 7, Vol. 26.

12 Quoted in *An Account of the Remarkable Occurrences in the Life and Travels of Col. James Smith* (Lexington, 1799), p. 58.

13 This was a small, temporary battalion consisting of grenadier companies detached from the 22nd, 40th and 45th regiments at Louisbourg.

14 ANQQ, Literary & Historical Society, P450/1, "General Wolfe, the soldier's friend," by Sergeant Thomson of the 78th.

15 The poor behaviour of the French regiments was often attributed to the inclusion of Canadian militiamen among their ranks. To protect themselves, these militiamen were accustomed to lying prone on the ground rather than standing to reload their muskets. It is true that a battalion's appearance would be changed as a result. When all is said and done, the Canadian militiamen's method did nothing to change the manoeuvre, because, whether prone or standing, they had to stop to reload their muskets. It was also alleged that some of the Canadian militiamen abandoned the line to rejoin those skirmishing on the flanks in order to fight in the manner to which they were accustomed. If this was true, one may wonder about the standard of training given the militiamen by the French sergeants. On the other hand, it is difficult to believe that militiamen, 300 at most, could have had a real influence on a battle involving some 3,000 veterans from France. In fact, as in many other formation battles that took place in Europe during the Seven Years' War, the French soldiers had been outclassed by the clearly superior tactics and discipline of the British and Prussian armies. Furthermore, the retreat of the French regiments in Quebec was covered by colonial militiamen and troops, and it was these troops which inflicted the greatest losses on the British.

16 Quoted by Captain John Knox of the 43rd Regiment in his diary, published in part in *The Siege of Quebec and the Campaigns in North America 1757-1760*, ed. Brian Cornell (London: 1976), p. 202. Wolfe's body was placed on the HMS *Lowestoft* at approximately 11 a.m. and taken to England, where he was buried in the family vault at Greenwich.

17 Montcalm was interred in a large hole made by an English shell in the Ursuline Chapel. His skull has been preserved at the Ursuline Museum.

18 Several authors have written that Fort Niagara surrendered on July 24, which is only partly true. On

the evening of July 24 Commander Pouchot and the British Captain Hervey agreed to a ceasefire and negotiated the terms of surrender. The surrender itself is dated the 25th, and that day the French garrison relinquished the fort. Dunnigan, Brian, *Siege - 1759: The Campaign Against Niagara*, Old Fort Niagara (Youngstown, N.Y., 1986), pp. 81-82.

19 NAC, MG18, K8, Vol. 12, p. 206. Army chart for the expedition to Quebec, April 1760. The army assembled by Lévis also included 356 non-combatants: 307 servants, 16 surgeons and 33 "Negro soldiers" belonging to the La Reine (10), Béarn (5), Royal-Roussillon (4), Guyenne (5) and Berry (9) regiments. In all, including non-combatants, Lévis' army totalled 7,266 men.

20 NAC, MG18, K8, Vol. 12. In his diary, Lévis estimated that his army at Sainte-Foy had "approximately 5,000 men, 2,400 of whom were militiamen; but there were over 1,400 men among these, such as the La Reine brigade [the La Reine and Languedoc regiments] and the cavalry, which were not in action, like the Amerindians who "having withdrawn, did not engage in battle." The latter reappeared at the end of the battle to take British prisoners. This unenviable fate was spared one officer of the 58th regiment, Henry Hamilton, by an officer of the Régiment de Berry, who, seeing that the Amerindians were arriving, offered him his coat and his white cockade, which Hamilton took with considerable gratitude. The disguised prisoner then turned towards the two French soldiers who were escorting him and said in French, with all the authority of one of their officers: "Allons mes enfants, marchez!" He was to become Governor of Bermuda, where he founded the city of Hamilton (NAC, MG23, GII, 11).

21 These eight Compagnies franches de la Marine were made up of soldiers who had been taken prisoner, mainly at Louisbourg, and then exchanged. The *Machault* scuttled itself. Most of the officers, seamen and soldiers, sacrificed in advance in this expedition, nevertheless managed to escape the British and return to France on small ships. Two centuries later, the *Machault* was studied by Parks Canada archaeologists.

22 "...it would be so scandalous...," *The Journal of Jeffery Amherst*, ed. J. Clarence Webster (Toronto & Chicago: 1931), p. 248.

23 Proclamation by General Amherst, Montreal, September 22, 1760, *Report of the Canadian Archives for 1918* (Ottawa: 1919), Appendix B, p. 86.

24 Spain entered the war in early 1762 to support France, but England had become so powerful that the large Spanish colonial towns of Havana in Cuba and Manila in the Philippines fell to the British. To recover them, Spain ceded Florida to the British and received Louisiana from France in return.

25 Sometimes spelled "Pondiac."

26 BL, Additional Manuscripts, Vol. 21666, Frederick Haldimand to James Murray, Trois-Rivières, March 6, 1764.

27 BL, Additional Manuscripts, Vol. 21666, Frederick Haldimand to James Murray, Trois-Rivières, March 23, 1764.

28 Sometimes called the Canadian Light Infantry. On the subject of the role played by the battalion in the Great Lakes area, see *Journals of Col. John Montrésor*, ed. G. D. Scull (New York: 1882).

29 Pontiac's confederation of nations fell apart in 1764, more precisely after two of the six Iroquois nations had said they supported the British. The peace arranged by Colonel Bouquet stated that the Amerindians were to release all Whites taken alive and adopted by their respective nations. As a result, hundreds of Whites were taken to Fort Pitt. The story of how they were reunited with their families is one of the most moving accounts in military history. See Bouquet, Henry, *An Historical Account of the Expedition Against the Ohio Indians in the Year MDCCLXIV* (London: 1766). This book was reprinted several times.

30 PRO, War Office 34, Vol. 74. James Abercrombie, major in the 78th Regiment, to Jeffery Amherst, London, January 10, 1764; Jeffery Amherst to Lord Halifax, London, January 14, 1764.

31 PRO, War Office 34, Vol. 41. Jeffery Amherst to Henry Bouquet, New York, August 31, 1763. For a favourable opinion of Rogers and his men, see Cueno, John R., *Robert Rogers of the Rangers* (New York: 1959).

32 PRO, Colonial Office 42, Vol. 28, Guy Carleton to Lord Shelburne, Quebec, November 25, 1767.

33 After the war, the British offered land to the soldiers of the disbanded regiments, without much success. Only the men of the 78th Scottish Regiment showed any interest. In the nineteenth century, a curious legend about the disbandment of this regiment entered our military heritage, to the effect that "a great portion of the soldiers" availed themselves of the offer and, marrying Canadian women, virtually regenerated the country while providing for its security – the British equivalent of the Carignan-Salières Regiment! Of course some Scottish officers had bought seigniories, and some soldiers of the 78th remained in this country, but in limited numbers. When it was disbanded, the regiment had only about 500 men. Of these, according to archival records, 358 returned to Great Britain and only 158 were demobilized in Quebec. See, for example, Lemoine, J. M., *Maple Leaves* (Quebec City: 1878), p. 142. The list of soldiers who remained was published in Harper, J. R., *The Fraser Highlanders* (Montreal: 1979), and the document giving the number of soldiers who returned to Great Britain may be found in PRO, War Office 34, Vol. 4, Embarcation Return of the 47th and 78th Regiments... Quebec, October 10, 1763.

34 *L'invasion du Canada par les Bastonnois, journal de M. Sanguinet*, ed. Richard Ouellet and Jean-Pierre Therrien (Quebec City: 1975), p. 47. According to a dispatch written in Montreal on July 10, which appeared in the *Maryland Journal and Baltimore Advertiser* of November 8, 1775, the company of English merchants was led by Major Robertson, Captain Porteous Grey and Lieutenant Todd.

35 Ibid., p. 63.

36 Ibid., p. 64.

37 Having received the approval of the King, Lord Dartmouth first asked for 3,000 men on July 1, then changed his mind and asked for twice as many on the 24th. The equipment required for all these people was collected in record time. On July 12, the weapons and uniforms for 3,000 men, as well as cannons, were on board the ship that was to transport them to Quebec. At the beginning of August, a second ship left England with equipment for another group of 3,000 men. The

coats sent were green, faced with red, and there wre some buff-coloured waistcoats and breeches. PRO, Colonial Office 42, Vol. 34. These shipments were also reported and described by a London correspondent of the *Maryland Gazette*, published in Annapolis on October 5, 12 and 19, 1775.

38 Figures concerning the number of men in the garrison are often contradictory, particulary for the militia. A report prepared on December 16, 1775, was reasonably accurate, except for the militiamen, who were estimated at only 500, 300 of whom were Canadians (PRO, Colonial Office 42, Vol. 34, Return of the men for the Defence of this town of Quebec). On the other hand, a report for the eight Francophone Canadian companies prepared on the same day gives 580 as the number of militiamen (NAC, RG8, C 1714, New Role of the Canadian Militia... Town of Quebec, December 16, 1775). The Anglophone British Militia had between 300 and 330 men, according to one of its captains. The Scottish soldiers, seamen and artificers all received a green coat with red collar, lapels and cuffs; the militiamen were issued an all-green coat without lapels. All wore buff-coloured waistcoats and breeches. The officers wore the same uniform as their men, but with epaulettes and silver lace on the tricorne. This was the first time that all the militiamen in a major Canadian town wore a military uniform.

39 According to the Americans, the official report of their losses gave 30 dead, 42 wounded and 389 prisoners, but in reality there were more dead (and no doubt also more wounded), as demonstrated by Stanley, George F. G., in *Canada Invaded* (Toronto: 1973), pp. 103-104. The Americans tend, even today, to minimize their losses and inflate those of their adversaries. British official reports are usually more reliable.

40 *L'invasion du Canada par les Bastonnois, journal de M. Sanguinet*, p. 78.

41 *Ibid.*, p. 85.

42 *Mills & Hick's British and American Register, with an Almanack for the Year 1774* (Boston: c. 1773). In the English colonies of the period, the companies of "cadets" had nothing to do with military training. They were prosperous bourgeois who usually served as an honour guard for the governors. Their members wore colourful uniforms, but the dress of the Halifax company is not known. The small above-mentioned book also refers to the existence of militia corps in King, Windsor, Queen's, Annapolis, Cumberland and Lunenburg counties.

43 Diary of the siege of Fort Cumberland by Joseph Goreham, published in *Report on Canadian Archives*, 1894, pp. 359-366. The garrison consisted of 171 officers and soldiers of the Royal Fencible Americans, four artillerymen from the Royal Artillery, 15 armed carpenters, one half-paid lieutenant (retired), three militia officers and nine inhabitants.

44 PRO, Colonial Office 42, Vol. 36, John Burgoyne to Lord Germain, Quebec, May 14, 1777.

45 *L'invasion du Canada par les Bastonnois, journal de M. Sanguinet*, p. 98.

46 PRO, War Office 1, Vol. 2, Guy Carleton to Lord Barrington, Chambly, June 8, 1776.

47 *L'invasion du Canada par les Bastonnois, journal de M. Sanguinet*, p. 107.

48 *Ibid.*

49 August Ludwig Schlözer, quoted in Wilhelmy, Jean-Pierre, *Les mercenaires allemands au Québec du XVIIIe siècle et leur apport à la population* (Beloeil, Qc: 1984), p. 162.

50 *Gazette de France*, October 29, 1782. Losses were estimated at 10 to 12 million French livres by the French – approximately a half million English pounds, according to the *Annual Register* for 1783. Whatever the amount, the loss was significant, because the company did not pay a dividend for three years.

51 A few items exchanged by Pérez and his men were sent to Spain. These exceptional records are kept in the Museo de América and the Museo Naval in Madrid. See in particular the excellent study by Cabello and Paz, "The Ethnographic Collections: A Special Legacy of the Spanish Presence on the Northwest Coast, 1774-1792," *Spain and the North Pacific Coast*, ed. Robin Inglis (Vancouver: Vancouver Maritime Museum, 1992), pp. 137-158.

52 "The Indians gazed at one another for some time with fright & silent astonishment," *Journals of Captain James Cook: The Voyage of the Resolution and Discovery, 1776-1780*, ed. J. C. Beeglehole (Cambridge: Hakluit Society, 1967), Vol. 3, p. 1350.

53 In the Nootka language: "Macuina, Macuina, Macuina; Asco-Tais, hua-cas; España, España, España; Hua-cas, Macuina, Nutka." In Spanish: "Macuina, Macuina, Macuina; es un gran príncipe, amigo nuestro; España, España, España; es amiga de Macuina y de Nutka." Quoted in Sanchez, Joseph, *Spanish Bluecoats: The Catalonian Volunteers in Northwestern New Spain, 1767-1810* (Albuquerque: University of New Mexico, 1990), p. 94.

54 *Loyalist Narratives from Upper Canada*, ed. James J. Talman (Toronto: Champlain Society, 1946), p. 229.

55 Aubert de Gaspé, Philippe, *Mémoires* (Quebec City: 1885; first ed. 1864), pp. 85-87.

56 Jean-Paul de Lagrave's study, *Fleury Mesplet (1734-1794) imprimeur, éditeur, libraire, journaliste* (Montreal: Fides, 1985), is the best work to consult on the spread of revolutionary ideas in French Canada.

57 Genêt attracted the antipathy of President George Washington, and was blamed by Robespierre. See Lagrave, pp. 420-421; see also Brunet, Michel, "La Révolution française sur les rives du Saint-Laurent," *Revue d'Histoire de l'Amérique française*, X (1957), pp. 155-162. From a military standpoint, it is not clear that the British authorities would have succeeded in mobilizing the French-Canadian militias against an invader from the mother country. A report prepared in May 1794 on the militias in the Quebec area concluded that most of the companies called would probably not take up arms against France. On the other hand, an assembly of militiamen held in Berthier near Montreal denounced the execution of Louis XVI and warned the citizens against "the diabolical doings of these inhuman men [the French Republicans]" – *Gazette de Québec*, May 16, 1793.

58 Mackay, Daniel S. C., "Les Royal Canadian Volunteers," *Journal de l'organisation des musées militaires du Canada*, VI (1977), pp. 1-17; Neilson, J. L. Hubert, *The Royal Canadian Volunteers 1794-1802: An Historical Sketch* (Montreal, 1895), pp. 1-8.

59 Much of the correspondence concerning this regiment, including the many types of dress, may be

found in NAC, RG8, volumes C792, C793, C794, C795. Volumes C1167 1/2 et C1203 1/2 are regimental order books. See also the "Prescott Papers" MG 23, K5. Lord Dorchester, in his January 31, 1795, request for uniforms from the Duke of Portland, mentioned round hats, but he received cocked hats – PRO, Colonial Office 42, Vol. 101.

[60] In 1810, the New Brunswick Fencibles offered to serve everywhere in the world, like the British regiments. The offer was accepted and it became the 104th Regiment, continuing for the moment its service in New Brunswick.

[61] "The acquisition of Canada...will be a mere matter of marching," quoted in White, Patrick C. T., *A Nation on Trial: America and the War of 1812* (New York: John Wiley, 1965), p. 126.

[62] *Gazette de Montréal*, April 13, 1812.

[63] NAC, RG9, Vol. 3, Jean-Baptiste Hertel de Rouville to François Vassal de Monviel, Chambly, May 17, 1812. There was so much red cloth used in 1812 that there was hardly any left when the time came to replace the uniforms, and in 1813 most of the militiamen wore green coats trimmed in red with white braid. Red was worn once again in 1814 and 1815, after uniforms arrived from England.

[64] PRO, Colonial Office 42, Vol. 146, George Prevost to Lord Liverpool, Quebec, May 18, 1812.

[65] Quoted in Hitsman, John Mackay, *The Incredible War of 1812: A Military History* (Toronto: University of Toronto Press, 1965), p. 61.

[66] Dunlop, William, *Recollections of the American War, 1812-14* (Toronto: Historical Publishing, 1905), p. 13.

[67] Long after Wilkinson's death in 1824, Louisiana historian Charles Gayarré discovered that prior to the War of 1812 he had accepted a fortune in gold from the Spanish, who secretly bought his cooperation and influence with the American authorities in connection with the drawing of the American boundaries with New Spain. See Archer, Christon, *The Army in Bourbon Mexico, 1764-1810* (Albuquerque: University of New Mexico, 1977) and Gayarré, Charles, *History of Louisiana* (New York: 1854), Vol. 2.

[68] The exercise did not concern only weapons handling, but also tactical manoeuvres and the movements of armies on the field of battle. It had considerable impact on the conduct of battle in the Napoleonic wars and was adopted with varying degrees of modification by most European armies. See Graves, Donald E., *The Battle of Lundy's Lane on the Niagara in 1814* (Baltimore: Nautical & Aviation Publishing, 1993).

[69] In August 1814 in Washington, British troops destroyed public buildings, including the Capitol and the President's residence, to avenge similar acts committed by the American army at York (Toronto) the preceding year. Before burning the residence of the President, the soldiers of the 21st British Regiment feasted on the presidential dinner that had been left hurriedly by Madison and his guests.

[70] This agreement nevertheless came too late to prevent the failure of a major British raid on New Orleans, which was defended by American General Andrew Jackson. The battle, which took place on January 8, 1815, had no strategic impact in spite of all the romanticism Americans have since attached to it.

[71] In 1830, President Andrew Jackson and Congress took away the land of the Amerindian nations to the south of the United States, whether friends or enemies, and ordered them to leave and settle west of the Mississippi. The Supreme Court was opposed to this, but Jackson overruled it and ordered the army to "get them out." About 30,000 people were rounded up by force and often chained, to follow what truly became "the trail of tears," more than a quarter of them dying along the way. See Cooke, Alistair, *America* (New York: Alfred A. Knopf, 1973), pp. 168-170.

[72] Pelletier, Oscar C., *Mémoires, souvenirs de familles et récits* (Quebec City: 1940), p. 50.

[73] A couplet from the play by George Farquhar, The Recruiting Officer, produced in April 1706 and quoted in *The Rambling Soldier: Life in the Lower Ranks, 1750-1900, Through Soldiers' Songs and Writings*, ed. Roy Palmer (London: Penguin, 1977), p. 9.

[74] PRO, War Office 34/2, James Murray to Jeffery Amherst, Quebec, August 27, 1763.

[75] In Grose, Frances, *A Dictionary of Buckish Slang, University Wit and Pickpocket Eloquence* (London: 1811), reprinted under the title *1811 Dictionary of the Vulgar Tongue* (Chicago: Follett, 1971), q.v.

[76] *Ibid.*, see for a detailed description. In some regiments, the newly married officers were also subjected to this tradition.

[77] The sergeants living in the barracks had a small room with a wooden partition at the end of the room.

[78] For example, between October 1826 and March 1827, 20,650 gallons of rum were sold in Montreal. This quantity no doubt corresponded to the rum ration occasionally given to soldiers and for supplies for the regimental canteens in the barracks. Yet the garrison in Upper and Lower Canada was only 3,000 soldiers. The alcohol consumed in bars also has to be taken into account. ANQM, registry of J.-M. Mondelet, Nos. 580, 587, 589, 594.

[79] Aubert de Gaspé, Philippe, *Mémoires* (Quebec City: 1885), pp. 32-33. After this punishment, the soldier was taken to the infirmary, where he stayed for at least three weeks recovering, his back covered in bandages soaked in sugar and lead oil (*plumbi acetas*). The surgeon could interrupt the punishment if he felt that the convicted man's life was in danger, because a few unfortunate ones did die. But an interruption is all that it was, and after the soldier was healed the rest of the sentence would be administered.

[80] PRO, War Office 34, Vol. 4, James Pitcher to Jeffery Amherst, Quebec, September 23, 1763.

[81] Based on a number of stereotypes, British officers of the period were for a long time depicted as ignorant and licentious. Nothing could be further from the truth, as demonstrated by John A. Houlding's excellent study, *Fit for Service: The Training of the British Army, 1715-1795* (Oxford: Clarendon, 1981).

[82] See Lacelle, Claudette, *La garnison britannique dans la ville de Québec d'après les journaux de 1764 à 1840* (Ottawa: Parks Canada, 1979), pp. 55-56.

[83] Cuthberston, Bennett, *A System for the Complete Interior Management and Oeconomy of a Battalion of Infantry* (London: 1769), p. 23.

[84] Garneau, François-Xavier, *Voyage en Angleterre et en France dans les années 1831, 1832 et 1833*, ed. Paul Wyczynski (Ottawa: University of Ottawa, 1968), p. 118. In 1831, Lieutenant Marlay and Garneau, the

French-Canadian man of letters, boarded the same ship at Quebec for London.

85 Hunter, Robert, *Quebec to Carolina in 1785-1786*, ed. Louis B. Wright and Marion Tinling (San Marino: Huntington Library, 1943), p. 108.

86 NAC, RG8, C1247, Duke of Richmond to the Secretary of State for War and the Colonies, Lord Bathurst, Quebec, November 10, 1818. The Duke of Richmond, an experienced military man, was appointed governor-in-chief of British North America in May 1818, and he personally inspected the border. He died accidentally the following year near present-day Ottawa while on a reconnaissance mission. His recommendations were ratified by the Duke of Wellington.

87 *Despatches, Correspondence, and Memoranda of Field Marshal Arthur Duke of Wellington*, edited by his son, the Duke of Wellington (London: John Murray, 1867), Vol. 1, p. 46.

88 Figures for the Rideau Canal are often contradictory. For some enlightenment, see Raudzens, George, *The British Ordnance Department and Canada's Canals, 1815-1855* (Waterloo: Wilfrid Laurier University, 1979). The budgets for the Royal Navy are based on Clowes, William Laird, *The Royal Navy: A History, From the Earliest Times to the Present* (London: Sampson, Low, Marston, 1901), Vol. VI, p. 190.

89 Jackman, Alonzo, "Journal of Alonzo Jackman's Excursion to Quebec, 1838," ed. Gary T. Lord, *Vermont History*, XLVI, No. 4, 1978, p. 256.

90 David, Laurent-Olivier, *Mélanges historiques et littéraires* (Montreal: Beauchemin, 1917), p. 267.

91 SRO, Dalhousie Papers, Confidential Report, Quebec, May 26, 1824.

92 SRO, Dalhousie Papers, Lord Dalhousie to Lord Bathurst, Quebec, December 19, 1823.

93 NAC, RG9, IA1, Vol. 82, François Vassal de Monviel to P.-H. Bédard, Esq. Quebec, December 5, 1823.

94 SRO, Dalhousie Papers, June 1, 1828, in which Dalhousie asks that the officers wear a grey or blue frock with a crimson sash. Several units reported having adopted blue frocks with sashes the following year - NAC, RG9, IA1, Vol. 34-35; the Beauce cavalry was mentioned in the *Quebec Mercury* on May 9, 1829.

95 NAC, RG4, A1, Vol. 620, British Rifle Corps, Montreal, December 16, 1835. This document, submitted to the governor, Lord Gosford, had 393 signatures on it. It would appear that these people preferred to form their own unit rather than join the Montreal Rifle Corps, which existed already, because this corps of volunteers was at the time commanded by Sabrevois de Bleury, a French-Canadian gentleman who was said to be a friend of Papineau and who had probably been appointed to reconcile the French population with the militia.

96 Papineau, Amédée, *Journal d'un Fils de la Liberté réfugié aux États-Unis par la suite de l'insurrection canadienne, en 1837* (Montreal: Étincelle, 1978), Vol. II, pp. 46-47.

97 Quoted in Senior, Elinor Kyte, *Redcoats & Patriotes: The Rebellions in Lower Canada, 1837-38* (Ottawa: Canadian War Museum, 1985), p. 137. The sacking of the Spanish city of Badajos, which was defended by the French in 1812, took place after a horribly bloody assault by the British army. Completely unhinged and made crazy by the violence of battle, the soldiers lost all discipline and went on a rampage of theft, sacking, drunkenness and rape. It took three days to restore order. No rapes were reported at Saint-Eustache because the women had vacated the town, with the children, prior to the battle.

98 Jean-Joseph Girouard to M. Morin, April 28, 1838, quoted in *Les Patriotes, 1830-1838*, ed. and compiled John Hare (Montreal: Libération, 1971), p. 144.

99 These were the Loyal St. Andrews Volunteers, some members of which successfully limited the pillage. Wales, B. A., *Memories of Old St. Andrews and Historical Sketch of the Seignory of Argenteuil* (Lachute: Watchman, 1934), p. 114.

100 *Mémoires de Robert S.-M. Bouchette, 1805-1840*, collected by his son and annotated by De Celles, A.-D., (Montreal: 1903), pp. 57-58.

101 This ploy was not as naïve as it may have appeared. It was used successfully by insurgents in India during the Indian Mutiny in 1857. From this period on British soldiers were ordered to attend religious services with their rifles.

102 Prieur, François-Xavier, *Notes d'un condamné politique de 1838* (Montreal: 1884), p. 11. The Patriotes also made a few cannons out of wood with steel bands around them, which did not work "because they could not withstand the demands of transportation," noted Prieur.

103 John Prince was investigated and acquitted. For more details about the battles of Pelee Island and Windsor, as well as the investigation that followed, see *John Prince: A Collection of Documents*, ed. R. Alan Douglas (Toronto: Champlain Society, 1980). It is worth noting that Prince's prejudices, to the effect that one could not trust the French Canadians at Windsor, proved to be totally unfounded. Some of the volunteers at the battle of Windsor were French Canadians under the command of Captain S.-J. Thebo (Thibault), of the 2nd Essex County Militia Regiment. This regiment consisted largely of French Canadians, including approximately 15 of its 35 officers.

104 NAC, RG4, B14, Vol. 2, Hawthornelock to Cathcart, D. Daly and Campbell, April 27, 1840. This organization was similar to the paramilitary constabulary force deployed in Ireland. See *Rules for the Government of the Rural Police* (Montreal: 1839). According to the *Bytown Gazette* of June 11, 1840, there were 30 constables in the Rural Police, 10 of whom were mounted, in each of its nine districts. The Montreal police had 106 men, four mounted, and the Quebec City police 83. Beginning in 1842, these two police corps were reduced by half. NAC, RG4, B14, Vol. 26, W. Coffin to the clerks of the cities of Montreal and Quebec, December 26 and 31, 1841.

105 PRO, War Office 1, Vol. 536, Memorandum upon the Canadian Frontier, November 1840.

106 PRO, War Office 1, Vol. 537, Memorandum on the Defence of Her Majesty's Dominions in North America, March 31, 1841.

107 In March 1840 police constables abandoned their sabres, firearms and military dress for a simple stick and a blue coat and top hat, the almost civilian uniform worn by policemen at the time so that they would look more like ordinary citizens. The Rural Police and the Quebec police were dissolved on January 1, 1843, and the Montreal police on the 23rd.

NAC, RG4, B14, Vol. 27, letters dated December 1842 and January 1843.

[108] NAC, RG9, IC1, Vol. 119, Lieutenant-Colonel Étienne-Pascal Taché to an unknown addressee, Montreal, September 8, 1846.

[109] Fréchette, Louis, *Mémoires intimes*, ed. George A. Klinck (Montreal: Fides, 1974), p. 121.

[110] Young, James, *Reminiscences of the Early History of Galt and the Settlement of Dumfries in the Province of Ontario* (Toronto: 1880), pp. 236-238.

[111] *La Patrie*, Montreal, November 10, 1854.

[112] In 1858 fears of an invasion by France became widespread among the people of the British Isles, although the two countries were at peace. In a tide of patriotic fervour inspired by Tennyson's verses of "Form! Riflemen, Form!," tens of thousands of men were raised in record time for the volunteer companies. In only a few months, this Volunteer Movement led to the creation of the British reserve army, which exists to this day.

[113] The subdivisions of the North Atlantic Squadron varied depending on the era. For example, at the time of the Fenian raids, throughout the 1860s, there were four permanent divisions (Barbados, Jamaica, Bermuda and Halifax, which was also the headquarters) and a temporary division that covered the St. Lawrence River and the Great Lakes.

[114] Breech-loading created a number of problems and the British returned to muzzle-loading in 1869. Technical progress solved these problems and breech-loading was adopted in the 1880s.

[115] The HMS *Erebus* had an unusual career. Built as a bomb galley in 1808, it was modified to a rocket-launching vessel and attached to the North Atlantic Squadron during the War of 1812. The rockets it fired against Fort McHenry during the night of September 13-14, 1814, inspired lawyer Francis Scott Key to write the American national anthem. One of the most celebrated verses of "The Star Spangled Banner" is "by the rocket's red glare...our Flag was still there"; indeed on that night the only way of knowing whether the fort was still resisting was if one could see the American flag by the light of the rockets. The Erebus, which was very solidly built, was occasionally assigned to Arctic exploration. It was part of the Ross expedition from 1841 to 1843 and, of course, the Franklin expedition as well. Since 1848, it has rested at the bottom of the Arctic, together with the HMS *Terror*.

[116] The actual Northwest Passage was crossed for the first time from east to west between 1903 and 1906, by Norwegian explorer Roald Amundsen on the *Gjoa*. The second time, it was by Sergeant Henry Larsen of the Royal Canadian Mounted Police on the *St. Roch*; he made the voyage from west to east from 1940 to 1942, and then from east to west in 1944. The *St. Roch* thus became the first Canadian vessel to cross the famous passage, the first ship to cross it in both directions, and the first to complete the task in less than a year. This outstanding small RCMP schooner is now kept by Parks Canada at the Vancouver Maritime Museum.

[117] This Fort Garry was not the first to be built at the junction of the Red and Assiniboine rivers. It was preceded by others, including Fort Rouge, built by La Vérendrye in 1738, and Fort Gibraltar, which was erected by the North West Company in 1804. Another Fort Garry, the first to be built of stone, was erected on this site in the early 1820s and abandoned some 10 years later. In 1835, construction, also in stone, began on the second Fort Garry, often called Upper Fort Garry, which was the administrative centre of the Hudson's Bay Company for several decades and which was to become the core of the city of Winnipeg. A stone gate, today located downtown, is the only vestige of Upper Fort Garry. Fortunately, Lower Fort Garry was not destroyed. This magnificent fort, one of the gems of our commercial and military heritage, is preserved by Parks Canada as an historic national site.

[118] Manitoba Archives, MG2, B7-1, Red River Volunteers attestations, Fort Garry, February and March 1835. The commander received £20 per year, each sergeant £10 and each volunteer £6.

[119] Quoted in McKelvie, B. A., and W. E. Ireland, "The Victoria Voltigeurs," in *British Columbia Historical Quarterly*, XX, 1956, p. 228.

[120] PRO, War Office 1, Vol. 551, note from Colonel Mundy, dated July 27, 1854, and letter from Governor James Douglas dated August 5, 1854.

[121] On November 16, 1863, 22 officers and soldiers along with eight women and 17 children departed for England. There was an emotional farewell ceremony. The band of the Royal Engineers played "Auld Lang Syne" and "Home Sweet Home," with the people and seamen assembled in the port as the ship left while joining in the singing. See Woodward, Frances M., "The Influence of the Royal Engineers on the Development of British Columbia," in *BC Studies*, No. 24, winter 1974-75.

[122] This was the same George Pickett who, after becoming a general in the Confederate army, commanded the famous "Pickett's Charge" at the battle of Gettysburg in 1863 during the American Civil War.

[123] The Treaty of Washington was signed in 1871, but the matter of San Juan Island was settled only after mediation by the German Emperor, who granted the island and the neighbouring archipelago to the United States on October 21, 1872.

[124] For details on the lesser-known campaigns, see the excellent study by Gough, Barry M., *Gunboat Frontier: British Maritime Authority and Northwest Coast Indians, 1846-1890* (Vancouver: University of British Columbia, 1984).

[125] PRO, Colonial Office 61, Vol. 1, "Laws of Britain to be in force in British Columbia," November 19, 1858.

[126] In 1864, the Victoria Volunteer Rifle Corps adopted a white and blue uniform similar to the one worn by the Austrian infantry! This uniform, which was criticized by the press, was changed the following year to an austere green-black one imported from England, which was similar to the one worn by the 60th King's Royal Rifle Corps. In December 1873, following British Columbia's union with Canada and the attendant reorganization of the corps of volunteers, the Victoria Volunteer Rifle Corps was disbanded to make way for the creation of two new companies of riflemen, which were to include some of its members. Lovatt, R., "Les voltigeurs, les fusiliers et les artilleurs de Victoria (C.-B,) 1851-1873," *Journal de l'organisation des musées militaires du Canada*, VI, 1977.

127 The New Westminster Home Guards disappeared around 1871, but the Seymour Artillery survived and was incorporated into the Royal Canadian Artillery.

128 Quoted in Stacey, C. P., *Canada and the British Army, 1846-1871: A Study in the Practice of Responsible Government* (Toronto: University of Toronto Press, 1963), p. 138.

129 Davis, R. H., *The Canadian Militia: Its Organization and Present Condition* (Caledonia: 1873), p. 11.

130 Spencer rifles were issued to a number of volunteer artillery and infantry units in Ontario, and Westley-Richards were issued to the Montreal volunteers. For additional details, see Chartrand, René, "American Breech-Loading Firearms in the Canadian Service, 1866-1872," *Arms Collecting*, XXIV, 1986.

131 A 10th district was created in 1870 for Manitoba, and an 11th for British Columbia the following year.

132 For example, the Halifax Battalion, created on May 14, 1860, was assigned the number 63 when it was really the third volunteer battalion to have been established in British North America. The 1st Battalion was created in Montreal on November 17, 1859, the 2nd in Toronto in April 1860, the 3rd, 4th, 5th and 6th in Montreal in January 1862, the 7th, 8th and 9th in Quebec in February and March 1862, the 10th in Toronto and the 11th in Saint-André d'Argenteuil on March 14, 1862, the 12th in Toronto on October 29, 1862, the 13th in Hamilton on December 11, 1862, the 14th in Kingston and the 15th in Belleville in January 1863, the 16th in Picton and the 17th in Lévis in February 1863, and so on. See Jackson, H. M., *The Roll of the Regiments* (The Active Militia), s.l., 1959.

133 NAC, RG9, Vol. 279, Adjutant-General to Captain James O'Reilly, March 10, 1857; Adjutant-General to Colonel Moffat, March 11 and 20, 1856. Captain O'Reilly's Kingston Irish Rifles company wore a green uniform with a pale-green collar, cuffs and shako feather, reminiscent of the national colour of Ireland.

134 From March 1 to August 31, 1858, 1,506 men enlisted. Most came from Ontario; fewer than 20 percent came from Quebec and there do not appear to have been any French Canadians among the recruits. It has sometimes been stated that the many sons of the veterans of the 100th regiment of the War of 1812 established along the Rideau River filled the ranks of the new 100th, which is erroneous; only three recruits from this group have been identified.

135 The number of French Canadians who served in the Union army remains very difficult to determine. In an 1868 speech, Georges-Étienne Cartier spoke of 50,000, which seems very high given that it represents almost the whole population of French Canadians in New England. Here, we are clearly speaking of Americans of Canadian descent already living in the United States, and not of volunteers who left from Canada. See Brault, Gérard-J., *The French-Canadian Heritage in New England* (Kingston and Montreal: McGill-Queen's University Press, 1986). There appear to have been few volunteers who left Canada to join the Union army.

136 Maximilian, brother of the Austrian Emperor, was crowned Emperor of Mexico, but it took a French garrison of some 35,000 men to keep him on the throne. Most Mexicans supported the republican forces of President Benito Juarez, who were fighting to restore their country's independence. For further details, see Chartrand, René, *The Mexican Adventure, 1861-1867* (London: Osprey Military, 1994).

137 Russel, W. Howard, *Canada: Its Defences, Condition, and Resources* (London: 1865, p. 219).

138 Quoted in Pariseau, Jean, and Serge Bernier, *Les Canadiens français et le bilinguisme dans les Forces armées canadiennes, Tome I, 1763-1969: le spectre d'une armée bicéphale* (Ottawa: Directorate of History, Department of National Defence, 1987), p. 50. The statutes and reports submitted to Parliament which were published in the records of the session, and the regulations which appeared in the Official Gazette were translated into French, but many other regulations and manuals, not to mention internal reports, were not. It was only in 1969, with the adoption of the Official Languages Act, that the use of French in federal departments became compulsory.

139 *Organisation militaire des Canadas. L'Ennemi! L'Ennemi!*, by A Rifleman (Quebec: 1862), p. 29.

140 NAC, RG9, IC8, Vol. 3. Commanding officer's reports, 4th Battalion, "Chasseurs canadiens" de Montréal, November 10, 1862.

141 In 1875, the matter of the Zouave uniform was submitted to the War Office, which deemed that the "national" colour of red was to be used by the Canadian militia. The question was again raised four years later and the proposal was rejected once again because, it was said, the Americans used grey (their uniform was dark blue with sky-blue trousers) and because it was not a French uniform. NAC, MG26, A, Vol. 307.

142 The century to follow was, moreover, all to the credit of the few Francophone Quebec units, who were able to promote French Canada's military heritage in spite of repeated harassment and humiliation. Many of those who were attracted to military life joined the companies of "Zouaves pontificaux canadiens" being established in many parishes in the 1870s, which were paramilitary organizations that they controlled and that enjoyed the enormous prestige the Church had at the time. Thus in this parallel volunteer militia, the red uniforms of the English were not worn, and its members did not have to put up with objections to their language, culture and faith. An incident that occurred in 1877 reflects the tensions between the communities and the values that underlay them. On a boat trip to Ottawa, a number of Pontifical Zouaves of that city caused a scandal by replacing the Union Jack with their own flag on the main mast of the ship. Captain Simmonds succeeded in having the Union Jack replaced, because it was required by law, and the Zouaves raised their flag on another mast. The incident was reported in the Ottawa *Daily Citizen* of July 3, 1877, and the Ottawa Loyalist Association awarded Simmonds a medal for upholding the honour of the British flag! The medal is kept in the Canadian War Museum.

143 For example, officers in the Canadian volunteer artillery went so far as to adopt not only the uniform of the British Royal Artillery, but the badges as well, in addition to its motto, "Ubique," in commemoration of its services around the world. This amused the British, and the wife of Governor-General Monck noted that the Canadian officers wearing these badges would be more aptly described as having been "nowhere"! Monck, Elizabeth, *My Canadian Leaves* (Dorchester:

Dorset County Express, 1873), pp. 139-140. The Adjutant-General of the militia took steps "in a quiet way" to have the Canadian officers remove the word "Ubique" from their badges. Col. P. L. McDougall to Captain R. H. de Montmorency, Ottawa, June 14, 1867. NAC, RG9, IC1, Vol. 286.

[144] The data on the number of Fenians who took part in this final invasion attempt vary considerably. Not only did Canadians overestimate their number, but there is still a significant gap between the number of contingents promised and those who in fact took part in the raids. Thus the 1st Vermont Fenian regiment mustered only 65 men instead of the 600 promised, the 2nd Massachusetts 140 instead of 1,000. See Toner, Peter M., "The Military Organisation of the 'Canadian' Fenians, 1866-1870," *The Irish Sword*, X, 1971, pp. 26-37.

[145] Several companies of volunteer militia were raised in Manitoba during October. See Tascona, Bruce, "The Independent Companies of Manitoba, 1871-1884," *Journal of the Military History Society of Manitoba*, 1992, pp. 5-12.

CHRONOLOGY OF MAJOR BATTLES 1755-1870

1755

June 3 – 16: 2,000 Anglo–Americans besiege and take Fort Beauséjour, New Brunswick.

June 8: The British fleet carries out a surprise attack on a French convoy off the coast of Newfoundland and takes two ships; the others manage to escape.

July 9: Battle of the Monongahela, Pennsylvania: 250 soldiers and militiamen, accompanied by 600 Amerindians, defeat 2,200 British soldiers.

August 8: The French ambush a corps of American troops near Fort Edward, New York.

September 8: An attack led by French General Dieskau at Lake George, New York, is repelled by American troops led by Colonel William Johnson.

1756

March 27: The French and the Canadians take Fort Bull, New York, with the help of Amerindians.

August 10 – 14: General Montcalm, leading 3,000 men, attacks and takes British forts at Oswego, New York, defended by Colonel Mercer and 1,800 men.

1757

March: François-Pierre de Rigaud de Vaudreuil leads 1,200 men on successful raids near Fort William Henry (Lake George, New York).

August 3 – 6: Montcalm, with 6,000 French and Canadians, supported by 1,600 Amerindians, attacks and takes Fort William Henry, defended by 2,500 men under the command of Lieutenant-Colonel George Monroe.

1758

June 2 – July 26: The British lay siege to and take the Fortress of Louisbourg.

July 8: The Battle of Carillon (Ticonderoga, New York): Montcalm, with 3,600 men, wards off an attack by a 15,000–man Anglo-American army commanded by Major-General James Abercromby.

August 25 – 28: Lieutenant-Colonel John Bradstreet, leading 3,000 Anglo-Americans, attacks and takes Fort Frontenac (Kingston, Ontario).

September 14: The French repulse a British attack near Fort Duquesne (Pittsburgh, Pennsylvania).

October and November: The French carry out victorious raids near Fort Ligonier, Pennsylvania.

1759

End of June – September 17: General James Wolfe attacks Quebec with 23,000 British seamen and soldiers; the city is defended by 15,000 soldiers and militiamen.

July 9 – 25: Successful siege of Fort Niagara, which is taken.

July 24: Battle of La Belle Famille (near Fort Niagara): the Anglo-Americans, supported by the Amerindians, crush French reinforcements from Ohio.

July 31: British troops attempt to disembark at Montmorency, near Quebec, and are repulsed by the French army.

September 13: Battle of the Plains of Abraham: Wolfe defeats Montcalm.

1760

April 28: The French and the Canadians rout the British at Sainte-Foy near Quebec City.

May 15: The French frigate the *Atalante* is taken near Cap Rouge, Quebec.

July: A fleet commanded by Lieutenant François Chenard de la Giraudais, consisting of four cargo vessels and the frigate Machault, is pursued all the way to Restigouche and defeated on July 8 by five British ships under the command of Captain John Byron.

August 17: The British take the French ship the *Outaouaise* at Pointe au Baril (near Prescott, Ontario).

August 18 – 25: The British lay siege to and take Fort Lévis (near Prescott, Ontario).

August 16 – 28: An Anglo-American army lays siege to Île-aux-Noix, Quebec; the French forces evacuate the island during the night of August 27-28.

1762

June 24 and September 13: A French fleet with 650 soldiers under the command of Chevalier de Ternay capture Bay Bulls and St. John's, Newfoundland, on June 24; on September 13 the British retake St. John's.

1763

May – June: A federation of the Amerindian nations of the Great Lakes area rally around Algonquin Chief Pontiac and takes several forts between Michilimackinac and Pittsburgh.

May – October: Some 1,000 Amerindians under Pontiac lay siege to Fort Detroit, defended by 450 men under the command of Major Henry Gladwyn.

July 29: At Ruisseau Parent (later renamed Bloody Run), James Dalyell, with 247 men, loses a night battle against Amerindians outside Fort Detroit.

August 6: Colonel Henry Bouquet's army crushes the Amerindians at Bushy Run, Pennsylvania.

1775

September 18 – November 3: 2,000 Americans led by General Richard Montgomery lay siege to and take Fort Saint-Jean (Saint-Jean, Quebec), which has in garrison 522 soldiers and 90 Canadian militiamen under the command of Major Charles Preston.

October 18: Fort Chambly surrenders to the Americans.

November 25: Canadian militiamen and British soldiers defeat an American army commanded by Ethan Allen at Longue-Pointe near Montreal.

December 6 – May 6, 1776: The Americans lay siege to Quebec.

December 31: American assaults on Quebec are repelled.

1776

June 8: The British fend off an American counterattack near Trois-Rivières, Quebec.

June 19 and 21: At Vaudreuil, to the west of Montreal, British soldiers, Canadian militiamen and Amerindians take Fort-aux-Cèdres and prepare an ambush, which defeats the Americans.

November 4: At Valcour Island, New York, the British fleet, commanded by Captain Thomas Pringle, defeats the American fleet on Lake Champlain, commanded by Benedict Arnold.

November 10 – December 28: American troops under the command of Jonathan Eddy lay siege to Fort Cumberland (formerly Fort Beauséjour), defended by Loyalist soldiers; the siege is lifted when British reinforcements arrive.

1777

August 6: At Oriskany, near Fort Stanwix (Rome, New York), a troop of Amerindians and Butler's Rangers defeats the Americans; the British then unsuccessfully lay siege to the fort during the month of August.

October 17: The British army is defeated at Saratoga, New York.

1778

July 3 – 4: Colonel John Butler carries out a series of raids in the Wyoming Valley, Pennsylvania, with his Rangers and with Amerindian support.

November 11: A troop of 520 men, consisting of Butler's Rangers and Amerindians, attacks Cherry Valley (near Albany, New York).

1781

July 21: Two French warships, the *Astrée* and the *Hermine*, under the command of Jean-François Galaup de Lapérouse, attack a British convoy near Cape Breton Island and take two ships.

1812

August 5 and 12: At Brownstown and Maguaga, Michigan, British and Canadian soldiers and Amerindians rout American reinforcements sent to defend Detroit.

August 15 – 16: British forces, commanded by General Isaac Brock, lay siege to and take Detroit.

October 9: The Americans take the *Caledonia* and destroy the *Detroit* near Fort Erie.

October 13: The Americans are warded off at the Battle of Queenston Heights (Ontario).

1813

January 22: The Americans are crushed at Frenchtown (Monroe, Michigan).

February 22: Lieutenant-Colonel George Macdonell takes Ogdensburg, New York, with detachments of the Glengarry Light Infantry and the 8th Regiment, as well as some militiamen.

April 27: The Americans take York (Toronto).

May 1 – 7: The British and Amerindians lay siege to Fort Meigs, Ohio; they do not succeed in taking it, but do crush the American reinforcements.

May 27: The Americans take Newark (Niagara-on-the-lake, Ontario) and Fort George.

May 28: A British attack on Sacket's Harbor, New York, fails.

June 3: British soldiers and Canadian militiamen take the American vessels the *Growler* and the *Eagle* at Île-aux-Noix.

June 6: The Americans are repulsed at Stoney Creek, Ontario.

June 24: The Amerindians defeat the Americans at Beaver Dam, Ontario.

July 2: The British and Amerindians are repulsed at Fort Stephenson, Ohio.

September 10: At Put-In-Bay, Ohio, an American squadron of nine ships defeats a squadron of six British ships.

September 28: The British fleet of Sir James Lucas Yeo is forced to retreat by the fleet of American Commodore Isaac Chauncey near Burlington, Ontario.

October 5: The British and Amerindians are defeated at Moraviantown, Ontario.

October 26: General Hampton's American army is defeated by an advance party of Canadians at Allen's Corners, along the Châteauguay River in Quebec.

November 11: General Wilkinson's American army is defeated at Crysler's Farm (Morrisburg, Ontario) by a British and Canadian corps.

December 16: The British take Fort Niagara.

1814

May 6: The British take Oswego, New York.

July 5: The Americans are victorious at Chippewa, Ontario.

July 19: The Amerindians are victorious over an American column at Rock River Rapids, Wisconsin.

July 25: An Anglo-Canadian army repels the American army at Lundy's Lane, Ontario.

August 4: An American attack on Mackinac, Michigan, is repulsed.

August 13 – September 21: The British and the Canadians unsuccessfully lay siege to Fort Erie, Ontario.

September 3: The British rout the Americans at Hampden, Maine.

September 3 and 6: The American ships the *Tigress* and the *Scorpion* are taken.

September 11: British and Canadian forces are defeated at Plattsburgh, New York.

1816

June 19: At Seven Oaks (Winnipeg), during a battle between the Métis and Amerindians of the North West Company, under the command of Cuthbert Grant, and the Scottish colonists of the Hudson's Bay Company, led by Governor Robert Semple, Semple and 20 colonists are killed.

1837

November 23: The Patriotes defeat British troops at Saint-Denis, Quebec.

November 25: British troops defeat the Patriotes at Saint-Charles, Quebec.

December 7: Militiamen repel the Patriots at Montgomery's Tavern, north of Toronto.

December 14: British troops and loyal volunteers defeat the Patriotes at Saint-Eustache, Quebec.

December 29: The Patriot ship the *Caroline* is taken and destroyed.

1838

January 8 – 9: The militia repel a Patriot attack on Amherstburg, Ontario.

March 3: A Patriot attack is repelled at Pelee Island, Ontario.

December 4: The Patriots are repelled at Windsor, Ontario.

December 7 and 9: The Patriotes are defeated at Lacolle and Odelltown, Quebec.

December 11 – 16: The Patriots are besieged in a windmill near Prescott, Ontario.

1851

July 19: An officer and some seamen of the HMS *Daedalus*, searching for Amerindian murderers, are injured by the Newittys at Bull Harbour, British Columbia; the seamen attack and raze the village.

1858

August: Ambushes and combats cause many deaths in the Okanagan and Fraser valleys (in British Columbia) between gold-diggers, mostly American, and Amerindians; the two sides make peace at the end of the month before the arrival of troops sent in to restore order.

1861

May 17: The HMS *Forward* shells the Haida camp of Cape Mudge as a form of reprisal against acts of piracy; the guilty are arrested.

1863

April – June: The HMS *Forward* shells an Amerindian village on Kuper Island, British Columbia, after some colonists are killed, and pursues Chief Acheewan for two months.

1864

April – August: Several workers and colonists die in ambushes by Chilcotin Amerindians in British Columbia during April and May; the HMS *Forward* and the HMS *Sutlej*, as well as volunteers, chase after them; after a few skirmishes, the Amerindians make peace and turn over the killers.

October 3 – 12: The Royal Navy shells and destroys nine Amerindian villages at Clayoquot, British Columbia.

1865

December 22: The Royal Navy shells and destroys an Amerindian village near Fort Rupert, British Columbia, to obtain the surrender of three Kwakiutl Amerindians who had killed a Newitty Amerindian.

1866

June 2: The Fenians defeat Canadian volunteers at Ridgeway and Fort Erie, Ontario.

June 8: The Fenians retreat at Pidgeon Hill, Quebec.

1869

May 3: The Royal Navy shells and destroys an Amerindian village at Hesquiat, British Columbia, because they pillaged a ship that had run aground and killed its survivors.

1870

May 25: Canadian volunteers repulse the Fenians at Eccles Hill, Quebec.

May 27: British troops and Canadian volunteers repulse the Fenians at Trout River, Quebec.

REGIMENTS AND UNITS SERVING IN CANADA 1755-1871

A large number of regiments and units were posted to locations in Canada and in what was to become the United States. Listed here are the names of the present-day Canadian provinces in which they served, as well as the years of service.

FRENCH ARMED FORCES
Army Troops
Artillery and Engineers

- Royal-Artillerie (detachments), 1756-60:Quebec, Ontario; 1762: Newfoundland.
- Corps royal du génie, 1755-60: Nova Scotia, Quebec, Ontario.

Infantry

- Régiment d'Artois (2nd Battalion), 1755-58: Nova Scotia.
- Régiment de Bourgogne (2nd Battalion), 1755-58: Nova Scotia.
- Régiment de Guyenne (2nd Battalion), 1755-60: Quebec, Ontario.
- Régiment de Béarn (2nd Battalion), 1755-60: Quebec, Ontario.
- Régiment de la Reine (2nd Battalion), 1755-60: Quebec, Ontario.
- Régiment de Languedoc (2nd Battalion), 1755-60: Quebec, Ontario.
- Régiment de la Sarre (2nd Battalion), 1756-60: Quebec, Ontario.
- Régiment Royal-Roussillon (2nd Battalion), 1756-60: Quebec, Ontario.
- Régiment de Berry (2nd and 3rd Battalions), 1757-60: Quebec, Ontario.
- Régiment de Cambis (2nd Battalion), 1758: Nova Scotia.
- Régiment des Volontaires-Étrangers (2nd Battalion), 1758: Nova Scotia.
- Detachments of the La Marine, Penthièvre, Beauvoisis and Montrevel regiments, 1762: Newfoundland.
- Detachments of the Armagnac and Auxerrois regiments, 1782: Manitoba.

Navy Troops

- Compagnies franches de la Marine (detached from ships), 1758: Nova Scotia.
- Bombardiers de la Marine (detachment), 1758: Nova Scotia.
- Corps royal d'infanterie de la Marine (detachment), 1782: Manitoba.

Colonial Troops

- Compagnies franches de la Marine of Canada, 1755-60: New Brunswick, Quebec, Ontario, Manitoba.
- Compagnies franches de la Marine of Île Royale, 1755-58, 1760: Nova Scotia, Prince Edward Island, New Brunswick.
- Canonniers-Bombardiers of Canada, 1755-60: New Brunswick, Quebec, Ontario.
- Canonniers-Bombardiers of Île Royale, 1755-58: Nova Scotia, New Brunswick.
- Canonniers-Bombardiers of Saint-Domingue (detachment), 1782: Manitoba.
- Ingénieurs des colonies, 1755-60: Nova Scotia, Quebec, Ontario; 1782: Manitoba.

Troops Raised in Canada

- Ouvriers d'artillerie, 1757-60: Quebec.
- Compagnie d'Irlandais (British deserters), 1757: Quebec.
- Corps de cavalerie, 1759-60: Quebec.

BRITISH ARMED FORCES
Army Troops
Cavalry

- 1st Dragoon Guards Regiment, 1839-43: Quebec, Ontario.
- 7th Hussars Regiment, 1838-43: Quebec.
- 13th Hussars Regiment, 1866-69: Quebec, Ontario.
- 19th Light Dragoons Regiment, 1813-16: Quebec, Ontario.

Artillery

- Royal Regiment of Artillery, 1755-1871: Newfoundland, Nova Scotia, New Brunswick, Prince Edward Island, Quebec, Ontario, Manitoba.
- Royal Irish Artillery, 1777: Quebec.

Engineers

- Corps of Royal Engineers, 1755-1871: Newfoundland, New Brunswick, Nova Scotia, Prince Edward Island, Quebec, Ontario; 1858-1863: British Columbia; 1870-1871: Manitoba.
- Company of sappers (to destroy Louisbourg), 1760-61: Nova Scotia.
- Royal Military Artificers, 1793-1812: Newfoundland, Nova Scotia, New Brunswick, Prince Edward Island.
- Royal Sappers and Miners, 1813-56: Quebec, Ontario; 1813-19, 1829-56: Nova Scotia; 1846-48: Manitoba; 1847-49: Northwest Territories.
- Royal Staff Corps. 1815-31: Nova Scotia, Quebec, Ontario.

Guards Infantry

- 1st Regiment (Grenadier Guards), 1838-42, 1862-63: Quebec.
- 2nd Regiment (Coldstream Guards), 1838-42: Quebec.
- 3rd Regiment (Scots Guards), 1862-64: Quebec.

Infantry

- 1st Regiment (1st Battalion), 1812-15: Quebec, Ontario; 2nd Battalion, 1757-63: Nova Scotia, Quebec, Newfoundland; 1836-51: Quebec, Ontario, Nova Scotia, New Brunswick; 4th Battalion, 1814-15: Quebec.
- 2nd Regiment, 1864-65: Nova Scotia.
- 3rd Regiment, 1814-15: Quebec.
- 4th Regiment, 1787-97: Nova Scotia, Quebec; 1866-68: Nova Scotia, Prince Edward Island.
- 5th Regiment, 1787-97, 1814-15: Quebec, Ontario.

- 6th Regiment, 1786-93: Nova Scotia; 1799-1806, 1814-15: Quebec, Ontario; 1846-48: Manitoba.
- 7th Regiment, 1773-76: Quebec; 1791-1802, 1808-10, 1848-50: Nova Scotia, Prince Edward Island.
- 8th Regiment, (1st Batallion) 1768-85: Quebec, Ontario; 1809-15: Nova Scotia, Quebec, Ontario; 1830-33, 1839-41: Nova Scotia, Prince Edward Island; (2nd Battalion) 1810-15: Nova Scotia, New Brunswick, Quebec.
- 9th Regiment, 1776-81: Quebec; 1814-15, 1856-57: Quebec, Ontario.
- 10th Regiment, 1767-68: Nova Scotia.
- 11th Regiment, 1838-40: New Brunswick, Quebec.
- 13th Regiment, 1813-15: Quebec.
- 14th Regiment, 1766-71, 1776: Nova Scotia; 1841-45: Quebec, Ontario, Nova Scotia, Prince Edward Island.
- 15th Regiment, 1758-61: Nova Scotia, Quebec; 1762-68: Quebec; 1817-21: Nova Scotia; 1827-40: Quebec, Ontario; 1862-68: New Brunswick; 1865-66: Prince Edward Island (detachment).
- 16th Regiment, 1790-91: Nova Scotia; 1814-15: Quebec, Ontario; 1861-70: Quebec, Ontario, Nova Scotia; 1865-66: Prince Edward Island (detachment).
- 17th Regiment, 1757-60 Nova Scotia, Quebec; 1762-67: Ontario; 1783-86, 1856-68: Nova Scotia, Quebec, Ontario.
- 19th Regiment, 1848-51: Quebec.
- 20th Regiment, 1776-77: Quebec; 1789-92: Nova Scotia; 1847-50: Quebec, Ontario.
- 21st Regiment, 1770-73, 1776-77: Quebec; 1789-93: Nova Scotia.
- 22nd Regiment, 1756-61, 1866-69: Nova Scotia, Quebec.
- 23rd Regiment, 1808-10: Nova Scotia; 1838-53: Nova Scotia, Quebec, Ontario, Prince Edward Island; 1866-67: Quebec.
- 24th Regiment, 1776-77: Quebec; 1789-1800: Quebec, Ontario, Nova Scotia; 1829-40: Quebec, Ontario.
- 25th Regiment, 1864-68: Quebec, Ontario.
- 26th Regiment, 1772-76: Quebec; 1787-1800, 1814-15: Quebec, Ontario; 1853-54: Quebec.
- 27th Regiment, 1759-61, 1763-67, 1814-15: Quebec.
- 28th Regiment, 1758-61: Nova Scotia, Quebec; 1764-67: Quebec.
- 29th Regiment, 1776-87: Quebec, Ontario; 1802-07, 1814-15: Nova Scotia; 1867-69: Quebec, Ontario.
- 30th Regiment, 1841-42: Nova Scotia, New Brunswick; 1861-69: Quebec, Ontario.
- 31st Regiment, 1779-87: Quebec.
- 32nd Regiment, 1830-41: Quebec, Ontario.
- 33rd Regiment, 1843-48: New Brunswick.
- 34th Regiment, 1776-87: Quebec; 1829-41: Nova Scotia, Prince Edward Island, New Brunswick, Quebec, Ontario.
- 35th Regiment, 1757-61: Nova Scotia, Quebec.
- 36th Regiment, 1839-42: New Brunswick.
- 37th Regiment, 1783-89: Nova Scotia, Newfoundland; 1814-25: Quebec, Ontario, Manitoba (small detachment in 1816); 1839-42: Nova Scotia, Prince Edward Island.
- 38th Regiment, 1783, 1848-51: Nova Scotia, Prince Edward Island.
- 39th Regiment, 1814-15, 1856-59: Quebec.
- 40th Regiment, 1755-64: Nova Scotia, Quebec, Newfoundland.
- 41st Regiment, 1799-1815: Quebec, Ontario.
- 42nd Regiment, 1759-61: Quebec; 1778-81: Newfoundland (detachment); 1782-89, 1851-52: Nova Scotia, Prince Edward Island.
- 43rd Regiment, 1757-61: Nova Scotia, Quebec; 1836-46: New Brunswick, Quebec, Ontario.
- 44th Regiment, 1758-65: Ontario, Quebec; 1780-86: Quebec.
- 45th Regiment, 1755-65: Nova Scotia, New Brunswick, Quebec (Grenadiers), Newfoundland.
- 46th Regiment, 1757-61: Nova Scotia, Ontario; 1763-67: Quebec; 1845-48: Nova Scotia, Ontario, Quebec.
- 47th Regiment, 1755-63: Nova Scotia, New Brunswick, Quebec; 1776-77: Quebec; 1790-91: Nova Scotia; 1861-68: Quebec, Ontario, Nova Scotia.
- 48th Regiment, 1757-61: Nova Scotia, Quebec.
- 49th Regiment, 1802-15: Quebec, Ontario.
- 52nd Regiment, 1765-74: Quebec; 1823-31: New Brunswick, Nova Scotia, Newfoundland, Prince Edward Island; 1842-45: New Brunswick, Nova Scotia, Prince Edward Island, Quebec.
- 53rd Regiment, 1776-89, 1866-69: Quebec, Ontario.
- 54th Regiment, 1783-91: Nova Scotia, New Brunswick; 1851-54: Quebec, Ontario.
- 55th Regiment, 1756-69: Nova Scotia, Ontario, Quebec.
- 56th Regiment, 1840-42: Quebec.
- 57th Regiment, 1783-91: Nova Scotia, New Brunswick; 1814-15: Quebec, Ontario.
- 58th Regiment. 1757-62: Nova Scotia, Quebec; 1814-15: Quebec.
- 59th Regiment, 1771-74: Nova Scotia.
- 60th Regiment, (1st Battalion) 1760-65: Quebec, Ontario; 1786-97: Nova Scotia, Newfoundland, Quebec, Ontario; 1820-24: Quebec, Ontario; 1867-71: Quebec, Ontario, Manitoba. (2nd Battalion) 1758-72: Nova Scotia, Quebec, Ontario; 1787-03, 1817-20, 1844-47: Quebec. (3rd Battalion) 1757-60: Nova Scotia, Quebec; 1816-24: Nova Scotia, Prince Edward Island, Newfoundland. (4th Battalion) 1758-63: Ontario, Quebec; 1858-68: Quebec, Ontario. (5th Battalion) 1803-05: Nova Scotia. (7th Battalion) 1814-17: Nova Scotia.
- 61st Regiment, 1870-72: Nova Scotia.
- 62nd Regiment, 1758-59: Nova Scotia, Quebec; 1776-77: Quebec; 1814-23: Nova Scotia, Prince Edward Island; 1856-64: Nova Scotia, New Brunswick, Quebec, Ontario.
- 63rd Regiment, 1856-65: Nova Scotia, New Brunswick, Quebec, Ontario.
- 64th Regiment, 1770-73, 1813-15: Nova Scotia; 1840-43: Nova Scotia, Prince Edward Island.
- 65th Regiment, 1769-76: Nova Scotia; 1785-93: Quebec, Ontario, New Brunswick; 1838-41: Nova Scotia.
- 66th Regiment, 1799-1802: Nova Scotia, Newfoundland; 1827-40: Quebec, Ontario; 1851-54: Quebec.
- 67th Regiment, 1840-42: Quebec.
- 68th Regiment, 1818-29: Quebec, Ontario; 1841-44: Quebec.
- 69th Regiment, 1839-42: Nova Scotia; 1867-70: Quebec, Ontario.
- 70th Regiment, 1778-83: Nova Scotia; 1813-27: Quebec, Ontario; 1841-42: Quebec.
- 71st Regiment, 1778-83 (detachment): Newfoundland; 1824-31, 1838-52: Quebec, Ontario.
- 72nd Regiment, 1851-54: Nova Scotia, Prince Edward Island.

- 73rd Regiment , 1838-41: Quebec, Ontario.
- 74th Regiment, 1778-79: Nova Scotia; 1818-28: Nova Scotia, New Brunswick, Prince Edward Island, Newfoundland; 1841-45: Quebec, Nova Scotia.
- 76th Regiment, 1814-27: Quebec, Ontario; 1841-42: Nova Scotia; 1850-57: New Brunswick, Prince Edward Island, Nova Scotia.
- 77th Regiment, 1758-61: Nova Scotia, Newfoundland, Ontario; 1846-48: Nova Scotia, Prince Edward Island, Quebec.
- 78th Regiment, 1757-63: Nova Scotia, Quebec, Newfoundland; 1867-71: Quebec, Nova Scotia.
- 79th Regiment, 1825-36: Quebec, Ontario; 1848-51: Quebec.
- 80th Regiment, 1758-63: Quebec, Ontario.
- 81st Regiment, 1814-15: Ontario; 1821-29: Nova Scotia, New Brunswick, Newfoundland, Prince Edward Island; 1843-47: Quebec, Ontario.
- 82nd Regiment, 1778-80, 1783: Nova Scotia; 1814-15, 1843-48: Quebec, Ontario.
- 83rd Regiment, 1834-43: Nova Scotia, Prince Edward Island, Quebec, Ontario.
- 84th Regiment (Royal Highland Emigrant, became the 84th in 1779); 1779-84: Quebec, Ontario, Nova Scotia, New Brunswick, Newfoundland; 1870-71: Nova Scotia.
- 85th Regiment, 1836-43: Nova Scotia, New Brunswick, Prince Edward Island, Quebec, Ontario.
- 88th Regiment, 1814-15: Quebec; 1850-51: Nova Scotia.
- 89th Regiment, 1812-15: Nova Scotia, Quebec, Ontario; 1841-47: Quebec, Nova Scotia, Prince Edward Island.
- 90th Regiment, 1814-15: Quebec, Ontario.
- 93th Regiment, 1815: Newfoundland; 1838-48: Nova Scotia, Prince Edward Island, Quebec, Ontario.
- 96th Regiment, 1824-35: Nova Scotia, Prince Edward Island; 1862-63: New Brunswick.
- 97th Regiment, 1814-15: Quebec, Ontario; 1848-53: Nova Scotia, Prince Edward Island.
- 98th Regiment, 1805-15: Nova Scotia, Quebec, New Brunswick.
- 99th Regiment, 1811-18: Nova Scotia, New Brunswick.
- 100th Regiment, 1806-18, 1866-68: Quebec, Ontario.
- 101st Regiment, 1807-16: Nova Scotia, Quebec, Ontario.
- 102nd Regiment, 1813-18: Nova Scotia.
- 103rd Regiment, 1812-17: Quebec, Ontario.
- 104th Regiment (New Brunswick Fencible Infantry, raised in 1803, numbered 104th in 1810), 1810-17: New Brunswick, Nova Scotia, Prince Edward Island, Ontario, Quebec.

Other Units from Great Britain

- Royal Marines, 1758-59: Nova Scotia, Quebec; 1813-14, 1838: Quebec, Ontario; 1859-72: British Columbia.
- Loyal Surrey Fencible Regiment, 1800-02: Nova Scotia.
- 10th Royal Veterans Battalion (renamed the 4th in 1815), 1807-16: Quebec, Ontario; 1814-15: Nova Scotia, Prince Edward Island (detachments).
- Royal Marine Artillery, 1813-16: Quebec, Ontario.
- The Rifle Brigade (95th Regiment until 1816), (1st Battalion) 1825-36: Nova Scotia, New Brunswick, Prince Edward Island; 1861-70: Quebec, Ontario; (2nd Battalion) 1843-52: Nova Scotia, New Brunswick, Prince Edward Island, Quebec, Ontario; (4th battalion) 1865-68: Quebec.
- Corps of Enrolled Pensioners, 1848-58: Manitoba; 1851-58: Ontario.

- Military Train, 1859-64: New Brunswick, Nova Scotia, Quebec, Ontario.

Rangers (1755-63)

- Nova Scotia Rangers (Goreham's; became Battalion of North American Rangers in 1761), 1755-62: Nova Scotia, Quebec.
- Corps of Rangers (Roger's), 1759-61: Quebec, Ontario.
- Queen's Royal American Rangers (Hopkin's), 1762-63: Ontario.

Foreign Troops in the British Army

- De Meuron's Regiment (Swiss), 1813-16: Quebec, Ontario.
- De Watteville's Regiment (Swiss), 1813-16: Quebec, Ontario.
- Independent Companies of Foreigners (French deserters), 1813: Nova Scotia.
- British Foreign Legion, 1855: Nova Scotia (detachment).

American Loyalists

- King's Orange Rangers, 1778-83: Nova Scotia.
- Independent Companies (Hierlihy's), 1778-82: Prince Edward Island.

German Troops in British Service

- Prinz Ludwig Dragoon Regiment (Brunswick), 1776-77, 1781-83: Quebec.
- Hesse-Hanau Artillery, 1776-83: Quebec.
- Hesse-Cassel Artillery, 1780-83: Quebec.
- Grenadier Battalion (Brunswick), 1776-77, 1781-83: Quebec.
- Von Barner Light Infantry Regiment (Brunswick), 1776-77: Quebec.
- Prinz Friedrich Infantry Regiment (Brunswick), 1776-83: Quebec.
- Von Riedesel Infantry Regiment (Brunswick), 1776-77, 1781-83: Quebec.
- Von Rhetz Infantry Regiment (Brunswick), 1776-77, 1781-83: Quebec.
- Von Specht Infantry Regiment (Brunswick), 1777, 1781-83: Quebec.
- Erb-Prinz Infantry Regiment (Hesse-Hanau), 1776-83: Quebec.
- Free Corps of Chasseurs (Hesse-Hanau), 1777-83: Quebec, Ontario.
- Von Seitz Infantry Battalion (Hesse-Cassel), 1778-83: Nova Scotia.
- Princess of Anhalt Infantry Regiment (Anhalt-Zerbst), 1778-83: Quebec.
- Von Ehrenbrook Infantry Battalion (Brunswick), 1778-81: Quebec.
- Von Barner Infantry Regiment (Brunswick), 1778-83: Quebec.
- Company of Chasseurs (Hesse-Cassel), 1780-83: Quebec.
- Von Lossberg Infantry Battalion (Hesse-Cassel), 1780-81: Quebec; 1781-82: Nova Scotia.
- Von Knyphausen Infantry Battalion (Hesse-Cassel), 1779-80: Prince Edward Island; 1780-83: Quebec.
- Company of Chasseurs (Anspach-Bayreuth), 1782-83: Nova Scotia.

CANADIAN CORPS 1764-1871

Listed here are only those corps on active duty for more than two years at the time of the 1837-38 Rebellions. The name of an American state is given in instances where the corps were raised in locations that are now in the United States.

Cavalry

- Provincial Cavalry (up to five companies with a variety of names) 1812-15: Quebec, Ontario.
- Provincial Light Cavalry (Queen's Light Dragoons & Royal Montreal Cavalry), 1837-50: Quebec.
- Huntington Frontier Cavalry, 1837-43: Quebec.
- Stanstead Frontier Cavalry, 1838-43: Quebec.
- Shefford Frontier Cavalry, 1837-43: Quebec.
- Incorporated Light Dragoons, 1837-43: Ontario.

Artillery

- Provincial Artillery, 1813-15: Quebec, Ontario.
- Kingston Incorporated Artillery, 1837-43: Ontario.

Engineers

- Artificiers and Labourers, 1778-80: Newfoundland.
- Provincial Artificiers, 1813-15: Ontario.

Infantry

- Canadian Volunteers Battalion, 1764: Quebec, Ontario.
- Royal Highland Emigrants Regiment, 1775-79 (later became the 84th Regiment): Quebec, Ontario (1st Battalion); Nova Scotia, New Brunswick, Newfoundland (2nd Battalion).
- Loyal Nova Scotia Volunteers Regiment, 1775-83: Nova Scotia.
- Loyal Fencible Americans Regiment, 1775-83: Nova Scotia, New Brunswick.
- Calbeck's Provincial Company, 1776-83: Prince Edward Island.
- King's Royal Regiment of New York, 1776-83: Quebec, Ontario.
- King's Loyal Americans (Jessup's), 1777-81: Quebec, Ontario.
- Canadian Militia, 3 companies mobilized, 1777: Quebec, Ontario.
- Loyal Volunteers (Leake's), 1777-81: Quebec.
- Queen's Loyal Rangers (Peter's), 1777-81: Quebec.
- American Volunteers (McAlpin's), 1777-81: Quebec.
- Company of Rangers (Adams's), 1777-79: Quebec.
- Butler's Rangers, 1777-84: Ontario.
- Detroit Volunteers, 1778-79: Michigan.
- King's Rangers (Roger's), 1779-83: Nova Scotia, Quebec.
- Newfoundland Regiment, 1780-83: Newfoundland.
- Loyal Rangers (Jessup's), 1781-83: Quebec.
- Queen's Rangers, 1791-1802: Ontario.
- Royal Newfoundland Regiment, 1793-1802: Newfoundland.
- Royal Nova Scotia Regiment, 1793-1802: Nova Scotia.
- King's New Brunswick Regiment, 1793-1802: New Brunswick.
- Island of St. John Volunteers, 1793-1802: Prince Edward Island.
- Royal Canadian Volunteers Regiment, 1795-1802: Quebec (1st Battalion), Ontario (2nd Battalion).

- Royal Newfoundland Regiment of Fencible Infantry, 1803-16: Newfoundland, Nova Scotia, Quebec, Ontario.
- Nova Scotia Regiment of Fencible Infantry, 1803-16: Newfoundland, Nova Scotia, Quebec, Ontario.
- New Brunswick Regiment of Fencible Infantry, 1803-10 (became the 104th Regiment): New Brunswick.
- New Brunswick Regiment of Fencible Infantry, 1812-16: New Brunswick.
- Canadian Voltigeurs Regiment, 1812-15: Quebec, Ontario.
- Glengarry Regiment of Fencible Light Infantry, 1812-16: Quebec, Ontario.
- 1st, 2nd, 3rd, 4th and 5th Battalions, Lower Canada Select Embodied Militia, 1812-15: Quebec. (The 5th became a battalion of Canadian Chasseurs in 1814.)
- Corps of Canadian Voyageurs (became Corps Commissariat Voyageurs in 1813), 1812-15: Quebec, Ontario.
- Frontier Light Infantry, 1813-15: Quebec.
- 6th Battalion, Lower Canada Select Embodied Militia, 1813-14: Quebec.
- Upper Canada Incorporated Militia Battalion, 1813-15: Ontario.
- Western Rangers, 1813-15: Ontario.
- Michigan Fencibles, 1813-15: Michigan.
- Royal Newfoundland Companies, 1824-62: Newfoundland.
- Red River Volunteers, 1835-c.46: Manitoba.
- Glengarry Light Infantry Company, 1837-43: Ontario, Quebec.
- Huntington Frontier Company, 1837-43: Quebec.
- Lacolle Frontier Company, 1837-43: Quebec.
- Sherbrooke Infantry Company, 1838-41: Quebec.
- Missisquoi Frontier Company, 1837-42: Quebec.
- Russeltown Frontier Company, 1838-43: Quebec.
- 1st, 2nd, 3rd, 4th and 5th Incorporated Militia Battalions, 1838-43: Ontario.
- Colored Infantry Company, 1838-50: Ontario.
- 1st Provincial Regiment, 1839-42: Quebec.
- Royal Canadian Rifle Regiment, 1840-70: Quebec, Ontario; 1857-61: Manitoba; 1862-70: Newfoundland.
- Victoria Voltigeurs, 1851-58: British Columbia.
- 1st, 2nd and 3rd Administrative Battalions, 1864-65: Quebec, Ontario.
- 1st Ontario Rifle Battalion, 1869-70: Manitoba.
- 2nd Quebec Rifle Battalion, 1869-70: Manitoba.
- Provisional Infantry Battalion, 1870-77: Manitoba.
- Canadian Artillery, batteries A and B, 1871 -: Quebec, Ontario.

AMERICAN ARMY

- 1st, 2nd, 3rd and 4th New York Regiments, 1775-76: Quebec.
- Warner Regiment (Green Mountain Boys - Vermont), 1775-76: Quebec.
- Pennsylvania Rifles Regiment, 1775-76: Quebec.
- New York Artillery Company, 1775-76: Quebec.
- Gardner's Regiment (Massachusetts), 1775-76: Quebec.
- Heath's Regiment (Massachusetts), 1775-76: Quebec.
- Paterson's Regiment (Massachusetts), 1775-76: Quebec.
- Bedel's Rangers Corps (New Hampshire), 1775-76: Quebec.
- 1st, 4th and 5th Connecticut Regiments, 1775-76: Quebec.
- Porter's Regiment (Massachusetts), 1776: Quebec.
- Elsmore's Regiment (Connecticut), 1776: Quebec.

- Burrall's Regiment (Connecticut), 1776: Quebec.
- 2nd, 5th and 8th New Hampshire Regiments, 1776: Quebec.
- Nicholson's Regiment (New York), 1776: Quebec.
- 1st and 2nd New Jersey Regiments, 1776: Quebec.
- 2nd, 4th and 6th Battalions of Pennsylvania, 1776: Quebec.

It would be futile to list the many American units that crossed the border during the War of 1812, because the vast majority of them were never more than a few weeks in Canada.

Canadian Units in American Service

- 1st Canadian Regiment (Colonel Livingston), 1775-76: Quebec.
- 2nd Canadian Regiment (Colonel Hazen), 1776: Quebec.
- Canadian Rangers (Dugan's), 1776: Quebec.
- Canadian Volunteers, 1813-14: Ontario.

SPANISH ARMY
Colonial Troops of New Spain

- Voluntarios de Cataluña (infantry, 1st Company), 1790-94: British Columbia.
- Compania fija de San Blas (infantry), 1794-95: British Columbia.

222

BIBLIOGRAPHY

The text and illustrations in this book are based on many different sources. The following bibliography is not exhaustive, but rather a guide to the main sources. The collections of artifacts at many historical sites and museums were also studied. Most of these are mentioned in the captions to the illustrations.

MANUSCRIPTS

National Archives of Canada
These archives are very important for Canadian researchers because they contain copies of virtually all manuscripts related to Canada in the British or French archives and national libraries. The collection of nineteenth-century military iconography is considerable. There is also an impressive collection of original records. The Northcliffe Collection (MG18) includes many records of the British and French armies from the Seven Years' War, including Montcalm's Diary. Series RG7, RG8, RG9, MG23, MG24 and MG26 contain thousands of volumes about the British army, the militias and the Canadian Volunteers.

Archives nationales de France
Colonies: Séries A (ordinances); B (In-letters); C11A (Canada); C11B (Île Royale); C13A and C13B (Louisiana); D2C (troops); E (personal files); F1A (finances); F3 (Moreau de Saint-Méry collection); Dépôt des fortifications des colonies.
Marine: Series A1 (ordinances); B4 (campaigns).

Archives nationales du Québec (in Montreal and Quebec City)
Court records; Quebec Literary & Historical Society, P450/1.

British Library
Series: Additional Manuscripts (Haldiman Papers).

Service historique de l'Armée de Terre, France
Archives de la Guerre. Series: A1 (general correspondence); XI (archives of the troop corps); Ordinances; Memoranda and surveys.

National Archives of the United States of America
Series: RG 92 (Quartermaster General); RG 94 (Adjutant General); RG 98 (U.S. Army Commands); RG 107 (Office of the Secretary of War); Service Records of Union Soldiers.

Public Archives of Nova Scotia
Series: MG 12 (General Orders); RG22 (Militia).

Public Records Office, Great Britain
Series: Colonial Office 5 (America and West Indies); 42 (Canada); 61 (Vancouver Island); 188 (New Brunswick); 194 (Newfoundland); 217 (Nova Scotia and Cape Breton); 226 (Prince Edward Island). Treasury 1 and 48. War Office 1 (In-letters); 3 (Out-letters, Commander in Chief); 7 (Out-letters, departemental); 17 (Monthly returns); 27 (Inspections); 28 (Miscellanea, Headquarters Records); 34 (Amherst Papers); 44 (Ordnance, In-letters); 55 (Ordnance - miscellanea).

In addition, we note the manuscripts kept at the following institutions: British Columbia Archives, Victoria; Clements Library, Ann Arbor; National Army Museum, London; Manitoba Archives, Winnipeg; Metropolitan Toronto Central Library; Museo Naval, Madrid; Musées de l'Armée, Paris and Salon-de-Provence; McCord Museum of Canadian History, Montreal; Library of Congress, Washington; Ontario Archives, Toronto; Royal Canadian Military Institute, Toronto; Scottish Records Office, Edinburgh.

REFERENCE WORKS

Atlas historique du Canada, volume I: Des origines à 1800. Montreal: Université de Montréal, 1987.

The Canadian Encyclopedia. 3 vols. Edmonton: Hurtig, 1985.

Corvisier, André. *Dictionnaire d'art et d'histoire militaire.* Paris: Presses universitaires de France, 1988.

Dictionnaire biographique du Canada. Vols. 3 to 12. Quebec City: Université Laval, 1974-90.

Johnson, Michael. *The Native Tribes of North America: A Concise Encyclopedia.* London: Windrow & Greene, 1993.

CONTEMPORARY PUBLISHED SOURCES AND WORKS

Amherst, Jeffery. *The Journal of Jeffery Amherst.* Edited by J. Clarence Webster. Toronto and Chicago: 1931.

Aubert de Gaspé, Philippe. *Mémoires.* Quebec City: 1885 (first edition 1864).

Bell, George. *Rough Notes by an Old Soldier.* 2 vols. London: 1867.

Bonnycastle, Richard H. *Canada, as It Was, Is, and May Be.* 2 vols. London: 1852.

Bouchette, Robert S.-M. *Mémoires de Robert S.-M. Bouchette, 1805-1840.* Collected by his son and annotated by A.-D. De Celles. Montreal: 1903.

Bougainville, Louis Antoine de. *Écrits sur le Canada: Mémoires - Journal - Lettres.* Edited by Roland Lamontagne. Sillery: Pélican, 1993.

Bouquet, Henry. *An Historical Account of the Expedition Against the Ohio Indians in the Year MDCCLXIV.* London: 1766.

Clode, Charles M. *The Military Forces of the Crown: Their Administration and Government.* 2 vols. London: J. Murray, 1869.

Cook, James. *Journals of Captain James Cook: The Voyage of the Resolution and Discovery, 1776-1780.* 3 vols. Edited by J. C. Beeglehole. Cambridge: Hakluit Society, 1967.

Cormier, Moïse. *The Journal of Moïse Cormier, Zouaves Pontificaux, 1868-1870.* Edited by David Ross. Winnipeg: Manitoba Museum of Man and Nature, 1975.

Cuthbertson, Bennett. *A System for the Complete Interior Management and Oeconomy of a Battalion of Infantry.* London: 1769.

Davis, R. H. *The Canadian Militia: Its Organization and Present Condition.* Caledonia: 1873.

Dennison, George T. *Soldiering in Canada.* Toronto: George Morang, 1901.

Desjardins, L. G. *Précis historique du 17ième Bataillon d'infanterie de Lévis depuis sa formation en 1862 jusqu'à 1872.* Lévis: 1872.

Documentary History of the Campaign upon the Niagara Frontier, 1812-1814. 9 vols. Edited by Ernest A. Cruikshank. Welland: Tribune, 1896-1908.

Faughnan, Thomas. *Stirring Incidents in the Life of a British Soldier.* Toronto: Hunter & Rose, 1884.

Knox, John. *The Siege of Quebec and the Campaigns in North America 1757-1760.* Edited by Brian Cornell. London: Folio, 1976.

Montrésor, John. *Journals of Col. John Montrésor.* Edited by G. D. Scull. New York: 1882.

Organisation militaire des Canadas. L'Ennemi! L'Ennemi! by A Rifleman. Quebec City: 1862.

Papineau, Amédée. *Journal d'un Fils de la Liberté, réfugié aux États-Unis par la suite de l'insurrection canadienne, en 1837.* 2 vols. Montreal: Étincelle, 1972-78.

Les Patriotes, 1830-1838. Edited and collected by John Hare. Montreal: Libération, 1971.

Pérez, Juan. *Juan Pérez on the Northwest Coast: Six Documents of His Expedition in 1774.* Edited by Howard K. Beals. Portland: Oregon Historical Society, 1989.

Preston, T. R. *Three Years' Residence in Canada, from 1837 to 1839.* 2 vols. London: 1840.

Prieur, François-Xavier. *Notes d'un condamné politique de 1838.* Montreal: 1884.

Prince, John. *John Prince: A Collection of Documents.* Edited by R. Alan Douglas. Toronto: Champlain Society, 1980.

Revolution Remembered: Eyewitness Accounts of the War for Independence. Edited by John C. Dann. Chicago: University of Chicago Press, 1980.

Richardson, K. S. F. *War of 1812. First Series. Containing a Full and Detailed Narrative of the Operations of the Right Division, of the Canadian Army.* s.l.: 1842.

Russel, W. Howard. *Canada: Its Defences, Condition, and Resources.* London: 1865.

Sanguinet. *L'invasion du Canada par les Bastonnois: Journal de M. Sanguinet.* Edited by Richard Ouellet and Jean-Pierre Therrien. Quebec City: Ministère des Affaires culturelles, 1975.

Select British Documents of the Canadian War of 1812. 3 vols. Edited by William W. Wood. Toronto: Champlain Society, 1920-28.

Simcoe, John Graves. *The Correspondence of Lieut. Governor John Graves Simcoe.* 5 vols. Edited by E. A. Cruikshank. Toronto: Ontario Historical Society, 1923-31.

Tolfrey, Frederic. *Tolfrey: Un aristocrate au Bas-Canada.* Translated and edited by Paul-Louis Martin. Montreal: Boréal, 1979.

Vancouver, George. *A Voyage of Discovery to the North Pacific Ocean and Round the World.* 3 vols. London: 1798.

Wolseley, Garnet. *The Story of a Soldier's Life.* 2 vols. Westminster: A. Constable, 1903.

Studies

Allen, Robert S. *His Majesty's Indian Allies: British Indian Policy in The Defence of Canada.* Toronto: Dundurn, 1993.

Barratt, Glynn. *Russia in Pacific Waters 1715-1825.* Vancouver: University of British Columbia, 1981.

Barnes, Leslie W. C. S. *Histoire illustrée de l'artillerie canadienne.* Ottawa: Canadian War Museum, 1979.

Bernard, Jean-Paul. *Les rébellions de 1837-1838.* Montreal: Boréal, 1983.

Blackmore, Howard L. *British Military Firearms, 1650-1860.* New York: Arco, 1968.

Brandani, Massimo, Piero Crociani and Massimo Fiorentino. *L'Esercito pontificio da Castelfirdardo a Porta Pia, 1860-1870.* Milan: Intergest, 1976.

Burt, A. L. *The United States, Great Britain and British North America from the Revolution to the Establishment of Peace after the War of 1812.* New Haven: Yale, 1940.

Cameron, Christina, and Jean Trudel. *Québec au temps de James Patterson Cockburn.* Quebec City: Garneau, 1976.

Carman, William Y. *British Military Uniforms from Contemporary Pictures.* New York: Arco, 1968.

Carmichael-Smyth, James. *Précis of the Wars in Canada from 1755 to the Treaty of Ghent in 1814.* London: Tinsley, 1862.

Castonguay, Jacques. *Les Voltigeurs de Québec: Premier régiment canadien-français.* Quebec City: Voltigeurs de Québec, 1987.

Chartrand, René. *The French Army in the War of American Independence, 1778-1783*. London: Osprey Military, 1991.
    – *Napoleon's Sea Soldiers*. London: Osprey Military, 1990.
    – *Napoleon's Overseas Army*. London: Osprey Military, 1989.
    – *Uniforms and Equipment of the American Forces in the War of 1812*. Youngstown, N.Y.: Old Fort Niagara, 1992.

Chambers, Ernest J. *The Canadian Militia: A History of the Origin and Development of the Force*. Montreal: Fresco, 1907.

Charbonneau, André. *Le plan-relief de Québec*. Ottawa: Parks Canada, 1981.

Clowes, William Laird. *The Royal Navy: A History, from the Earliest Times to the Present*. Vols. 2 to 6. London: Sampson, Low, Marston, 1901.

Cruikshank, Ernest J. *Butler's Rangers*. Welland: 1893.
    – *The King's Royal Regiment of New York*. Toronto: Ontario Historical Society, 1931.

Cueno, John R. *Robert Rogers of the Rangers*. New York: Oxford, 1959.

D'Arcy, William. *The Fenian Movement in the United States: 1858-1886*. New York: Russel & Russel, 1971.

Deschênes, Gaston. *L'année des Anglais: La côte-du-sud à l'heure de la conquête*. Sillery: Septentrion, 1988.

Desloges, Yvon. *Les forts de la pointe Lévy*. Ottawa: Canadian Parks Service, 1991.

Dickinson, R. J. *Officers' Mess: Life and Customs in the Regiments*. Tunbridge Wells: Midas, 1973.

Dunnigan, Brian. *Siege - 1759: The Campaign Against Niagara, Old Fort Niagara*. Youngstown, N.Y.: Old Fort Niagara, 1986.

Eelking, Max von. *The German Allied Troops in the North American War of Independence, 1776-1783*. Translated from the German by J. G. Rosengarten. Albany: Munsell, 1893.

Elting, John R. *Amateurs, To Arms! A Military History of the War of 1812*. Chapel Hill: Algonquin, 1991.

Egan, Thomas J. *The Halifax Volunteer Battalion and Volunteer Companies, 1859-1877*. Halifax: 1888.

Facey-Crowther, David. *The New Brunswick Militia, 1787-1867*. Fredericton: New Brunswick Historical Society, 1990.

Filion, Mario. *Le blockhaus de Lacolle: Histoire et architecture*. Quebec City: Ministère des Affaires culturelles, 1983.

FitzGibbon, Mary Agnes. *A Veteran of 1812*. Toronto: William Briggs, 1894.

Forbes, A. *A History of the Army Ordnance Services*. Vols. 1 and 2. London: Medici Society, 1929.

Forester, C. S. *The Age of Fighting Sail: The Story of the Naval War of 1812*. Garden City: Doubleday, 1956.

Fortescue, John W. *A History of the British Army*. Vols. 3 to 12. London: Macmillan, 1911-23.

Fortin, Réal. *La guerre des patriotes le long du Richelieu*. Saint-Jean-sur-Richelieu: Milles Roches, 1988.

Fosten, D. S. V. and B. K. *The Thin Red Line*. London: Windrow & Greene, 1989.

Frégault, Guy. *La guerre de la conquête*. Montreal: Fides, 1967.

Fry, Bruce W. *"Un air de fort": Les fortifications de Louisbourg*. 2 vols. Ottawa: Parks Canada, 1984.

Fryer, Mary Beacock. *Volunteers & Redcoats, Raiders & Rebels: A Military History of the Rebellions in Upper Canada*. Toronto: Dundurn, 1987.

Graham, Gerald. *Empire of the North Atlantic: The Maritime Struggle for North America*. Toronto: University of Toronto, 1950.

Graves, Donald E. *The Battle of Lundy's Lane on the Niagara in 1814*. Baltimore: Nautical & Aviation Publishing, 1993.

Greenhous, Brereton. *Semper Paratus: The History of the Royal Hamilton Light Infantry (Wentworth Regiment), 1862-1977*. Hamilton: RHLI Historical Association, 1977.

González Claverán, Virginia. *La expedición científica de Malaspina en Nueva España 1789-1794*. Mexico: El Colegio de México, 1988.

Gooding, S. James. *An Introduction to British Artillery in North America*. Ottawa: Museum Restoration Service, 1965.

Gough, Barry M. *Distant Dominion: Britain and the Northwest Coast of North America, 1579-1809*. Vancouver: University of British Columbia, 1980.
    – *Gunboat Frontier: British Maritime Authority and Northwest Coast Indians, 1846-1890*. Vancouver: University of British Columbia, 1984.
    – *The Royal Navy and the Northwest Coast of America, 1810-1914*. Vancouver: University of British Columbia, 1971.

Gravel, Jean-Yves. *L'armée au Québec (1868-1900): Un portrait social*. Montreal: Boréal, 1974.

Guitard, Michelle. *Histoire sociale des miliciens de la bataille de la Châteauguay*. Ottawa: Parks Canada, 1983.

Hardy, René. *Les Zouaves*. Montreal: Boréal, 1980.

Harper, J. R. *The Fraser Highlanders*. Montreal: Military and Maritime Museum, 1979.

Haythornthwaite, Philip J. *The Napoleonic Source Book.* New York: Facts On File, 1990.
– *Nelson's Navy.* London: Osprey Military, 1993.

Higueras, Maria Dolores. *NW Coast of America: Iconographic Album of the Malaspina Expedition.* Madrid: Museo Naval, 1991.

Hitsman, J. Mackay. *The Incredible War of 1812.* Toronto: University of Toronto, 1965.

Houlding, John A. *Fit for Service: The Training of the British Army, 1715-1795.* Oxford: Clarendon, 1981.
– *French Arms Drill of the 18th Century.* Bloomfield: Museum Restoration Service, 1988.

Irving, L. Homfray. *Officers of the British Forces in Canada during the War of 1812-15.* Toronto: Canadian Military Institute, 1908.

Jackson, H. M. *The Queen's Rangers in Upper Canada, 1792 and After.* s.l., s.d.
– *The Roll of the Regiments (The Active Militia).* s.l., 1959.

Jarret, Dudley. *British Naval Dress.* London: J. M. Dent, 1960.

Johnston, A. J. B. *La défense de Halifax: Artillerie, 1825-1906.* Ottawa: Parks Canada, 1981.

Kendrick, John. *The Men with Wooden Feet: The Spanish Exploration of the Pacific Northwest.* Toronto: NC Press, 1985.

Lacelle, Claudette. *La garnison britannique dans la ville de Québec d'après les journaux de 1764 à 1840.* Ottawa: Parks Canada, 1979.
– *La propriété militaire à Québec de 1760 à 1871.* Ottawa: Parks Canada, 1982.

Lagrave, Jean-Paul de. *Fleury Mesplet (1734-1794): Imprimeur, éditeur, libraire, journaliste.* Montreal: Fides, 1985.

Lavery, Brian. *Nelson's Navy: The Ships, Men and Organisation, 1793-1815.* London and Annapolis: Naval Institute, 1989.

Lee, David. *La bataille du moulin à vent: Novembre 1838.* Ottawa: Parks Canada, 1979.

Low, Charles Rathbone. *Her Majesty's Navy.* London: J. S. Virtue, 1893.

Mann, Michael. *A Particular Duty: The Canadian Rebellions, 1837-1839.* Salisbury: Michael Russel, 1986.

McConnell, David. *L'Artillerie lisse britannique: Une étude technologique.* Ottawa: Canadian Parks Service, 1989.

Military Uniforms in America. The Era of the American Revolution 1755-1795. Composite work under the direction of John R. Elting. San Rafael: Presidio Press, 1974.

Moogk, Peter N. *Vancouver Defended: A History of the Men and Guns of the Lower Mainland Defences, 1859-1949.* Surrey: Antonson, 1978.

Morton, Desmond. *A Military History of Canada.* Edmonton: Hurtig, 1985.

Neuburg, Victor. *Gone for a Soldier: A History of Life in the British Ranks from 1642.* London: Cassel, 1989.

Nicholson, G. W. L. *The Gunners of Canada: The History of the Royal Regiment of Canadian Artillery.* Vol. 1. Toronto: McClelland and Stewart, 1967.
– *The Fighting Newfoundlander.* Government of Newfoundland, 1964.

Pariseau, Jean, and Serge Bernier. *Les Canadiens français et le bilinguisme dans les Forces armées canadiennes. Tome I, 1763-1969: Le spectre d'une armée bicéphale.* Ottawa: Directorate of History, Department of National Defence, 1987.

Proulx, Gilles. *Entre France et Nouvelle-France.* Ottawa: Marcel Broquet and Parks Canada, 1984.

Le Québec et la guerre. Composite work edited by Jean-Yves Gravel. Montreal: Boréal, 1974.

Raudzens, George. *The British Ordnance Department and Canada's Canals, 1815-1855.* Waterloo: Wilfrid Laurier University, 1979.

Riling, Joseph R. *The Art and Science of War in America: A Bibliography of American Imprints.* Bloomfield: Museum Restoration Service, 1990.

Rioux, Christian. *La présence du régiment Royal Artillery à Québec de 1759 à 1871.* Ottawa: Parks Canada, 1982.

Ross, David, and Grant Tyler. *Canadian Campaigns, 1860-1870.* London: Osprey Military, 1992.

Ross, David. *Military Uniforms - Uniformes militaires.* Saint John: New Brunswick Museum, 1980.

Sarty, Roger F. *Coast Artillery 1815-1914.* Bloomfield: Museum Restoration Service, 1988.

Sanchez, Joseph. *Spanish Bluecoats: The Catalonian Volunteers in Northwestern New Spain, 1767-1810.* Albuquerque: University of New Mexico, 1990.

Senior, Elinor Kyte. *Redcoats & Patriotes: The Rebellions in Lower Canada, 1837-38.* Stittsville: Canada's Wings, 1985.

Senior, Hereward. *The Last Invasion of Canada: The Fenian Raids, 1866-1870.* Toronto: Dundurn, 1991.

Snider, C. H. J. *Under the Red Jack: Privateers of the Maritime Provinces of Canada in the War of 1812.* London: Martin Hopkinson, 1928.

Squires, W. Austin. *The 104th Regiment of Foot (The New Brunswick Regiment) 1803-1817.* Fredericton: Brunswick Press, 1962.

Stacey, C. P. *Canada and the British Army, 1846-1871: A Study in the Practice of Responsible Government*. Toronto: University of Toronto, 1963.
  – *Quebec, 1759: The Siege and the Battle*. Toronto: Macmillan, 1959.

Stanley, George F. G. *L'invasion du Canada 1775-1776*. Quebec City: 1975.
  – *La guerre de 1812: Les opérations terrestres*. Ottawa: Canadian War Museum, 1983.
  – *New France: The Last Phase, 1744-1760*. Toronto: McClelland and Stewart, 1968.
  – *Nos soldats: Histoire militaire du Canada de 1608 à nos jours*. French version of *Canada's Soldiers*. Under the direction of Serge Bernier. Montreal: Éditions de l'homme, 1980.
  – *Toil & Trouble: Military Expeditions to Red River*. Toronto: Dundurn, 1989.

Steele, I. K. *Guerillas and Grenadiers*. Toronto: Ryerson, 1971.

Stewart, Charles H. *The Service of British Regiments in Canada and North America*. Ottawa: Department of National Defence Library, 1964.

Stotz, Charles Morse. *Outposts of the War for Empire*. Pittsburgh: Historical Society of Western Pennsylvania, 1985.

Strachan, Hew. *From Waterloo to Balaclava: Tactics, Technology, and the British Army, 1815-1854*. Cambridge: Cambridge University, 1985.

Sulte, Benjamin. *Histoire de la milice canadienne-française, 1760-1897*. Montreal: 1897.

Summers, Jack L., and René Chartrand. *L'uniforme militaire au Canada, 1665-1970*. Ottawa: Canadian War Museum, 1981.

Trudel, Marcel. *Le régime militaire dans le gouvernement de Trois-Rivières 1760-1764*. Trois-Rivières: Bien public, 1952.

Tucker, Gilbert Norman. *The Naval Service of Canada: Its Official History*. Vol. 1. Ottawa: National Defence, 1952.

Vincent, Elizabeth. *Le Génie royal au Canada: Matériaux et techniques de construction*. Ottawa: Environment Canada, Canadian Parks Service, 1993.

Watteville, H. de. *The British Soldier: His Daily Life from Tudor to Modern Times*. New York: Putnam, 1955.

Webber, David. *A Thousand Young Men: The Colonial Volunteer Militia of Prince Edward Island, 1775-1874*. Charlottetown: Prince Edward Island Museum & Heritage Foundation, 1990.

Whitfield, Carol M. *Tommy Atkins: The British Soldier in Canada, 1759-1871*. Ottawa: Parks Canada, 1981.

Wilhelmy, Jean-Pierre. *Les mercenaires allemands au Québec du XVIIIe siècle et leur apport à la population*. Beloeil: Maison des mots, 1984.

Wright, Robert K. *The Continental Army*. Washington: U.S. Army Center of Military History, 1983.

ARTICLES

Archer, Christon I. "Spanish Exploration and Settlement of the Northwest Coast in the 18th Century," *Sound Heritage*, VII, 1978.

Allen, Robert S. "The British Indian Department, 1755-1830," *Canadian Historic Sites*, No. 14. Ottawa: Parks Canada, 1975.

Beattie, Judith, and Bernard Pothier. "La bataille de Restigouche," *Lieux historiques canadiens*, No. 16. Ottawa: Parks Canada, 1978.

Blanco, Richard L. "Attempts to Abolish Branding and Flogging in the Army of Victorian England Before 1881," *Journal of the Society for Army Historical Research*, XLVI, 1968.
  – "The Attempted Control of Venereal Desease in the Army of Mid-Victorian England," *Journal of the Society for Army Historical Research*, XLV, 1967.
  – "Army Recruiting Reforms, 1861-1867," *Journal of the Society for Army Historical Research*, XLVI, 1968.

Chartrand, René. "The Garrison at Nootka: Spanish Colonial Troops at the End of the Eighteenth Century," in *Spain and the North Pacific Coast*. Composite work edited by Robin Inglis. Vancouver: Vancouver Maritime Museum, 1992.
  – "Winter Uniforms in Canada, 1665-1871," *Military Collector & Historian, Journal of the Company of Military Historians*, XLIII, 1991.

Davidson, J. A. "The Preposterous Fortress of the North: The Story of Fort Prince of Wales," *Canadian Geographical Journal*, October 1960.

Edwards, Joseph P. "The Militia of Nova Scotia, 1749-1867," *Collections of the Nova Scotia Historical Society*, XVII, 1913.

Gough, Barry M. "Nootka Sound in James Cook's Pacific World," *Sound Heritage*, VII, 1978.

Greenough, John Joseph. "La Citadelle d'Halifax, 1825-1860: histoire et architecture," *Lieux historiques canadiens*, No. 17. Ottawa: Parks Canada, 1977.

Haarmann, Albert A. "Notes on the Brunswick Troops in British Service during the American War of Independence 1776-1783," *Journal of the Society for Army Historical Research*, XLVIII, 1970.

Hancock, J. T. "The First British Combat Engineers," *Royal Engineers Journal*, LXXXVIII, 1974.

Lovatt, R. "Les Voltigeurs, les Fusiliers et les Artilleurs de Victoria (C.-B), 1851-1873," *Journal de l'Organisation des musées militaires du Canada*, VI, 1977.

Luvaas, Jay. "General Sir Patrick MacDougall, the American Civil War and the Defence of Canada," *Canadian Historical Association Report*, 1962.

Mackay, Daniel S. C. "Les Royal Canadian Volunteers," *Journal de l'Organisation des musées militaires du Canada*, VI, 1977.

McKelvie, B. A., and W. E. Ireland. "The Victoria Voltigeurs," *British Columbia Historical Quarterly*, XX, 1956.

McGee, Timothy J. "An Elegant Band of Music: Music in Canada in the 18th Century," *International Journal of Canadian Studies/Revue internationale d'études canadiennes*, V, 1992.

Morrison, William R. "The Second Battalion, Quebec Rifles, at Lower Fort Garry," *Canadian Historic Sites*, no 4. Ottawa: Parks Canada, 1970.

Nasatir, A. P. "The Anglo-Spanish Frontier in the Illinois Country During the American Revolution, 1779-1783," *Journal of the Illinois State Historical Society*, XXI, 1929.

Nicolai, Martin L. "A Different Kind of Courage: The French Military and the Canadian Irregular Soldier during the Seven Years' War," *Canadian Historical Review*, LXX, 1989.

Tascona, Bruce. "The Independent Companies of Manitoba, 1871-1884," *Journal of the Military History Society of Manitoba*, 1992.

Toner, Peter M. "The Military Organisation of the 'Canadian' Fenians, 1866-1870," *The Irish Sword*, X, 1971.

Whitfield, Carol M. "Barrack Life in the Nineteenth Century; or How and Why Tommy's Lot Improved," *Material History Bulletin*, XV, 1982.
    – "Tommy Atkin's Family," *Bulletin for the Preservation of Technology*, V, 1973.

THESES AND DISSERTATIONS

Dubé, Timothy D. "The Enrolled Pensioner Scheme in Canada West, 1851-1858, with Specific Reference to the Plan at Amherstburg." Master's thesis, University of Windsor, 1982.

Graves, Donald E. "Joseph Wilcocks and the Canadian Volunteers: An Account of Political Disaffection in Upper Canada." Master's thesis, Carleton University, 1982.

Hartley, Gerald M. F. "Years of Adjustment: British Policy and the Canadian Militia, 1760-1787." Master's thesis, Queen's University, 1993.

Henderson, James L. "A Study of the British Garrison in London, Canada West (Later Ontario), 1838-1869." Master's thesis, University of Windsor, 1967.

Hitsman, J. Mackay. "Defence of Canada, 1763-1871: A Study of British Strategy." Ph.D. diss., University of Ottawa, 1964.

Jones, Oakah L. "The Spanish Occupation of Nootka Sound, 1790-1795." Master's thesis, University of Oklahoma, 1960.

Lépine, Luc. "La participation des Canadiens français à la Guerre de 1812." Master's thesis, Université de Montréal, 1986.

INDEX*

A

Abercromby, Major General James: 28, 29-30
Acadia: 19, 22-23, *23*, 58-59, 89
Acapulco: 71
Accommodation (steamship): 170
Activa (ship): 83
Active Militia: 166
Adelaide Peninsula: 174
Agamemnon (warship): 171
Alaska: 71, 73, 75-77, 82, 177, 178
Albany: 21, 27, 37, 52, 60, 62, 170
Alberni, Lieutenant-Colonel Pedro de: 80, 82
Alcalá-Galiano, Dionisio: 83, *84*, 93
Alcide (ship): 18
Alcohol: 126, 129-130
Allan's Corners: 109
Allen, Ethan: 53
Alta California: 72
American Artillery Regiment: 99
American Civil War: 187-189, 193, 199
American Revolution: 51-52, 58, 123
American War of Independence: 89, 90, *90*
Amherst, General Jeffery: 28, 29, 36-37, 41-42, 46, 47, 49
Amherstburg: 89-90, 155
Amiens (treaty at): 91, 92
Ancaster: 101
Anhalt-Zerbst Regiment: 64, *65*
Annapolis: 59, 60
Antietam: 187, 199
Appomattox: 193
Aranzazu (ship): 83
Argonaut (ship): 79
Armagnac regiment: 67, *68*
Armstrong, General John: 101
Armstrong, William G.: 172
Army List: 92
Arnold, Benedict: 52, 54, 55-56, 58
Aroostook War: 161-162, 167
Arteaga, Lieutenant Ignacio de: 77
Artois regiment: 18
Astoria, Fort: 177. *See also* George (fort)
Atalante (ship): 39, *40*
Atrevida (corvette): 78
Aubert de Gaspé, Philippe: 87, 131
Aubry, Captain: 30-31
Australia: 78, 159, 160, 197
Austria: 15, 91, 187
Auxerrois regiment: 67, *69*

B

Baffin (bay): 174
Baffin (island): 172
Bagot, Ambassador Charles: 141
Bahama (ship): 93
Baie des Chaleurs: 40
Baie Saint-Paul Militia: *87*
Baker's farm: 158
Baltimore: 117
Bands, military: *61. See also* Musicians, regimental
Bank of Montreal: 146
Banks Island: 172, 174
Barclay, Captain Robert Heriot: 101

Bay Bulls: 91
Baynes, Rear-Admiral Robert Lambert: 180
Béarn regiment: *17*, 18
Beaufort, Sir James: 173
Beaugrand, Honoré: 199
Beauharnois: 157, 158, *158*
Beaujeu: *See* Villemonde, Louis Liénard de Beaujeu de
Beaumont: 57
Beauport: 34, 36
Beauséjour, Fort (Fort Cumberland): 18, *21*, 59, *59*
Beaver Dams (Thorold): 107
Beaver, HMS: 178
Beechey Island: 174
Belgium: 118, 199
Bell, Captain George: 147
Bella Coola River: 84
Belle Famille: *See* La Belle Famille
Bering, Vitus Jonassen: 71
Bering Strait: 76, 174
Bermuda: 117, 170
Berryer (Minister of the Navy): 32
Berry regiment: 25, *25*, 34, 39
Bigot, Intendant François: 25
Blackfoot (Amerindians): *176*
Black people: *61*, 118, 185, *186*, 187
Black Rock: 111
Bodega y Quadra, Lieutenant Juan Francisco de la: 74-75, *75*, 77, 83
Boerstler, Colonel Charles: 107
Bonaventure: 197
Bond Head, Lieutenant-Governor Sir Francis: 146
Booker, Lieutenant-Colonel Alfred: 194
Boothia, Gulf of: 173
Boscawen, Admiral Edward: 18
Boston: 52, 58, 169
Bougainville, Louis-Antoine de: 31-32, 41, 75
Bouquet, Colonel Henry: 46-47, *47*
Bourget, Monseigneur Ignace: 200, 201-202
Bourgogne regiment: 18
Bourlamaque, General François-Charles de: 36-37
Braddock, General Edward: 17-18, 19, 20, 23-24, 30, 47
Bradstreet, Lieutenant-Colonel John: 31
Brant, Joseph (Chief Thayendanegea): 65, 66, 70, 89
Brantford: 70
Brest: 18
Briand, Monseigneur: 52
British Light Cavalry: *153*
British Light Dragoons: *165*
British Party: 145
British Rifles: 145, 202
Brock, General Isaac: 96-100
Brown, General Jacob: 107, 112-114
Brown, Thomas Storrow: 148
Bruce, Gaspard: 175
Brunel, Marc Isambard: 170
Brunswick von Riedesel Regiment: *64*
Bucareli (bay): 75
Bucareli y Ursua, Viceroy Antonio Maria: 72, 74, 77
Buffalo (town): 111, 114
Buies, Arthur: 199
Bull, Fort: 24
Burgoyne, General John: 60-63

*The page numbers in Italic type indicate illustrations.

229

HUDSON
BAY

Fort Prince of Wales

York Factory

Fort Severn

JAMI

Reindeer River

Churchill

Nelson River

Hayes R.

Severn River

Saskatchewan R.

Cedar L.

Albany River

Lake Winnipegosis

Lake Winnipeg

Lake Manitoba

Abi

Assiniboine R.

Lower Fort Garry

Lake Nipigon

Fort Garry

Red River

Lake of the Woods

Fort William

Lake Superior

Sault Ste Marie
Fort St. Jo

Fort Mackinac
Fort Michilimackinac

Little Missouri River

Green Bay

Le H

Prairie du Chien

Lake Michigan

Détroit
Fort Malden

Chicago
(Fort Dearborn)

Fort St. Joseph

Fort Meigs

Mississippi River

Illinois River

Wabash R.

Fort Vincennes

Ohio

Missouri River

St. Louis

Mississippi River

Tennessee River

THE WEST COAST

| 0 | 50 | 100 | 150 mi |
| 0 | 100 | 200 km |

Sitka

Stikine

N

Queen Charlotte Islands

Bella Coola

Fraser

Vancouver Island

Nootka

New Westminster
Fort Langley

Esquimalt/Victoria

San Juan Islands

PACIFIC
OCEAN

Fort Astoria

Columbia

Fort Vancouver

M
POSTS AN

| 0 | 100 |
| 0 | 100 | 20 |

Citadel . . . .
Posts and Forts . .